Modern Critical Views

Edward Albee
Maya Angelou
Asian-American
Writers
Margaret Atwood
Jane Austen
James Baldwin
Samuel Beckett
Saul Bellow
The Bible
William Blake
Jorge Luis Borges
Ray Bradbury
The Brontës
Gwendolyn Brooks
Robert Browning
Italo Calvino
Albert Camus
Lewis Carroll
Willa Cather
Cervantes
Geoffrey Chaucer
Anton Chekhov
Kate Chopin
Agatha Christie
Samuel Taylor
Coleridge
Joseph Conrad
Contemporary Poets
Stephen Crane
Dante
Daniel Defoe
Charles Dickens
Emily Dickinson
John Donne and the
17th-Century
Poets
Fyodor Dostoevsky
W. E. B. DuBois
George Eliot
T. S. Eliot
Ralph Ellison
Ralph Waldo
Emerson
William Faulkner
F. Scott Fitzgerald

Sigmund Freud
Robert Frost
George Gordon,
Lord Byron
Graham Greene
Thomas Hardy
Nathaniel
Hawthorne
Ernest Hemingway
Hispanic-American
Writers
Homer
Langston Hughes
Zora Neale Hurston
Henrik Ibsen
John Irving
Henry James
James Joyce
Franz Kafka
John Keats
Jamaica Kincaid
Stephen King
Rudyard Kipling
D. H. Lawrence
Ursula K. Le Guin
Sinclair Lewis
Bernard Malamud
Christopher Marlowe
Gabriel García
Márquez
Carson McCullers
Herman Melville
Arthur Miller
John Milton
Toni Morrison
Native-American
Writers
Joyce Carol Oates
Flannery O'Connor
Eugene O'Neill
George Orwell
Sylvia Plath
Edgar Allan Poe
Katherine Anne
Porter
J. D. Salinger

Jean-Paul Sartre
William Shakespeare:
Histories and
Poems
William Shakespeare's
Romances
William Shakespeare:
The Comedies
William Shakespeare:
The Tragedies
George Bernard
Shaw
Mary Wollstonecraft
Shelley
Percy Bysshe Shelley
Alexander
Solzhenitsyn
Sophocles
John Steinbeck
Tom Stoppard
Jonathan Swift
Amy Tan
Alfred, Lord
Tennyson
Henry David
Thoreau
J. R. R. Tolkien
Leo Tolstoy
Mark Twain
John Updike
Kurt Vonnegut
Alice Walker
Robert Penn Warren
Eudora Welty
Edith Wharton
Walt Whitman
Oscar Wilde
Tennessee Williams
Thomas Wolfe
Tom Wolfe
Virginia Woolf
William Wordsworth
Richard Wright
William Butler Yeats

Modern Critical Views

ALEKSANDR SOLZHENITSYN

Edited and with an introduction by
Harold Bloom
Sterling Professor of the Humanities
Yale University

CHELSEA HOUSE PUBLISHERS
Philadelphia

Printed and bound in the United States of America

10 9 8 7 6 5 4 3 2 1

∞ The paper used in this publication meets the minimum
requirements of the American National Standard for
Permanence of Paper for Printed Library Materials,
Z39.48-1984

Library of Congress Cataloging-in-Publication Data

Alexander Solzenhitsyn / editor, Harold Bloom.
     p. cm. — (Modern Critical views)
   Includes bibliographical references.
   ISBN 0-7910-5918-9 (alk. Paper)
    1. Solzenhitsyn, Aleksandr Iseavich, 1918–   —Criticism
and interpretation.
  I. Bloom, Harold.   II. Series.

   PG3488.O4 Z5537 2000
   891.73'44—dc21   00-060319
                                     CIP

Chelsea House Publishers
1974 Sproul Road, Suite 400
Broomall, PA 19008-0914

The Chelsea House World Wide Web address is
http://www.chelseahouse.com

Contributing Editor: Tenley Williams

Produced by: Robert Gerson Publisher's Services, Santa Barbara, CA

Contents

Editor's Note

My Introduction wonders whether Solzehenitsyn's importance may prove to be more historical than aesthetic, and questions also whether he has been able to transcend Tolstoy's influence upon him.

The chronological sequence of criticism begins with Edmund E. Ericson Jr.'s consideration of the short novel *One Day in the Life of Ivan Denisovich*, which is seen as a tribute to humanity's endurance.

In a very challenging essay, James M. Curtis analyzes Solzhenitsyn's complex relation to his great precursor, Tolstoy, after which Kenneth N. Brostrom finds in the poem *Prussian Nights* Solzhenitsyn's insistence that morality resides in our actions, and not in our feelings.

The Gulag Archipelago is regarded by John B. Dunlop as a "positive" statement, despite the horrors it depicts, because it represents a triumph over ideology.

Edward J. Brown examines Solzhenitsyn's polemical literary satire *The Calf and the Oak*, finding in it a crucial document of Russian cultural history, while Mikhail S. Bernstam sees Solzhenitsyn as an original Liberal without precedent in Russian tradition, and therefore doomed to be misunderstood both in Russia and the West.

Q. D. Leavis defends Solzhenitsyn both as a literary stylist, and as an advocate of individual rights, after which Anna Diegel compares Pasternak and Solzhenitsyn as such advocates.

Dostoevsky is contrasted to Solzhenitsyn, as novelistic visonaries of detention by the state, in Sophie Ollivier's essay, while Caryl Emerson views Solzhenitsyn as a prophet whose Word warns us against the "relentless cult of novelty."

Hugh Ragsdale emphasizes what is still Solzhenitsyn's political dilemma: how to preserve the folk ethos of Russian culture while the nation recoils from Soviet Marxism towards Western capitalism.

In this volume's final essay, Svitlana Kobets finds a hidden pattern of Christian asceticism in *One Day in the Life of Ivan Denisovich*, the Tolstoyan tale that marked Solzhenitsyn's true inception.

Introduction

Solzhenitsyn is a central figure in the Great Russian narrative tradition whose titans include Tolstoy, Dostoevsky, and Leskov, all of whom were crucial influences upon Solzhenitsyn's own fiction. Tolstoy, the largest of these presences in Solzhenitsyn, seems to have had as profound an effect upon the later writer's life as upon the work. The heroic stance against a corrupt and brutal government, the patriotic Russian reaffirmation of the Old Believer Faith: these passed from Tolstoy to Solzhenitsyn. Count Tolstoy, aristocrat and heresiarch, was untouchable by the awed Czarist regime. Solzhenitsyn, an uncommon commoner, served in the Gulag despite his heroism in battle, and finally was sent into exile by a perplexed and frightened Politboro. Returning from his New England exile when Communism fell, the aging Solzhenitsyn at 81 is scarcely at home in the quasi-democratic Russia of Putin, where as writer he is all but totally isolated. Tolstoy, in his darkest moments, was supported by thousands of Tolstoyans, literary and religious, but Solzhenitsyn seems to have lived beyond his time. As a prophet crying out against moral depravity in his beloved Russia, he is ignored, or dismissed as a relic. Jeremiah-like, he denounces Russian yielding to Western consumerism, but the consumers are not moved. He came out neither for nor against Yeltsin and Putin, but declared again for Jesus, the Russian Jesus of Tolstoy and (with many differences) of Dostoevsky.

It is difficult to judge Solzhenitsyn's major works—*August 1914, Cancer Ward, The First Circle, The Gulag Archipelago, One Day in the Life of Ivan Denisovich*—apart from their context, his magnificent struggle against the Stalinist legacy. The judgment of his younger Russian contemporaries is that all these are now, at best, admirable Period Pieces. Will that now fashionable judgment prevail?

Clearly, there is no *War and Peace* nor *Anna Karenina*, no *The Brothers Karamazov* nor *Crime and Punishment*, among Solzhenitsyn's narratives. Are

1

we to say that he is doomed to be remembered only in the category of the writer-as-witness, a much larger version of the sincere but limited Elie Wiesel? If one looks for his American equivalent, one finds not Faulkner nor even Hemingway but John Dos Passos, a grand camera eye, or even Steinbeck, whose *The Grapes of Wrath* seems not unworthy of Solzhenitsyn's populist religiosity.

We do Solzhenitsyn's novels a kind of violence by attempting to read them apart from their central, historical position as polemical testimonies against Stalin and his heirs. Yet it is the year 2001. Do these books sustain themselves aesthetically by their own internal strength? Can we read *The First Circle* as we read *The Charterhouse of Parma* and *The Magic Mountain*, as another great instance of the classic European novel?

The answer seems to me a touch mixed: yes and no, no and yes. *The First Circle* derives from *War and Peace*, a dangerous origin for any novel whatsoever, and also from Tolstoy's great short novel, *Hadji Murad*. Several critics have noted the clear relation between Czar Nicholas I in *Hadji Murad* and Stalin in *The First Circle*; both rulers are accurately portrayed as vicious egomaniacs. But a generally Tolstoyan atmosphere pervades all of *The First Circle*, and becomes disconcerting. Solzhenitsyn tends to be a laconic writer, more like Hemingway (whom he had read closely) than like Tolstoy. A persistent Tolstoyanism demands Tolstoy's own power to freshly re-perceive natural reality, as though he were a new Homer. Solzhenitsyn is a writer of a wholly different order, driven by anger and heroic endurance but lacking Tolstoy's superbly natural grace.

Fiction writers of the century now ending in Russia have included Isaac Babel, permanently memorable for his short stories, and Mikhail Bulgakov, whose fantasy-novel *The Master and Margarita* is an astonishment. Solzhenitsyn does not provide the pure pleasure of reading they do, at least for me. And he may not have the absolute aesthetic eminence of the great modern Russian poets: Alexander Blok, Anna Akhmatova, Osip Mandelstam, Marina Tsvetayeva. Yet Solzhenitsyn, who cannot be said to have triumphed in his aesthetic *agon* with Tolstoy (but then, who could?), has an eminence *in time* so strong that it may prevail over time. His life and his work alike are exemplary, and scarcely can be distinguished, one from the other.

EDWARD E. ERICSON JR.

Humanity In Extremis:
One Day in the Life of Ivan Denisovich *and*
The Love-Girl and the Innocent

The short novel *One Day in the Life of Ivan Denisovich* is a very important work, both for Solzhenitsyn's artistic reputation and for the unfolding story of his career. The play *The Love-Girl and the Innocent* is considerably less important on both scores. What links them together is their setting in similar (not identical) hard-labor prison camps; they reflect on the same general period and experiences of Solzhenitsyn's life. Both were composed shortly after the author's release into freedom.

The story of the publication of *One Day in the Life of Ivan Denisovich* is one of the exciting literary stories of our time. When, in 1961, Solzhenitsyn hoped that the Soviet cultural climate might possibly have thawed enough to allow his novel to be published, he sought to get it through to Alexander Tvardovsky, editor of *Novy Mir*. His middleman was Lev Kopelev (the real-life model for the character Lev Rubin in *The First Circle*.) Solzhenitsyn knew that he risked his life in seeking to be published. He knew also that if any Soviet periodical would publish his story, *Novy Mir* would be the one. Tvardovsky stuffed this work by a total unknown into his briefcase and took it home; and, as was his wont, he propped himself up comfortably in his bed to page through newly received manuscripts. He opened *One Day*. The work immediately overwhelmed him: "I realized at once that there was something

From *Solzhenitsyn: The Moral Vision* by Edward E. Ericson Jr. © 1980 by Wm. B. Eerdmans Publishing Co.

important, and that in some way I must celebrate the event. I got out of bed, got fully dressed again in every particular, and sat down at my desk. That night I read a new classic of Russian literature."

Anticipating the knee-jerk response of the Soviet literary establishment to this searing indictment of Stalin's prison camps, Tvardovsky, the supreme literary diplomat, using his powerful position and connections, went right to the top and sought from Nikita Khrushchev permission to publish the novel. Khrushchev apparently decided that this novel would help him consolidate his base of power, which he was building partly on a denunciation of Stalin's corruption of total control. Khrushchev's fellow members of the Politburo felt that they had little choice but to allow *Novy Mir* to publish the controversial novel.

It appeared in the November 1962 issue, in an overrun of 95,000 which sold out immediately. A separate run of nearly a million copies also sold out quickly. An unknown small-town teacher was, at one stroke, on the center stage of Russian literature. The whole world took note. For his "liberalism" Khrushchev was praised widely.

Early reviews, even in the most orthodox of Soviet sources, were overwhelmingly favorable. *Pravda* remarked on Solzhenitsyn's "profound humanity, because people remained people even in an atmosphere of mockery." Zhores Medvedev, who was later to write *Ten Years after Ivan Denisovich*, emphasized the artistry of the novel. But most responses, in keeping with Khrushchev's motivation for allowing publication, centered on the book's political significance. Importantly, most Western reviews also emphasized the political dimension; the book's publication was viewed as an event illustrating the increasing thaw within the Soviet Union, thus auguring well for future East-West relations. So from the beginning Solzhenitsyn's work was viewed through the wrong lens.

A political approach does not penetrate to the heart of *One Day*. The novel is not, in its essence, about Stalin's inhumanity to man; it is about man's inhumanity to man. Stalin is not some aberration in an otherwise smooth progression of humaneness in history. The evil of the human heart is a universal theme: this is Solzhenitsyn's approach.

Perhaps never has the political appropriation of a work of art by state authorities backfired so dramatically and totally as in the case of *One Day*. Once having been catapulted into the limelight of world attention, Solzhenitsyn would not be silent. Now he had a platform, and his sense of duty urged him on. Khrushchev had let out of the bottle a genie which his successors could not put back in. The high visibility afforded by Khrushchev's decision provided Solzhenitsyn with all the protection of world opinion which he needed in order to escape the brutalities which almost certainly would otherwise have been visited upon him for saying what he went on to say.

Despite the fact that some critics consider *One Day in the Life of Ivan Denisovich* the best piece Solzhenitsyn ever has written, he seems to have felt that he was still at a kind of apprenticeship stage. He had already laid plans for much larger novels; first he had to perfect his craft by working in units of smaller scope.

One Day nevertheless has many traits in common with one or more of the longer novels. Of course, it keeps its eye on those universal issues of human suffering, of good and evil, of life and death. Like *The First Circle* and *Cancer Ward*, it is based on persons and events which Solzhenitsyn experienced and observed in his own life. It has Solzhenitsyn's characteristically tight setting in time—one day in this case. It has a large number of characters, giving us something like a cross section of Soviet society—another Solzhenitsyn trait.

If *One Day* was part of a period of apprenticeship, it stands near the end of that period. The author was about to embark on those long novels of his maturity. And this novel is a piece of such consummate artistry that to call it the work of an apprentice seems ultimately inadequate. Had Solzhenitsyn written nothing after *One Day*, his reputation as an author of note would have been secure. With this short novel he had arrived, whatever his further ambitions. His literary situation at this stage is interestingly parallel to that of Milton: had Milton written nothing after "Lycidas," he would still be an anthologized poet; but he went on to *Paradise Lost, Paradise Regained*, and *Samson Agonistes*.

The novel depicts a single day in the life of a simple peasant, Ivan Denisovich Shukhov, who has been unjustly thrown into a prison camp. While we see many of his fellow zeks, the focus remains rather tightly fixed on Shukhov. It is a day in which not much, certainly nothing momentous, happens. The zeks eat their pitifully inadequate gruel, work hard as bricklayers and foundrymen (Solzhenitsyn himself worked as both), are counted and recounted, and finally retire—to prepare for another day, and other days, of the same.

Solzhenitsyn shows great respect for his title character. Shukhov is not at all an authorial alter ego, as are Oleg Kostoglotov in *Cancer Ward* (somewhat) and Gleb Nerzhin in *The First Circle* (considerably). The clearest sign of respect is in the mere naming of the hero. The combination of given name (Ivan—significantly, the most common of Russian names) and patronymic (Denisovich—son of Denis) is a polite form most readily used for persons of high station or intrinsic importance. Solzhenitsyn applies it to a simple peasant. The author deems his character worthy of the respect usually reserved for "important" people.

The most memorable technical trait of *One Day* is its understatement. The novel depicts horrors which might well elicit white-hot anger—or, if not that, a kind of sentimentality over the suffering of innocents. Then novel makes no such explicit claim on our emotions. Rather, it describes the day of Shukhov and his fellows as not too bad, as almost a good day. The final passage of the novel, capped by a brilliantly conceived final sentence, highlights the device of understatement:

> Shukhov went to sleep, and he was very happy. He'd had a lot of luck today. They hadn't put him in the cooler. The gang hadn't been chased out to work in the Socialist Community Development. He'd finagled an extra bowl of mush at noon. The boss had gotten them good rates for their work. He'd felt good making that wall. They hadn't found a piece of steel in the frisk. Caesar had paid him off in the evening. He'd bought some tobacco. And he'd gotten over that sickness.
>
> Nothing had spoiled the day and it had been almost happy.
>
> There were three thousand six hundred and fifty-three days like this in his sentence, from reveille to lights out.
>
> The extra ones were because of the leap years. . . .

This concluding passage also allows us to check on the important technical matter of narrative point of view. It is a matter handled delicately but consistently in this novel. The author is always telling the story; Shukhov is always in the third person. Yet, by a clever sleight of hand, the author keeps making his readers feel as if they are inside the mind of the main character; truly, Ivan Denisovich is the one who thinks that this is not the worst of days. Readers are left with the impression that they see and experience Shukhov's day through his own eyes, though in technical fact they never do. In this, Solzhenitsyn has shown considerable skill as a fiction writer.

As is typical of Solzhenitsyn's works, *One Day* shows us suffering humanity *in extremis*. But because of Shukhov's limited perspective, suffering here is depicted as primarily physical. In *The First Circle* the more sophisticated Gleb Nerzhin shows that suffering is also psychological and even spiritual. Yet both of these novels—in contrast with *Cancer Ward*, which deals with the *mystery* of suffering—treat a suffering the perpetrator of which is no mystery at all. Still, even in *One Day* the suffering of the body takes on a metaphysical dimension—through the mediation of the author, who can go beyond the ken of the main character. The inhospitably cold climate becomes a symbol of the inhumane setting for human life in general, and the reader comes away feeling moral outrage rather than mere vicarious physical pain. When a medical assistant finds the feverish Ivan not ill enough to exempt from the day's work, the author queries, "How can you expect a man who's warm to understand a man who's cold?" It is one of those microcosmic remarks from which ray out large symbolic meanings. The warm man is the one open to perpetrating injustice. Solzhenitsyn devotes his life to making warm men feel the cold.

Any such "big" thoughts are as far beyond Shukhov as they are beyond the prison guards. Shukhov, now yearning after a handful of oats that once he would have fed only to his horses, thinks, as he gets his pittance of food for the day, "This was what a prisoner lived for, this one little moment." But even here the stomach is cheated and the soul, thereby, troubled. And what do these guards of the "animals" care? "Every ration was short. The only question was—by how much? So you checked every day to set your mind at rest, hoping you hadn't been too badly treated."

The arbitrariness of the life of the zeks is all-governing. The guards are not allowed to recognize the diversity and unpredictability of life; only two zeks may be sick per day; only two letters per zek may be mailed out per year. "Soviet power," Solzhenitsyn satirizes, has decreed that the sun stands highest in the sky not at noon but an hour later. Being dehumanized entails being denatured.

Given the collectivist ideology of the Soviets, an ironic effect of their prison regimen is that it breaks down the sense of human solidarity. Solzhenitsyn, who speaks consistently on behalf of individual dignity, always speaks with equal consistency on behalf of human solidarity. So he laments that in a zek's mind it is another zek who is one's worst enemy. Occasional displays of solidarity, which should be a natural outflowing of the zeks' common humanity and their shared plight, usually succumb to the camp attitude, "You croak today but *I* mean to live till tomorrow."

Nevertheless, however much the grim environment and the need to adapt somehow to it may reduce the basic humanity of the zeks, such pressures can never eradicate the human essence. To be sure, Shukhov is constantly and instinctively concerned with self-preservation. When he was accused, absurdly, of high treason for surrendering to the Germans with the intention of betraying his country, he coolly calculated: "If he didn't sign, he was as good as buried. But if he did, he'd still go on living a while. So he signed." But there is more. A man will assert his wants as well as his needs. For instance, he wants to smoke; it is an unnecessary small pleasure, but he will find a way. Then, there is satisfaction in work. Ivan works poorly only when given meaningless tasks. Laying bricks well pleases him, even if in prison. Constructive work brings out in him the ennobling quality of self-validation through creative effort. And what truly human being can remain forever silent when he is treated as mere flesh and bones? When, on the way to work, Ivan is frisked by the camp guards, he thinks, "Come on, paw me as hard as you like. There is nothing but my soul in my chest." The camp system would grant him the status only of an animal, a workhorse. It is up to him to insist, however inaccurately, that he is more than that, that he is spiritual, too, and not only material.

The greatest of all human capacities demonstrated by Ivan Denisovich is his capacity to absorb pain and yet to endure with at least some vestiges of humanity intact. This enduring humanity is one of Solzhenitsyn's most important themes, and it is his great consolation as he weeps for mankind. The best efforts to reduce humanity to the level of the animal are never entirely successful; and, by definition, a process of dehumanization which is not totally successful is a failure: some humanity remains. "There's nothing you can't do to a man . . ."—except that you cannot do away with his humanity altogether. Longsuffering, Solzhenitsyn thinks, is a peculiarly strong trait of the Russian peasantry. The peasant may be patient, but he is also durable; and ultimately he will overcome.

Ivan Denisovich's attitude toward religion is much like Matryona's in "Matryona's House." Both show little interest in formal religion, either ecclesiastical or credal. Yet both breathe a kind of natural piety, and religious references pepper their everyday talk. Ivan's ready response to his tribulations in prison is, "As long as you're in the barracks—praise the Lord and sit tight." At day's end, grateful that he is not in the cells and thinking that it is not "so bad sleeping here," he murmurs, "Thank God." When he forgets until the last moment before he is frisked that he has a hacksaw blade on him, he almost involuntarily prays as "hard as he could": "God in Heaven, help me and keep me out of the can!" Afterwards, however, this down-to-earth peasant "didn't say a prayer of thanks because there wasn't any time and there was no sense in it now."

Ivan's faith is naive and unreasoned, and includes a sizeable dose of superstition. He believes in God: "When He thunders up there in the sky, how can you help believe in Him?" He also believes, as folk in his village do, that each month God makes a new moon, because he needs the old one to crumble up into stars: "The stars keep falling down, so you've got to have new ones in their place." Atheistic rulers may curtail the growth of religion ("The Russians didn't even remember which hand you cross yourself with"), but it is beyond their power to shake the faith of the Matryonas and Ivans.

While Solzhenitsyn clearly admires Ivan's faith, Ivan does not represent his religious ideal. A character who comes closer to doing so is Alyosha (or Alyoshka) the Baptist. It is intriguing that Solzhenitsyn, who has returned to his ancestral Russian Orthodox Church, gives the deepest religious sentiments in this novel to a character who is hostile to Orthodoxy. This depiction is of a piece with the novel's high praise of two Estonian zeks—and this from an author sometimes called chauvinistic and nationalistic. The fact is that the author is simply being faithful to the quality of the persons whom he knew in the camps. In addition, Solzhenitsyn's handling of Alyosha shows that his primary religious concerns are not with the particularities of Orthodoxy but with those central aspects of the Christian faith held in common by all Christians.

The climactic conversation of the novel is between Ivan and Alyosha. Alyosha's prominence here has been prepared for by frequent earlier depictions of him as a good worker and kind person. Alyosha's faith does not incapacitate him for survival. On the contrary, it is a source of the inner strength that so often characterizes Solzhenitsyn's little heroes, the small people who somehow are able to withstand everything that a soulless bureaucracy inflicts on them. While he allows anyone to order him about, he is still clever enough to have hidden his New Testament in a chink in the wall so that it has survived every search. The regular Sunday fellowship of Alyosha and his fellow Baptists allows them to cope with the hardships of camp life "like water off a duck's back." He is sustained by biblical passages of consolation: "Yet if any man suffer as a Christian, let him not be ashamed; but let him glorify God on this behalf."

The climactic conversation begins when Alyosha, reading his Bible, overhears Ivan's routine, day's end prayer and says, "Look here, Ivan Denisovich, your soul wants to pray to God, so why don't you let it have its way?" Ivan, the naive Orthodox, associates this Baptist with high devotion and thinks that Alyosha's eyes glowed "like two candles." But Ivan, for whom camp experience is a microcosm of all of life, doubts the efficacy of praying: " . . . all these prayers are like the complaints we send in to the higher-ups— either they don't get there or they come back to you marked 'Rejected.'" Alyoshka scolds Ivan for not praying "hard enough," and adds, "if you have faith and tell the mountain to move, it will move." This bold confidence is too much for literal-minded Ivan, who has never seen a mountain move (though he then allows that he has never seen a mountain at all!). For his part, Ivan, unlike those zeks who have lost their capacity for compassion, pities the Baptists as "poor fellows": They were in no one's way, and "all they did was pray to God"; yet "they all got twenty-five years. . . ." On the question of mountain-moving, Alyosha asserts the supremacy of the spiritual realm over the material, since of all physical things, the Lord commanded them to pray only for their daily bread; beyond that, "We must pray about things of the spirit—that the Lord Jesus should remove the scum of anger from our hearts. . . ."

Ivan does not want to be misunderstood. Although disillusioned by a bad priest, he insists that he believes in God. "But what I don't believe in is Heaven and Hell." The afterlife, after all, is not open to empirical verification, as are monthly new moons and falling stars. When he prays, he says, it will be for something real, like release from prison. This attitude scandalizes Alyosha, who consciously suffers for Christ. He counters, "What do you want your freedom for? What faith you have left will be choked in thorns. Rejoice that you are in prison. Here you can think of your soul." This spiritual focus, which Solzhenitsyn elsewhere asserts in his own person, affects Ivan: "Alyosha was talking the truth. You could tell by his voice and his eyes he was glad to be in prison."

Solzhenitsyn admires the Baptist's ability to give a positive meaning to his prison experience; Alyosha is the only character in the novel who can do so. Ivan admires that, too. But it just will not do for him. "It was Christ told you to come here, and you are here because of Him. But why am *I* here? Because they didn't get ready for the war like they should've in forty-one? Was that *my* fault?"

Although he cannot believe everything Alyosha can, Ivan's actions are as good as anyone's. Considering Alyosha impractical, always giving and never getting, Ivan gives him a biscuit, though that gesture leaves the giver with nothing for himself. Solzhenitsyn comments, "We've nothing but we always find a way to make something extra." Ivan gives the cup of cold water, though not always knowingly in God's name. If Alyosha has the best words, no one has better deeds than Ivan.

Ivan and Alyosha are brothers under the skin. Both are models of humanity in the midst of inhumanity; both care for others as much as for themselves. Ivan represents the best possible from a man without an articulated faith; a man can act very well without faith in a transcendent reality. Such a one is in no position, however, to explain the mystery of suffering. This crucial matter, which Ivan deeply needs, is what Alyosha can add. Without Alyosha, the novel would be much diminished. Ivan, as good as he is, needs Alyosha's insight to complete the picture.

The Love-Girl and the Innocent is one of Solzhenitsyn's two published plays, neither of which ranks among his top literary successes. In this case, the large cast of characters in a brief work is especially problematical (fifty-seven individuals, plus others in groups—in a play of 133 pages). It shares with *One Day in the Life of Ivan Denisovich* the setting of a prison camp, though this time a mixed camp of "politicals" and thieves. It also shares the themes of suffering, injustice, and dehumanization. Campland, that "invisible country," is the place "where ninety-nine men weep while one man laughs."

The two memorable characters are the title characters: Lyuba Nyegnevitskaya, the love-girl, and Rodion Nemov, the newly arrived innocent. Her view is that all men are "only after one thing." So she adapts. She, a so-called kulak from a land-owning family, had been married off at fourteen years of age. Nemov, not the adapter Lyuba is, feels "sorry for everyone" in the cruel camp setting. He carries within him the staple Solzhenitsyn conviction that conscience is more important and valuable than life itself. Formerly a cavalry captain, Nemov upon his arrival there is named production chief of the camp. But quickly the professional thieves, whom Stalin considered "social allies," persuade the camp commandant to get rid of this circumspect man and to replace him with a man of their own ilk, the engineer Khomich. Lyuba, despite her compromises, has enough insight to know a good man when she sees one, and she feels sorry for Nemov; she recognizes that he is not camp-wise.

After Nemov is demoted to foundryman, he and Lyuba discover a strong mutual attraction. They live for a week in a courtship-like arrangement. But the camp doctor, Mereshchun, wants Lyuba for his live-in "camp wife." Now in love with Nemov, she suggests that he and the doctor share her; she can manage that much. But the idealistic Nemov cannot tolerate such an arrangement.

Shortly thereafter, Nemov is struck on the head by a falling lump of coal. First word is that he is dead, but it turns out that he is not. The final scene shows Lyuba returning to the doctor's cabin, sad but reconciled to her demeaning fate.

This drama, especially given Solzhenitsyn's elaborate stage directions, would probably be better in the playing than in the reading. The background, picturing Stalin and flowers and children, as well as posters ("Work ennobles man," "He who does not work does not eat," and later "People are the most valuable capital—J. Stalin"), provides a striking contrast with the foreground and its unmitigated misery and injustice.

The Love-Girl and the Innocent shows as clearly, if not so effectively, as *One Day in the Life of Ivan Denisovich* the dehumanization of the Soviet camps. Little of Solzhenitsyn's religious outlook comes through in this play, although his moral vision remains constant. In that light, this play could be seen as the most directly anti-Stalinist, or anti-Soviet, of all Solzhenitsyn's full-length works—the others always rising rather clearly to more universal themes. Still, the dual vision of human nature, with good and evil warring in each human heart, remains prominent. The struggle is seen more sharply in Lyuba than in any other character.

It is possible to read this play allegorically, though care must be exercised here, since Solzhenitsyn's writings generally do not invite such an interpretation. Yet it is easy enough to see Lyuba as Mother Russia, who submits unhappily to the demeaning yoke of servitude; repressing her best moral instincts, she turns her back, regretfully, on the high but hard way—to private freedom within public bondage—offered by the example of Nemov.

JAMES M. CURTIS

Solzhenitsyn's Traditional Imagination: Tolstoy

> *Which of the Russian writers has not secretly*
> *measured for himself Pushkin's Frock coat? . . .*
> *Tolstoy's peasant shirt?*
> —Galakhov, in The First Circle

In the essay which begins part 3 of *War and Peace*, calculus—although the word itself never appears—is applied to the problems of history:

> This new branch of mathematics, unknown to the ancients, by admitting infinitely small quantities, that is, those by which the principal condition of motion (absolute continuity) is re-established, in the examination of movement by this very thing corrects that inevitable error which the human mind cannot help making in examining disparate units of motion instead of incessant motion.
>
> In finding laws of historical motion precisely the same thing takes place.
>
> The movement of mankind, flowing from an innumerable quantity of human whims, occurs incessantly. . . . Only by

admitting the infinitely small unit for observation—the differential of history, that is, homogeneous inclinations of people—and by achieving the art of integrating (taking the sums of these infinitely small units), can we hope to comprehend the laws of history.

This passage exemplifies better than anything else in Tolstoy's fiction what Eichenbaum meant when he commented that in the 1860s "Tolstoy became infected by philosophizing." Just as Chernyshevsky, in *What Is to Be Done?*, attempted to apply Newtonian physics to people by making them discrete units free of jealousy, so Tolstoy attempted to apply Newtonian physics to history. He wished to think of the people of a country as discrete units of space, and then integrate them to achieve an understanding of historical laws which, he wanted to believe, had the same nature as physical laws. The social application of these simple, consistent physical laws had great appeal for Tolstoy in a world in which the emancipation of the serfs had complicated both economic and personal relationships. Moreover, Tolstoy shared with Lenin the need to simplify social relationships; both men wished to suppress the significance of personalities in history by treating Newtonian physics and Euclidean geometry as models of social organization. This affinity, and Lenin's appreciation of Tolstoy as a "mirror of the revolution," endeared Tolstoy to Soviet critics; in the twenties they exhorted writers to emulate him as tirelessly as they denounced Dostoyevsky.

The official interpretation of Tolstoy emphasizes the patriotism of his characters. It notes, for instance, Natasha's almost hysterical insistence that the Rostovs leave behind their furniture in order to free carts for wounded soldiers during the evacuation of Moscow, but it would ignore her indifference to the sight of Moscow on fire a little later. That is to say, Soviet critics generally neglect one pole of the dialectic between public commitment and private happiness that structures so much of Tolstoy's work. Yet one of Mandelstam's pithy remarks, about the actress Vera Komissarzhevskaya, applies to Tolstoy as well, and explains how Tolstoy lends himself so well to the official Soviet version of Russian history: "In essence, the Protestant spirit of the Russian intelligentsia, a unique Protestantism from art and from the theater, found its expression in Komissarzhevskaya." A great deal about the late Tolstoy—his doubts about art and the theater, his fear of sensuality, his moralizing—make sense if we understand him as another example of "the Protestant spirit of the Russian intelligentsia," of the same process which later produced Lenin.

Solzhenitsyn surely had such considerations in mind when he linked Tolstoy and Lenin by saying that Tolstoyanism "led to the Revolution." The full meaning of this extraordinary and seemingly paradoxical statement will become clear only in an analysis of Solzhenitsyn's use of Tolstoy, but it must refer to, among other things, the way Tolstoy anticipated Lenin's secularization of asceticism and his distrust of technology. Thus, in dealing with the relationship between Tolstoy and Solzhenitsyn, one must consider Tolstoy's work, the development of Russian history since 1850, and the way both of them are encoded into Solzhenitsyn's work. The fact that Tolstoy's work embodies certain features of the Russian historical process that have found their fullest expressions (as Mandelstam would have put it) only since the Revolution means that this cannot be a purely esthetic problem. The ease with which Tolstoy lends himself to propaganda gives Solzhenitsyn's relationship to him an ambiguity which resembles that of some of Virginia Woolf's contemporary admirers, who denounce *Anna Karenina* as a blatant instance of the male chauvinist mentality at work, while admitting that it may be the greatest novel ever written.

In this chapter I wish to treat this crucial, complex problem by assimilating it to the patterns in the relationships between poets that Harold Bloom sets forth in his book *The Anxiety of Influence*, a work that has many implications for the history of Russian literature. When Bloom uses so dramatic a phrase as "the Cartesian engulfment," we realize that he is explicating the effects of the dissociation of the poetic sensibility since the seventeenth century. And, since Pushkin was born in 1799, the year in which Wordsworth wrote his Lucy poems, all of the Russian classics belong to what Bloom calls the "modern" period. I agree whole-heartedly with his statement of the principles that should govern the study of literary influence.

> The profundities of poetic influence cannot be reduced to source-study, to the history of ideas, to the patterning of images. Poetic influence, or as I shall more frequently term it, poetic misprision, is necessarily the study of the life-cycle of the poet-as-poet. When such study considers the context in which that life-cycle is enacted, it will be compelled to examine simultaneously the relations between poets as cases akin to what Freud called the family romance, and as chapters in the history of modern revisionism, "modern" meaning here post-Enlightenment.

In his hermetic way, Bloom develops a Freudian-cum-Nietzschean interpretation of the Oedipus myth as a paradigm for creativity by assuming that Oedipus, the "strong poet" (which is to say, any major creative artist), must encounter, and overcome, the Sphinx of a strong precursor. He avoids biographical reductionism by using only the poetic texts as evidence, thus effectively and ingeniously merging psychology and esthetics.

Slavicists will recognize that Bloom is unconsciously continuing Yury Tynyanov's pioneering work on the way Dostoyevsky was able to overcome Gogol's influence, which threatened to become paralyzing, by parodying him. But whereas Tynyanov did not develop a general statement of the problem, Bloom offers six "revisionary ratios," of which three present particular interest here.

> *Tessera*, which is completion and antithesis; . . . A poet antithetically "completes" his precursor, by so reading the parent-poem as to retain its terms but to mean them in another sense, as though the precursor had failed to go far enough.

> *Kenosis*, which is a breaking-device similar to the defense mechanisms our psyches employ against repetition compulsions; *kenosis* is then a movement towards discontinuity with the precursor.

> *Apophrades*, or the return of the dead; I take the word from the Athenian dismal or unlucky days upon which the dead returned to reinhabit the houses in which they had lived. The later poet, in his own final phase, already burdened by an imaginative solitude that is almost a solipsism, holds his own poem so open again to the precursor's work that at first we might believe the wheel has come full circle. . . . But the poem is now *held* open to the precursor, where once it *was* open, and the uncanny effect is that the new poem's achievement makes it seem to us, not as though the precursor were writing it, but as though the later poet himself had written the precursor's characteristic work.

As usual, Bloom's cryptic utterances require a word or two of explication; this holds especially with regard to apophrades. If what I have called the critic's tradition exists in any meaningful way, it exists as a juxtaposition of the past and the present. If I read Solzhenitsyn, and if my reading of him affects me with sufficient force, then it will affect my reading of Tolstoy. I may have the sensation that Solzhenitsyn has influenced Tolstoy, because Solzhenitsyn has influenced my reading of Tolstoy. It is, then, through the intermediary of the critic that the poetic son can encounter and overcome the poetic father. Many of Bloom's remarks make much more sense if we interpolate the critic as a third party into his accounts of poetic oedipal complexes.

Bloom tells us that "Milton is the central problem in any theory and history of poetic influence in English." Likewise, as Galakhov observes,

Pushkin and Tolstoy are the central problems in any theory of history of literary influence in Russia. Bloom's insistence that poetic influence takes the form of a struggle between a son and a father gives the lie to much of the sentimentalizing about Pushkin that goes on in Russia; the incessant praise of Pushkin actually masks filial fear of the omnipotent father. (Compare the analogous distinction between public statements and reality during Stalin's lifetime.)

Pushkin may seem to us influenced by Mandelstam, although hardly by anyone else. Nabokov's fantasy (in *The Gift*) about what he would have been like had he lived in the 1860s, like the parodistic translation and commentary of *Yevgeny Onegin*, certainly attests to an anxiety of influence. Even more eerie is the case of Tynyanov, who looked like Pushkin, learned to imitate his handwriting, and imaginatively recreated him in his unfinished novel *Pushkin*.

As with Pushkin, so with Tolstoy; Russian veneration masks great anxiety about his awesome power. It is as hard for Russians to be tough-minded about Tolstoy as it is for Germans to be tough-minded about Goethe. Tolstoy's extraliterary significance poses particular problems for Solzhenitsyn and requires from him great self-consciousness as a writer. As we shall learn, Solzhenitsyn proves equal to the tasks, as he creates the relationships with Tolstoy that Bloom terms tessera and apophrades.

Finally, there is the matter of kenosis, which Bloom defines as "the movement toward discontinuity with the precursor"; Solzhenitsyn hints at his kenosis with Tolstoy when he stated in the Nobel Lecture, "The twentieth century has turned out to be more cruel than the preceding ones." Tolstoy always had great difficulty in treating the problem of evil and suffering in the world and tended to resort to melodrama whenever he tried it, as in his play *The Power of Darkness*. This is Dostoyevskian material, and Solzhenitsyn completed his kenosis with Tolstoy by drawing on Dostoyevsky.

One Day in the Life of Ivan Denisovich

In her pioneering article on Solzhenitsyn's relationship with Tolstoy, Kathryn B. Feuer says:

> Since a writer's first published work is usually significant of his elective affinities, it is worth noting that the account of a day in the life of Ivan Denisovich recalls [Tolstoy's] "The Woodfelling" [1855] in its chief organizing devices: men of various class and attitude, caught in a common situation of stress which belongs to and is yet outside the ordinary life of their society, joined together by membership in a group within the larger whole, conducted

through a day which begins before dawn and ends in moonlight, with the position and heat of the sun used to define forward movement and also to demarcate shifts in mood or focus.

A further generalization also suggests itself. Both Solzhenitsyn and Tolstoy drew on their own experiences in large groups of men who lived in isolation from society when they wrote these stories. Thus, in using autobiographical material Solzhenitsyn is writing in a way that is more characteristic of Tolstoy than of Dostoyevsky. A detailed analysis of *One Day* will show that Solzhenitsyn is working with, and against, the historical dynamics, characterizations, and style of Tolstoy's works— primarily *War and Peace*, of course.

In terms of literary history, both "The Woodfelling" and *One Day* relate to the past in similar ways. "The Woodfelling" takes place in the Caucasus, and its style contrasts with that of Lermontov and Marlinsky, who had written about that exotic area in florid, rhetorical styles. Place has less significance for Solzhenitsyn than for Tolstoy, however, and we need to read *One Day* not against previous Soviet literature on Siberia but against the glorification of work in Soviet literature. Presumably, one of the things which Khrushchev liked about *One Day* was its positive attitude toward work, as the Soviet phrase has it; Gary Kern even calls *One Day* a *"celebration of labor."* But whereas the workers in socialist realism are happy because they work for the good of the state, Ivan Denisovich is happy in his work because through it he maintains his pride. Kern is surely right when he says that Ivan Denisovich's "moment of . . . greatest freedom" comes when he runs back to look at the wall that he has laid and finds that it is straight. Like Lily Briscoe, he has had his vision—and it sustains him.

Ivan Denisovich himself resembles Captain Khlopov, a character from Tolstoy's "The Raid," a short story closely related in style and setting to "The Woodfelling." Khlopov, a veteran soldier, dismisses the narrator's eager questions about the nature of bravery: "'Brave? brave?' The captain repeated with the appearance of a man presented with a similar question for the first time. '*He who behaves as one should is brave.*'" Similarly, Ivan Denisovich pities, rather than admires, Buynovsky for his attempt to challenge the guards' right to make the zeks take off their jackets while being frisked at the gate. And he does not mind wearing his number on his cap, jacket, and pants because he accepts unflinchingly the knowledge that resistance would have no practical effect and would only waste some of his precious energy, which—like Captain Khlopov—he refuses to expend on Romantic actions.

Historical similarities generally give rise to stylistic similarities, and *One Day* also resembles "The Woodfelling" in its use of unusual vocabulary.

Following Lermontov and Marlinsky for once, Tolstoy uses a number of slang expressions, which he italicizes, as in the sentence, "The company commander Bolkhov was one of the officers called *bonjours* [*bonzhurami*] in the regiment." He also supplies explanatory notes for unusual words that the ordinary Russian reader might not know. Likewise, Solzhenitsyn italicizes camp slang: "Although he, as a shy man, did not dare to make a fuss and *sway the rights*." While Solzhenitsyn did not include footnotes in *One Day*, he did include a brief glossary of prison slang in the definitive edition of his works.

Considering these general similarities, we are not surprised to find a borrowing from "The Woodfelling" in *One Day*, in an incident that occurs at the end of the zeks' grueling work day. When the zeks line up to be counted so they can begin the long trek back to camp, it turns out that one prisoner is missing. Two men from his work brigade search him out and return with him. As it happens, the man is a Moldavian and a "real" spy. When the man returns, the assistant leader of the brigade feigns more anger than he really feels, in order to shield him from the guards: "The bastard, he crawled out onto the scaffolding, hid from me, and got warm, and went to sleep." When the zeks return to camp, the guards lead the man away and charge him with an attempt to escape.

This incident from the end of *One Day* may derive from one at the beginning of "The Woodfelling," in which the young officer who narrates the story tells us that as the troops prepare to move out, somebody discovers that a soldier named Velenchuk is missing. The officers send one Antonov to find him, and the rest set off.

> But we did not have time to go a hundred paces before both soldiers caught up with us.
> "Where was he?" I asked Antonov.
> "Sleeping in the park."
> "Was he drunk?"
> "Not at all."
> "Then why did he go to sleep?"
> "I don't know."

No one mentions the incident again, and Velenchuk proves to be a faithful, brave soldier, but a lucky shot kills him.

In both stories, a large group of men waits in the cold for an absent member; soon another member of the group finds him and brings him back. The different treatment of the incident points up some contrasts between Tolstoy's age and Solzhenitsyn's. The Moldavian is punished, whereas Velenchuk is not. More significantly, we do not know why Velenchuk oversleeps, but we know very well that the Moldavian's exhaustion caused him to doze off.

This contrast raises the question of Tolstoy's treatment of the peasantry, and hence the relation of his work to Romanticism. Tolstoy's treatment of Napoleon in *War and Peace* has given rise to the belief that he was anti-Romantic. Yet in order to debunk the myth of the Romantic hero, he created the even more Romantic myth of the spontaneous uprising of the people. To do so, he suppressed many facts about the War of 1812, as Eichenbaum and Shklovsky have shown, and even transferred certain positive features of the *French* army onto the Russian army, as Feuer has shown. Yet while this information helps us to understand the process of myth making, the cultural dynamics of the myth have more significance here.

By this I mean that Tolstoy's myth of the War of 1812 became the history of the War of 1812 for many Russians. Lenin, for example, completely believed it, as the obituary which he wrote on the occasion of Tolstoy's death makes clear: "And Tolstoy not only gave artistic works which will always be valued and read by the masses when they create humane conditions of life for themselves, having brought down the yoke of the landowners and capitalists—he was able with remarkable force to convey the mood of the broad masses, oppressed by the contemporary order, to draw their position, to express their elemental feeling of protest and resentment."

Since Lenin did not exactly believe in the close reading of artistic texts, he did not realize that there is hardly anything in Tolstoy to support these generalizations. He needed to believe them, though, because they denied the isolation of the artist from the people and thus corresponded to his own need to deny his isolation. However, media theory allows a more general interpretation of Tolstoy's presentation of peasant life.

One of McLuhan's key principles states that "each new technology . . . turns its predecessor into an art form." Applied to the problem at hand, this principle means that the railroad boom in Russia in the 1860s and 1870s was speeding up the disintegration of manorial life in rural Russia that the emancipation of the serfs had begun. While real peasants were abandoning the traditional order of rural life, they appeared in Tolstoy's art as symbols of the psychic and social integration which Tolstoy saw disappearing all around him, and which he often characterizes as "mysterious." As a result, narrative commentary in Tolstoy hardly ever gives us insight into the peasants' thought or emotions; to do so would endow them with an individual consciousness that would destroy their effectiveness as symbols. In *War and Peace* we learn that Platon Karatayev (to take the obvious example) has no individual consciousness and is not separated from the archetypes that structure the life of oral societies:

Every word of his and every action was a manifestation of an activity unknown to him, which was his life. But his life, as he himself looked upon it, had no meaning as a separate life. It had meaning only as a particle of the whole, which he constantly felt. His words and actions poured out of him as regularly, inevitably, and immediately as a fragrance comes from a flower. He could not understand either the value or the meaning of an action or a word taken separately.

Karatayev's spiritual self-sufficiency contrasts with Pierre's doubts and anxieties, of course; it is his function to offer Pierre wholeness in the form of advice and symbolic food, as the old peasant in *Anna Karenina* tells Levin to live "in God's way" and offers him symbolic water.

When Karatayev offers Pierre half a baked potato, "it seemed to Pierre that he had never eaten food more delicious than this." He experiences such joy at his release from alienation that he hardly feels "that which even he later called suffering":

The horse meat was delicious and nourishing, the salt-peter smell of the powder used in place of salt was even pleasant; there was no great cold, and during the day it was always warm while walking, and at night there were bonfires; the lice which ate his body had a pleasantly warming effect.

Even Tolstoy's contemporaries scoffed at this passage, which represents Tolstoy's most extreme denial of the body. No matter how much sense this reaction makes for Pierre psychologically, it must seem like the sheerest Romanticism to those who have passed through the meat-grinder of the Gulag Archipelago: those who have been cold and hungry for ten years or more cannot create characters who make light of the body's demands.

In Bloom's terminology, "tessera" means completion and antithesis, since the precursor did not go far enough; for Solzhenitsyn, Tolstoy did not go far enough in presenting the varieties of prison experience, and a tessera relationship between Karatayev and Ivan Denisovich results. Ivan Denisovich resembles Karatayev in that both are peasants who have gone from the farm to the army to prison while remaining essentially peasants who know how to fend for themselves. We learn of Karatayev that

he had only to lie down, to immediately go to sleep like a rock, and he had only to stretch up, to set about something immediately, without a second of delay, as children take up their toys when they get up. He knew how to do everything, not very well, but not badly either. He was always busy and only at night allowed himself conversations, which he liked, and songs.

Solzhenitsyn translates this passage into twentieth-century style, omitting the paternalistic condescension:

> Shukhov never slept past wake-up; he always got up with it—there was an hour and a half of one's own, not government, time before work, and someone who knows camp life can always do some work: sew someone a glove-cover from an old lining; put a rich brigade member's boots right at his cot so he won't have to stamp bare-footed around the pile, and pick his out.

Unlike Karatayev, Shukhov lives in, and reacts to, a world of cause and effect; while both Shukhov and Karatayev sew, Shukhov does so more frequently because he continually has to fight hunger and cold.

Platon Karatayev and the other peasants who appear sporadically in *War and Peace* do no farming to speak of, but the peasants in *Anna Karenina* do. Although they try to cheat Levin and often cause him frustration, they are just as symbolic and even allegorical as Karatayev. In a most indicative scene in book 3 of *Anna Karenina*, Levin admires a young peasant couple who are healthy and happy, as peasants uncontaminated by city ways always are in Tolstoy. Levin finds out from the man's father that they have been married for over two years, and asks whether they have any children. "'What children! For a year he didn't understand anything, and was too shy to ask,' answered the old man." Tolstoy's peasants are not interested in sex, and they do not drink to excess, if at all. (Nikita, the patriarch in *The Power of Darkness*, is a teetotaler and refuses an offer of a drink.) Tolstoy's peasants, in short, do not suffer from malnutrition or infectious diseases, do not wish to leave the land, and are not intemperate; and they thus do not constitute "realistic," "truthful," or "lifelike" images of actual Russian peasants in the 1870s. They represent something like wish fulfillment, and not just on Tolstoy's part. These highly conventionalized characters have satisfied the need of Lenin and many other Russians who have wished to believe in the peasantry as the embodiment of goodness and the Russian soul.

The conventions Tolstoy obeys in creating his peasants derive from the eighteenth century, like so much else in his work, and they have continued to evolve in the twentieth century. Tolstoy's peasants clearly hark back to those of earlier pastorals. (Tolstoy's swerve is to omit the love theme.) This realization helps us to understand something that might otherwise seem startling: the continuity between Tolstoy's masterpieces and the many cliché-ridden works of socialist realism. Like Tolstoy's peasants, happy Soviet workers find complete fulfillment in physical labor, and it never occurs to them to find fault with, or even discuss, their living and working conditions. Socialist realists have written a number of variants of this narrative comment about the peasants whom Levin admires: "The whole work day left no trace but merriment." William Empson's comment in *Versions of Pastoral* that proletarian literature is simply covert pastoral enables us to find the coherence of tradition in almost everything Tolstoy wrote about the peasants; the Soviet idolatry of Tolstoy, as opposed to Dostoyevsky, is an expression of the resurgence of the pastoral in Soviet literature.

This subject of the continuity between the presentation of work in Tolstoy and Soviet attitudes toward work obviously deserves more detailed treatment than I can give it here, but one example may indicate the nature of the problem. Early in *One Day*, Ivan Denisovich is sitting in the camp clinic, mulling over his chances for getting excused from work. He realizes that even if he is allowed to stay in the clinic, he won't be able to rest. The new doctor at the clinic, Stephan Grigorich, makes the ambulatory patients go outside and work in the prison compound. "He says that work is the best medicine for illness," Ivan recalls. Ah yes, we think, another example of Soviet cynicism and exploitation. We think this that is, until we realize that the belief that physical labor cures illness comes—directly or indirectly—from *Anna Karenina*, After the famous hay-mowing scene, Levin tells his brother Sergei Koznyshev, "You wouldn't believe how useful this regimen is against any nonsense. I want to enrich medicine with a new term: *Arbeitscur*." Just as Pierre's denial that he suffered physically while a prisoner makes sense for him, so Levin's statement makes sense for him. But we notice that Levin may hay only once; he doesn't have to do it every day, and he is well fed. But in the twentieth century, his belief in the health benefits of physical labor lent itself to distortion as a justification for Stalin's work camps.

Reacting against the pastoral conventions which govern the presentation of peasants both Tolstoy and in social realism, Solzhenitsyn narrates *One Day* through Ivan's consciousness, thus making him less symbolic and more individual. (We never have insight into the thoughts and feelings of Tolstoy's happy peasants.) In this sense, Ivan is more complicated than Platon Karatayev, or the peasants in *Anna Karenina*. Several paragraphs after we read "Shukhov never slept past wake-up," we read "Shukhov did not get up." His awareness of the difficulties of surviving the camp makes it impossible to characterize him as "always" doing one thing or another. He has no real awareness of, or interest in, anything beyond his own skill and integrity. He never denies the reality of the cold, the hunger, and the exhaustion, for he knows that those who do will not survive a "tenner."

Karatayev's real descendant in *One Day* is Alyoshka the Baptist, who prays frequently and endures the deprivations of camp life easily. "The camp goes over them [the Baptists] like water off a duck's back," Ivan thinks to himself. We must accept this as true, for we have no narrative insight into Alyoshka's mind, as we have none into Katatayev's. Ivan completes the reversal of Karatayev when he passes on to Alyoshka one of the cookies Caesar Markovich has given him, since he realizes that Alyoshka "can't earn."

Like Alyoshka, Spiridon in *The First Circle* also resembles Karatayev in that he is a peasant who often speaks in proverbs. Although Nerzhin's camp experiences have burned away his Romantic populism, he enjoys talking to Spiridon, as Pierre enjoys talking to Karatayev. But here, too, we find a tessera, an antithesis, and an explicit one at that. Nerzhin asks himself about Spiridon's long and difficult life, "Did this not agree somehow with the Tolstoyan truth that no one in the world is right and no one is guilty?" As Feuer notes, Spiridon denies that "truth," with his proverb-criterion (which rhymes in Russian), "The wolfhound is right, but the cannibal is not." Just as no Tolstoyan peasant could wish for the destruction of his own country, as Spiridon does later in this scene, so no Tolstoyan peasant could make a statement that implies an acceptance of violence as inherent in the human experience but also states a criterion for judging it.

Tolstoy's presence affects the narrative techniques of *One Day* as well as the characterizations. Although a great deal of the narration in *One Day* consists of Ivan Denisovich's thoughts and perceptions, we very soon find another authorial voice whose diction differs from that of this shrewd, semiliterate peasant, and is usually marked with parentheses. Solzhenitsyn takes over this narrative mode from Tolstoy, uses it frequently in *One Day*, occasionally in *The First Circle*, and the sporadically in *Cancer Ward* and *August 1914*. A few examples from *War and Peace* and *One Day* will suffice to demonstrate the effects.

In both works, parentheses often relate a general situation to a specific action or attitude. During the campaign of 1805, we learn,

> the senior officers [in Nikolay Rostov's regiment] occupied themselves with obtaining straw and potatoes, and in general with obtaining the means to feed the men; the junior officers occupied themselves, as always, some with cards (there was a lot of money, although there were no provisions), and some with innocent games—*svayka* and *gorodki*.

Analogously, when Shukhov returns to the warder's quarters to wash the floor,

> the Tarter was not there, but there were four warders; they had given up checkers and sleep, are were arguing about how much millet they would be given in January (the situation with produce was bad in the compound, and although potatoes had long since given out, the warders were sold certain produce separately from that of the compound, at a discount).

In the same scene, Ivan goes for water to wash the floor: "He picked up the bucket even without gloves (in his haste he had forgotten them under his pillow) and went to the well." Likewise, when Count Rostov dances with Marya Dmitryevna at Natasha's name-day, "Her enormous body stood straight, with her mighty arms lowered (she had given her reticule to the countess); only her stern, but beautiful, face alone danced."

Occasionally, this authorial voice appears without parentheses, to point out the self-deception of which people are capable. When Nikolay Rostov is telling Boris Drubetskoy and Berg about the battle at Schöngraben,

> he recounted to them his feat at Schöngraben precisely as people who have taken part in battles recount them, that is, as they would wish it had been, but not at all the way it was. Rostov was a truthful young man; he would not have said an untruth deliberately for anything.

Analogously, when Shukhov and the other zeks believe that the Moldavian is still working and is forcing them to wait in the cold, Shukhov becomes angry, like everyone else. "And it was strange to Shukhov that someone could work like that, without noticing the bell. Shukhov had quite forgotten that he himself had just been working like that—and had been annoyed that he had left for the watchtower too early."

The opposite of this technique, the narration of an event exclusively through the perception of a character who does not understand that event, also occurs in *War and Peace* and has become well known since Viktor Shklovsky gave it the name of *ostraneniye*, "estrangement." Natasha Rostov's visit to the opera provides a classic example. She has just come to the city from the country and has been treated rudely by Andrey's father and sister. She is depressed and impatient for Andrey's return, and she longs to see him. Hence, she perceives the opera in this way:

On the stage there were some boards in the middle; at the sides
there stood painted cardboards representing trees; in the back a
cloth was stretched on boards. In the middle of the stage sat
some girls in red bodices and white skirts. One very fat one, in
a white silk dress, sat to the side, on a low bench, to which a
green piece of cardboard was glued in the back. They were all
singing something.

This account of the opera continues for another paragraph, and then a
narrative commentary tells us, "After the country and in that serious mood
that Natasha was in, all this was strange and amazing to her." Her state of
mind makes her a temporary *naif*, but the recognition that the *naif* cannot
survive in the twentieth century is essential to Solzhenitsyn's clinamen with
Tolstoy, Bloom's term for the ephebe's swerve from his precursor. Hence,
estrangement occurs only once in Solzhenitsyn's work, presumably as an
experiment. As Natasha does not perceive the conventions of opera, so
Shukhov cannot recognize the conventions of poetry when he goes to the
camp clinic.

Shukhov took off his cap, as though before the authorities, and,
by the camp habit of letting his eyes go where they shouldn't,
couldn't help noticing that Nikolay was writing in real even lines,
and, going in from the edge, was beginning one line under
another with a capital letter. It was immediately comprehensible
to Shukhov, of course, that this was not work, but something on
the sly, which did not concern him.

Whereas Natasha's perceptions result from her state of mind, and are
temporary, Shukhov's express a more permanent fact, his lack of education.
    A final example of similarity in narrative technique involves the style of
the narrative itself, without regard for characterization. For moments of
particular intensity, Tolstoy uses anaphora to convey an experience to the
reader. As Andrey's regiment passes Bald Hills, we have this account:

The wagons, the artillery went along soundlessly up to the hub,
and the infantry up to the ankle, in the soft, suffocating, hot sand,
which had not cooled off overnight. One part of this sandy dust
was kneaded by legs and wheels; another part rose and stood like
a cloud over the army, getting into the eyes, into the hair, into the
ears, into the nostrils, and, mainly, into the lungs of the men and
animals that were moving along the road.

This passage provided the stylistic model for the following passage, in which the Tartar leads Ivan Denisovich to the barracks where he is to wash the floor. Note the analogous repetition of the same preposition with a series of different objects.

> Then when past the high board fence around the BUR [high security barracks]—that stone inner prison; past the barbed wire that protected the camp bakery from the prisoners; past the corner of the staff barracks where the frost-covered railroad tie, caught on a thick wire, hung on a pole; past another pole, where in a sheltered area, so as not to show too low, hung the thermometer.

In both cases, the heavy repetition reinforces our sense of the way the men's suffering goes on and on.

Even more significant than the presence of these borrowings from Tolstoy is their rarity. Something like estrangement occurs once in "Matryona's House," when the simple peasant woman listens to Chaliapin and says, "He sings funny, not in our way" but nowhere else in Solzhenitsyn. Likewise, the heavy, repetitive style occurs only three more times in Solzhenitsyn's fiction to date, and he uses it for highly charged material, such as Stalin's first appearance in *The First Circle*:

> On the little ottoman lay a man whose image had been sculpted, painted with oil, aquarel, gouache, sepia, sketched in charcoal, chalk, ground brick, composed of roadside pebbles, from sea shells, poured plate, from wheat grain and soy beans, carved on bone, grown from grass, woven on rugs, composed of airplanes, recorded on film—as no one else's has ever been over the three billion years of the existence of the earth's core.

The effects of Stalin's rule appear later, when we learn that at night boxcars took prisoners

> to Pechora, to Inta, to Vorkuta, to Sov-Gavan, to Norilsk; to the Irkutsk, Chita, Krasnoyarsk, Novosibirsk, Central Asian, Karadini, Dzhezkazgan, Pribalkashiya, Irtyshsk, Tobolsk, Ural, Saratov, Vyatsk, Vologda, Perm, Solvychegodsk, Rybinsk, Potma, Sukhobezvodnoya, and many other nameless little camps. In small groups, a hundred and two hundred at a time, they were taken during the day in truck beds to Serebryany Bor,

to New Jerusalem, to Pavshino, to Khovrino, to Beskudnikovo,
to Khimki, to Dmitrov, to Solnechnogorsk.

The final instance occurs in *Cancer Ward*, during Kostoglotov's first
x-ray treatment.

> And through the square of the skin of the belly left bare, and
> then through the layers and organs whose names the owner
> himself did not know, through the body of the tumor-toad,
> through the stomach or intestines, through the blood, going
> along the arteries and veins, through the lymph, through the
> cells, through the spine and the small bones, and through still
> more layers, vessels and the skin there on the back, then
> through the covering of the cot, the four-centimeter-thick
> boards of the floor, through the joists, through the fill, and
> further, further, going to the very stone foundation or into the
> earth—poured the unyielding x-rays, the quivering vectors of
> the electrical and magnetic fields unimaginable to the human
> mind, or the more understandable shell-quanta tearing apart
> and mincing everything in their way.

One Day thus begins the interplay of comparison and contrast with
Tolstoy which permeates Solzhenitsyn's major fiction. The setting in the
prison camp resembles the setting of Tolstoy's early war fiction in that it
presents a group of men isolated from society. The handling of the narrative,
which recounts events through the perception of a character, yet which also
includes authorial commentary, also has an unmistakably Tolstoyan quality.
Without this affinity, Solzhenitsyn's clinamen, or swerve, from his precursor
would have less effect and less meaning.

With few exceptions, Tolstoy limits his use of narrative insight to
nobles; he does not give us the thoughts of peasants (or of Napoleon or
Hélène Kuragin, for that matter), because he wants them to function as
symbols. Solzhenitsyn simply extends the use of narrative through a
character's perception to a peasant and will continue to extend that use of
insight to Stalin in *The First Circle* and Rusanov in *Cancer Ward*. It is difficult
to exaggerate the historical significance of Solzhenitsyn's persistent
psychologizing, since it works against the abstractions and symbols which
Tolstoy and Lenin created.

Other features of *One Day* seem more experimental, as though
Solzhenitsyn was clarifying to himself which features of Tolstoy he could
exploit for his own purposes. Solzhenitsyn never uses estrangement after *One*

Day, for example, and the heavy rhetoric of Tolstoy's sustained anaphora appears rarely in the major novels.

If Solzhenitsyn was using *One Day* to take stock of his relationship to Tolstoy, this may explain why he broke off work on *The First Circle* to write it; he couldn't both solve the novel's intimidating technical problems and come to terms with Tolstoy at the same time. He needed the more manageable demands of a novella with only one major character, for this purpose. Having written *One Day*, he could return to *The First Circle* and complete it.

The First Circle

Despite Tolstoy's importance in *One Day*, Solzhenitsyn never mentions him by name. He does mention Tolstoy by name in *The First Circle*, but the references have no particular consistency or structural significance. When, for instance, Gleb Nerzhin is arguing with Lev Rubin early in the novel, he comments approvingly, "When Lev Tolstoy hoped that he would be put in prison, he was reasoning like a real, seeing man with a healthy spiritual life." While Nerzhin admires the late Tolstoy, Shchagov has only contempt for him; annoyed at hearing a song that glorifies war correspondents, Shchagov says that they, like the late Tolstoy, were merely playing a role: "Even the boldest of the correspondents differed from the man at the front as irrevocably as a count plowing the earth from the peasant plowman." In still another place, when Professor Chelnov mentions Pierre's disdain at the French guard who would not let him go outside he does raise an important, Tolstoyan issue in *The First Circle*, but in doing so he also characterizes himself as a man who thinks seriously about the meaning of prison life in general; he later refers to Boethius's *On the Consolation of Philosophy*. Thus the meaning of the discussions of Tolstoy varies according to the speakers; the explicit comments tell us more about them than about Tolstoy's meaning for the novel as a whole. Only close analysis of the implicit references to Tolstoy in the characterization and narrative technique of *The First Circle* will deal with this more general issue.

It seem appropriate to begin consideration of the characters in *The First Circle* with Stalin. In his combination of egotism and brutality, he resembles Tolstoy's Nicholas I in *Hadji Murad*, of course, but he also resembles several characters in *War and Peace*. Feuer mentions one similarity to Napoleon in that both are *poseurs*; both believe that they create history with their slightest movement and thought. Moreover, both lack the common soldier's skills. "Having ridden up to Aleksandr, he [Napoleon] tipped his hat, and with this motion Rostov's cavalry man's eye couldn't help noticing that Napoleon sat poorly and uneasily on his horse." As for Stalin, he served briefly in the tsarist army, "but he had still not learned to roll up a greatcoat roll and load a rifle (he also didn't know how to later as commissar or marshal, and it was awkward to ask)." Stalin wears a field jacket, like Napoleon, and, planning World War III, thinks that "neither Napoleon nor Hitler could take Britain because they had an enemy on the Continent. But he would not have one."

Napoleon waits in vain for a delegation of *les boyards* on the outskirts of Moscow, and Stalin speaks fractured Russian; neither man knows or understands Russian life. This similarity suggests a continuity from Tolstoy to Solzhenitsyn in the opposition of Russians and non-Russians, between innocence and experience. But it is essential to Solzhenitsyn's tessera with Tolstoy that he break down the oppositions of nineteenth-century Russian literature—Russia and the West, Moscow and St. Petersburg, or the city and the country. In the electric age such oppositions do not exist, and in this respect Andrey Bely's *Kotik Letayev* (1918) forms a middle stage in the thematic development of the Russian novel from Tolstoy to Solzhenitsyn. *Kotik Letayev* was the first major Russian novel that generalized to Moscow the treatment of urban spaces as threatening and disturbing which previous Russian writers— and even Bely himself, in *Petersburg*—had reserved for St. Petersburg.

Since the opposition of Russians to non-Russians does not hold in Solzhenitsyn's work, Stalin resembles not only Napoleon, but also various Russians in *War and Peace*, such as Arakcheyev. When, for example, Andrey is waiting to see Arakcheyev in 1807, we learn that the faces of those in the reception room showed various emotions, "but as soon as the door [to Arakcheyev's office] opened, only one was momentarily expressed—fear." Abakumov waits alone to see Stalin in *The First Circle*, but he, too, experiences a common fear: "Coming here, this strapping, powerful man died from fear every time no less than citizens at night in the frenzy of arrests when they heard steps on the stairs."

Stalin resembles Andrey's father, Prince Nikolay Bolkonsky, in several respects. Both have, and exercise, great power; Bald Hills runs according to the prince's schedule, as Russia runs according to Stalin's. Both he and Stalin bully others and treat them capriciously because they are cowards, of course; but they cannot avoid their fear of sleep.

> One thing which disturbed Princess Marya was that he [old Prince Bolkonsky] slept little, and, having changed his habit of sleeping in his room, changed the place of his lodging every

night. Now he ordered his campaign bed set up in the gallery; now he remained on the divan or in the Voltaire arm chair in the living room and dozed without undressing while, not Mlle Bourienne, but the boy Petrushka read to him; now he spent the night in the dining room.

The first description of Stalin lying fully dressed on an ottoman and reading his own biography (old Bolkonsky writes his memoirs in *War and Peace*) surely derives from this passage, as does the statement that Stalin took various security measures: "And he had several bedrooms furnished, and he indicated where to make his bed just before he went to sleep." Bolkonsky's and Stalin's fear of other people expresses an alienation from the self, a sense notoriously difficult to avoid at night. As we will learn, *all* of the representatives of the government *apparat* have difficulty sleeping at night.

At the next level of power stand the Makarygins; their dinner party is played off against Natasha's name-day party in *War and Peace* and ultimately changes our perception of that scene. As Feuer points out, Makarygin insists that his male guests "must bow to the 'tobacco altar'—a collection kept in his study"; as in *War and Peace*, "Count [Rostov] led his male guests to his study, offering them his choice collection of Turkish pipes." In case the reader misses that clue, the narrative commentary offers another one; the Makarygins have records with patriotic songs, "but to listen to them here would have been as improper, as to talk seriously about the biblical miracles in the living rooms of nobles."

The Makarygins and the Rostovs spend their evening with their guests in remarkably similar ways. The older and younger generations separate; there is dancing, popular songs, and ice cream; there is talk of war, and of the glories of the past. One can interpret Natasha's name-day party as the last expression of the great days of the Russian aristocracy; when Count Rostov and Marya Dmitryevna dance the Daniel Cooper, "'That's how people danced in our time, *ma chere*,' the count said." Makarygin contrasts the past and the present, too, but in a different way. After describing a scene in which Klara questions whether he is a worker, Makarygin asks, "When we were chasing Kolchak, could we have thought that we would have such gratitude from our children?" Like the Rostovs, the Makarygins—the father and mother at least—accept unquestioningly the mores and standards of their society. Since this is the case, Makarygin can only respond to any questioning of the status quo with rage and threats. When Klara brings up the injustice of the large salary he makes and tells him that he is not really a worker, "barely restraining himself, in order not to hit his daughter, he ripped her shoe out of her hands, and slammed it on the floor: And *how* can you

compare! The party of the working class and the Fascist rabble?!"
Likewise, when Dushan Radović, a Serb, compares Yugoslavia and Russia,
he again becomes angry and threatens: "So the quasi-Fascist regime in
Yugoslavia is socialism? Does that mean that we have a degeneration? Old
phrases! We heard them long ago, only those who pronounced them are in
the next world."

Money and patriotism also cause anxiety for the Rostovs when they
have to think about them. When Count Rostov tells his clerk to bring five
hundred rubles, Mitenka first objects. "'Your excellency, when shall I get
them?' Mitenka said. 'Please know that . . . However, please don't get upset,'
he added having noticed that the count had already begun to breathe heavily
and often, which was always a sign of beginning anger. 'I was about to forget
. . . Shall I get them this minute?'" While in the army, Nikolay Rostov buys
a horse for twice what it is worth, gives away Denisov's money, and, of
course, loses forty-three thousand rubles to Dolokhov.

Potentially more ominous when we think of the subsequent evolution
of Russian history is Nikolay's need for approval and his inability to question
authority. When we first meet him at Natasha's name-day dinner, he is so
eager to conform to the spirit of the times that he overdoes it. When a
German colonel affirms his Russian patriotism and asks Nikolay's opinion,
Nikolay responds, "I completely agree with you," and adds, "I am convinced
that Russians must die or triumph." However, a narrative comment
undercuts this confident tone, adding that, like the others present, he felt
that "after the word had been said, . . . it was too solemn and overdone for
the present occasion and therefore awkward." Nikolay often feels this
conflict between his instincts and the attitudes of the people around him. As
Tolstoy's men often do, he needs to impose clearcut dichotomies on
experience; but experience keeps frustrating this need.

As a nation, the Russians neither die nor triumph in 1805, and the
ambiguities of the Peace of Tilsit therefore disturb Nikolay greatly.

> Now he remembered this self-satisfied Bonaparte with his white
> little hand who was not an emperor whom the emperor Aleksandr
> liked and respected. What were the torn-off arms, legs, the men
> killed for? Now he remembered Lazarev who had gotten a
> reward, and Denisov, punished and unforgiven. He found himself
> at such strange thoughts that he was afraid of them.

When two officers express just these "strange" thoughts, he becomes furious,
as Makarygin does, and replies in the same tone.

"How can you judge what would be better!" he shouted with a face that had suddenly become flushed. "How can you judge the acts of the emperor; what right have we to judge?! We cannot understand either the goal or the acts of the emperor!" The thing for us to do is do our duty, cut, and not think, that's all," he concluded.

There can be no doubt about the Russian here, for Nikolay says, "*Nashe delo . . . ne dumat'.*" Nikolay wishes to act spontaneously, without thinking, as his forebears had done; in effect, he is resisting what Eliot called the dissociation of sensibility into the dichotomy of thinking and feeling. Like the other Rostovs, Nikolay is committed to feeling. But he also needs the approval of others more than he cares to admit, and when "feeling," that is, traditional, formulaic responses to events, fails to evoke similar responses in his peers, he becomes violent. The problem, of course, is that as technology transformed the world in the nineteenth century, destroying traditional social structures, it became ever more necessary to "think." We now understand that the refusal to think renders a people incapable of opposing despotism, and that the nineteenth-century Romantic cult of feeling, which Nikolay represents here, is thus related to the rise of twentieth-century totalitarianism.

Makarygin offers a case in point. He would have wholeheartedly agreed with Nikolay's belief that "the thing for us to do is not think" and would have repeated it to Klara, if he had ever read *War and Peace*. Like Nikolay's fellow officers, Klara is guilty of thinking—of judging for herself and expressing openly the dichotomies that Russian official propaganda, both tsarist and Soviet, has always purported to resolve. People who lack the stability and emotional depth to confront these dichotomies can only resort to violence when others disagree with them, thereby voicing their own inner fears.

Thus, Nikolay Rostov and Pyotr Makarygin have a family resemblance, and thus, however much it goes against our tendency to think of Tolstoy as a champion of individual freedom, we must understand that he created in Nikolay the most representative apologist for Stalinism in Russian classical literature. To be sure, some of Dostoyevsky's characters are more eloquent, but they are discussing philosophical issues like freedom and morality. Nikolay is so very important because he represents the ordinary Russians who could not understand such intellectualizing, but whose attitudes allowed Stalinism to flourish.

In the first epilogue to *War and Peace*, which takes place in 1820, it becomes more difficult not to "think," and the Rostovs feel even more hostile towards those who do. A true Rostov, Natasha expresses her attitude toward Pierre's Decembrist activities like this: "'It's all nonsense, all trifles,' said Natasha. 'All his thoughts which lead to nothing, and all these foolish societies.'" And after Nikolay listens to Pierre's concerns about the government, he bursts forth with the most bloodthirsty attack on the right to individual conscience in Tolstoy.

> I can't prove it. You say that everything is bad with us and that there will be a revolution; I don't see it; but you say that the path [of allegiance] is a crime, and to that I'll say to you: That you are my best friend, you know that, but you create a secret society, you begin to act against society, whatever it may be like, I know that my duty is to obey it. And let Arakcheyev order me to attack you with a squadron and cut—I won't stop to think for a second and I'll go. And now judge as you wish.

The Rostovs' fear of thinking and judging as an individual is, in historical terms, a fear of fragmentation. But Rostov, like most Russian nationalists, ignores the fact that it was precisely the government which was carrying out a program of fragmentation, and had been doing so for a long time. These are the "strange" thoughts which he cannot admit to himself, but which Solzhenitsyn's characters can no longer avoid. Although Nikolay Rostov raves about cutting people up, he does not in fact do so (he beats the peasants, though); Makarygin has no such compunctions. The difference between them comes to the difference between a proto-Stalinist and a Stalinist; thus Solzhenitsyn works out the logical implications of the attitude that made Stalin possible, as Tolstoy himself could not do.

The *sharashka* in *The First Circle* represents a high degree of the fragmentation and mechanization of life which St. Petersburg society symbolizes in *War and Peace*. This mechanization appears most clearly in the salon of Anna Pavlovna Scherer, who regulates the conversation among her guests in the following manner:

> Like the foreman of a spinning mill who has placed the workmen at their places, and goes around the plant, noticing a spindle which has stopped, or the unusual, loudly speaking sound of a spindle, rushes over to check it or set it in proper motion—thus Anna Pavlovna went around her drawing-room, went up to a circle that had fallen silent, or was talking too much, and with a single word of rearrangement adjusted the steady, proper conversation machine.

In keeping with the more laconic style of *The First Circle*, and the absence in it of clear-cut oppositions, this simile appears in an abbreviated form when Solzhenitsyn takes it over:

> From this half-empty office, where the means of production consisted only of an iron book case with the prison *cases*, half a dozen chairs, a telephone and a call button, Lieutenant Colonel Klimentyev, without any visible linkage, control rods, or gear-wheels, successfully directed the external course of three hundred prisoners' lives, and the work of fifty guards.

Whereas Anna Pavlovna's salon represents only one of the poles in *War and Peace*, Klimentyev's office represents a microcosm of all of Russia; this fact surely helps account for the sustained intensity of *The First Circle*.

Despite the high intellectual level of the conversation and the presence of black bread on the tables, the *sharashka* is still a prison—Moscow Special Prison No. 1, to be precise. We therefore need to read Gleb Nerzhin's experience of prison against Pierre's in *War and Peace*. The effects of Nerzhin's prison experiences appear primarily in two places, in his meeting with his wife in the Lefort Prison and at the end of the novel. Gleb's wife "saw him quite new, quite unknown."

> "It agrees with you," she nodded sadly.
> "What agrees?"
> "In general, here. All this. To be here."

Mulling this over later, Nerzhin thinks:

> "It agrees with you here," she had said.
> It agreed with him to be in prison!
> It was the truth.
> Essentially he was not sorry for the five years spent in prison.
> Still not even moving away from them, Nerzhin had already recognized them as right for him, necessary for his own life.

Similarly, people notice that Pierre's prison experience has changed him for the better. "The change that had occurred in Pierre was noticed in their own way by his servants—Terenty and Vaska—as well. They found that he had become much simpler." We also have Natasha's testimony; she tells Princess Marya, "He has become pure, smooth, fresh; like from the bath, do you understand—morally from the bath. Right?"

However, the new Pierre differs in two ways from the new Nerzhin. Different as Pierre is from Nikolay, he, too, is a *naif*. "How good they all are," he thinks as he looks around him. He has food, servants, and money; he can easily think this, as Nerzhin never would. After the *sharashka*, it is not a life of ease but only something worse that awaits Nerzhin and the other zeks who are sent off:

> Yes, the taiga and the tundra; the cold pole of Oi-Myakon and the copper mines of Dzhezkazgan: The pick and the wheel barrow; the inadequate ration of soggy bread, the hospital, death awaited them.
> Only something worse awaited them.
> But in their souls there was peace with themselves. The fearlessness of people who have lost *everything* completely—a fearlessness which is achieved with difficulty, but permanently—possessed them.

It would never occur to Nerzhin to look around and say, "They are all good," because he has too much experience of the power of evil.

A satisfactory understanding of the context of Solzhenitsyn's use of prison requires a brief digression on the prison literature of nineteenth-century France. Although Solzhenitsyn himself knows very little about French literature, Tolstoy certainly knew, and drew on, Fabrice's experience of prison as a place of rebirth in Stendhal's *The Charterhouse of Parma*. And a reading of Victor Brombert's study *The Romantic Prison* makes it clear that many motifs from Stendahl and his contemporaries appear in *The First Circle*.

Although there is a reference in *The First Circle* to Hugo's *Ninety-three*, and Rubin is thrilled when he gets a chance to borrow a copy of *The Count of Monte Cristo*, most of the commonplaces of prison literature which Brombert conveniently lists derive from prison's dialectic of confinement and liberation, and do not require a specific source.

> The sordid cell and the hospitable cell, the cruelty of the jailors (but also the presence of the "good" jailor), glimpses of the landscape and the sky, the contrast between the ugliness of the "inside" and the supposed splendor of the surrounding scenery, prisons within the prison (the image of the iron mask), . . . the symbolism of the wall as an invitation to transcendence. . . . On the one hand, mental prowess and experimentation (geometric formulations formulated without the help of paper, imaginary

chess games); on the other hand, an outward reach, love at a distance (often for the jailor's daughter), conversations with the beloved (in fairy tales the beloved may be changed into a bird!), a movement of the mind toward the outside which makes the prisoner reinvent communication.

Virtually all of these motifs appear in various ways in *The First Circle*. Nerzhin, for instance, experiences love at a distance from both his wife and from Simochka; both he and Rubin certainly exert their "mental prowess," and so forth.

The following comment by Brombert about prison literature deserves particular attention: "The image of the bird seems favored, perhaps because it lends itself to a fundamental ambiguity. For the bird, in its free flight, brings to mind the cage from which it might have escaped, the cage that awaits it, the cage that it perhaps regrets." Although this is not the place to discuss in detail Solzhenitsyn's frequent use of bird imagery in *The First Circle*, a couple of quotations may give a sense of his skillful use of this highly traditional image. With regard to the vain attempt of the prisoners' wives to seek legal aid: "The helpless women walked back and forth in front of the concrete wall of the law as they did before the wall of Butyrka, four times as thick as a man is tall—there were no wings to take off and flutter across it; it remained only to bow at any little gate which opened." And, as Innokenty Volodin is led off to his first interrogation, "Innokenty put his hands behind him and with his head thrown back, as a bird drinks water, came out of the box."

Yet, to continue a tradition, one must renew it. For Brombert's nineteenth-century Romantics, prison meant isolation and idleness. Stalin's prisoners had to exert themselves totally to earn a little gruel and a slice of bread, and they were kept in isolation only during the investigation, sometimes not even then. Consider this scene from *The Gulag Archipelago* which Solzhenitsyn recounts from the memoirs of Ivanov-Rasumnik. The year is 1938.

> In Lubyanka's reception "dog cell," he calculated that for whole weeks, there was 1 square meter for THREE persons (try it, stand like that!); in the dog cell there was no window or ventilation, from the bodies and breathing the temperature was 40–45 degrees [C.] (!); everyone had on only their underwear (having put their winter things under them); the naked bodies were pressed together, and from the sweat of others, the skin developed eczema.

The constant experience of feeling part of a herd made the nineteenth-century experience of prison as isolation meaningless for Russians. Nerzhin needs to be alone after seeing his wife,

> but it was precisely the chance to be alone that there was none of in the *sharashka*, as in any camp. Always, there were cells, and freight cars for prisoners, and cattle cars, and camp barracks, and hospital wards—and people, people, everywhere you went; strangers and people close to you, subtle people and crude people, but always people, people.

Thus, a little later, the narrative commentary gives us his musings on the irrelevance of nineteenth-century prison literature in the age of the banality of evil:

> In the description of prisons people have always tried to lay the horrors on thick. But is it not more horrible when there is no horror? When the horror is in the grayish methodicalness of weeks? In the fact that you forget: the only life given to you on earth is broken. And you're ready to forgive; you've already forgiven the blockheads. And your thoughts are occupied with grabbing, not a middle piece, but an end piece of bread from the prison tray, how to get underwear that isn't torn and isn't too small in the periodic prison bath.

> It is necessary to experience all this. One cannot make it up. In order to write
>
> > I sit behind bars, in a damp dungeon
>
> or—open the dungeon, give me the dark-eyed maiden—it's hardly necessary to be in prison at all; it's easy to imagine everything. But this is primitive. Only with the continuous, endless years is the true feeling of prison acquired.

The line "I sit behind bars, in a damp dungeon" comes from Pushkin's "The Prisoner" (1822), and the line "Open the dungeon" and the reference to the "dark-eyed maiden" come from Lermontov's poem of the same name (1837). These, then, are works contemporary with those which Brombert discusses, and they emphasize still further the irrelevance for *The First Circle* of the nineteenth century's use of prison as isolation, which is so consistent with the Romantic cult of the individual. This matter of the "true feeling" has to do with the psychology of the prison experience and does not exhaust Solzhenitsyn's treatment of prison, which also has a metaphysics. But a consideration of the metaphysics of the prison experience will have its proper place in the discussion of Solzhenitsyn's relationship to Dostoyevsky.

Let us now return to the specific affinities between *War and Peace* and *The First Circle* by considering the first three sentences of Solzhenitsyn's novel:

> The fretwork hands showed 4:05.
> In the dying December afternoon the bronze of the clock on the little étagère was quite dark. The panes of the high window began right at the floor.

These three simple declarative sentences state the three major motifs in the presentation of Andrey Bolkonsky in *War and Peace*—darkness, clocks, and windows. Their appearance in the description of Volodin's office makes him a prime example of Solzhenitsyn's tessera with Tolstoy. By tessera, we recall, Bloom means completion and antithesis: "A poet antithetically 'completes' his precursor, by so reading the parent-poem as to retain its terms but to mean them in another sense, as though the precursor had failed to go far enough." In Volodin, Solzhenitsyn retains the terms, or motifs, of Tolstoy's presentation of Andrey, but means them in another sense by making Volodin less haughty and brittle then Andrey.

As part of old Bolkonsky's rigidity, "His appearances at the table took place under one and the same unchangeable conditions, and not only at one and the same hour, but minute as well." Hence, when Andrey and his wife arrive at Bald Hills, "he looked at his watch, as though to check whether his father's habits had changed during the time he hadn't seen him, and, convinced that they hadn't changed, turned to his wife." A window or door often frames Andrey, and often does so at night, as when he listens to Natasha sing or when he broods on history before the Battle of Borodino. Andrey is associated with the darkness because he is doomed, of course.

The motifs of the window, the darkness, and the watch reappear in the excruciatingly minute accounts of Innokenty's first night in Lubyanka, which is all the more excruciating since, as with the descriptions of Ivan Denisovich's day, we realize that it represents the experience of millions. In one of the numerous "boxes" which he occupies, Innokenty thinks, "How necessary a window was here;—even the smallest one, even one such as they put in opera sets for prison cellars—but there was not even that." And, while he is rethinking Epicurus,

> a foolish thought now wedged itself into his head, pushing out the serious ones: his watch was put in storage; it would run until it ran down, then stop—and no one would wind it anymore, and

with this position of the hands it would wait either for the death of the owner or its confiscation along with the rest of his property. The interesting thing was, what time would it then show?

Like Andrey, Innokenty is doomed from the beginning, and he interests us, as Andrey does, because he is half in, and half out of, his society, an attitude which his posture at the window succinctly images: "Seeing all this, and not seeing all this, state councillor of the second rank Innokenty Volodin, leaning against the edge of the window molding, whistled something subtle and long." Although Innokenty's father was a revolutionary, his mother was an esthete; he has succeeded in Soviet society, but he is not entirely of it. "A state councillor of the second rank, which meant a lieutenant colonel of diplomatic service, tall, thin, not in a uniform, but in a suit of supple cloth, Volodin seemed more a well-to-do young idler than a responsible member of the ministry of foreign affairs."

As with Andrey, the ambiguity within him manifests itself in his discomfort with his wife, who cannot understand it. The wives enjoy the social gatherings, while their husbands do not; Andrey goes unwillingly to Anna Pavlovna's soiree, as Innokenty goes unwillingly to the Makarygin's dinner party. Both men undertake something dangerous (a military campaign, a phone call) that radically changes their lives, not simply to avoid their wives, but to assuage a deeper malaise. Andrey's trip to the Rostov's estate gives him a spiritual rebirth, if only a temporary one; but Innokenty's trip to the countryside with Klara in the chapter "In the Open" has no effect at all. After death comes through the door in Andrey's famous death scene, he belongs to the next world, not this one; as Innokenty's long night in Lubyanka comes to an end, he begins a new life, but one that we know well, and one that is definitely of this world.

Since he married a Makarygin, Volodin has a tenuous connection to the Rostovs, and we need to read the chapter "An Uncle in Tver" against the visit that Nikolay and Natasha make to their uncle in the countryside. Nikolay and Natasha visit their uncle after the hunt scene; when we read, "In the entranceway there was a smell of fresh apples, and wolf and fox skins were hanging," we realize that his house is the most complete symbol of the natural life in the novel. Natasha enjoys food intensely, as Tolstoy's characters always do when a natural man offers it. (Their uncle refuses government service and lives with his peasant housekeeper.) Natasha also sings while he plays the balalaika. But whereas Tolstoy's characters search for nature (with varying degrees of success), Solzhenitsyn's discover the past in the form of the printed word. Whereas Nikolay and Natasha's uncle hangs wolf and fox skins in his house, Innokenty's uncle hangs newspapers in his: "The 'rugs' were old yellowed dusty newspapers for some reason, they were hung everywhere, in many layers: the panes of the cabinets and the buffet niche, the tops of the windows, the areas behind the stove were covered with them."

Nikolay and Natasha's uncle refuses government service, the only employment possible for a noble at that time, so that he can live with nature; Innokenty's uncle refuses government service, the only employment available to anyone, so that he can live with history. "These yellow newspapers, hung in many layers as though against the sun or dust, were a means of noncriminal preservation of the most interesting old pronouncements." Over the stove, for example, hangs a statement by Stalin from 1940: "'I know that the German people loves its *Führer*; therefore, I raise a toast to his health!'"

In the preceding chapter, "But Conscience Is Given Only Once, Too," which prepares Innokenty for the encounter with his uncle, he discovers his mother's letters, diaries, and books from the period just before the Revolution. 'Innokenty discovered that he was a savage who had grown up in the cave of social studies, in the skins of the class struggle." He also finds out that his mother had loved another man, which is consistent with his uncle's hint that his father raped his mother. Discussing the Bolsheviks' use of force at the Constituent Assembly, in which Innokenty's father participated, the uncle says, "And almost at the very time when [your] mama . . . gave in to him . . . They very much liked to enjoy nice girls from good houses. It was in that they saw the sweetness of the Revolution." Thus, personal history and political history merge in Innokenty's life.

It is appropriate that his uncle's question, paraphrased from Herzen, "Why must the love of one's country be extended to any of its governments?" is Innokenty's last thought given in the novel. As he goes off to his first interrogation, he thinks, "Why must the love of one's native land be exten . . . ?" This unfinished question, meaningful to him now that he has disavowed his former life, and the epicureanism that justified it, occurs to him in Lubyanka; this question in turn implies another of his uncle's searching questions, the one that concludes the chapter "An Uncle from Tver": "And have you never felt the rightness of the truth: the sins of the parents fall on their children?" When Nikolay and Natasha visit their uncle, they find a reinforcement of what they are and an anticipation of their future married lives in the countryside. By completion and antithesis, Innokenty visits his uncle, only to find evidence of his own ignorance and guilt.

Throughout the chapters that recount Volodin's arrest and first night in Lubyanka, there appears a less explicit but more strongly ironic version of the authorial voice that called attention to Shukhov's inconsistencies in *One Day*. When a confused and disordered Volodin looks at the ventilation hole in the ceiling of his cell, he thinks of the Nazi concentration camps.

> And suddenly it clearly occurred to him that this ventilation hole was not a ventilation hole at all, but [that] poison gas was slowly being admitted, perhaps processed by that buzzing machine, that the gas had been coming in since the very minute he had been locked in here, and that such a restrictive cell with a door fitting flush to the threshold was intended for no other purpose!

Although the absence of quotation marks means that this statement is not a quotation, the exclamation mark gives it an emotional intensity. Thus we have here a narrative mode that Wayne Booth did not consider in *The Rhetoric of Fiction*—not an unreliable narrator but narration that has itself become unreliable. The narration has merged with the thoughts of the character, but our knowledge of his naïveté prevents us from giving full credence to it, as we ordinarily would. It turns out, of course, that Volodin's fear of being gassed is post–World War II paranoia, and his assumptions, such as his assumption that he will be interrogated immediately, repeatedly prove false. This set of chapters has a certain grim black humor about it, as his depersonalizing experiences disabuse him of his Romantic notions about prison.

The authorial voice, marked by parentheses, appears frequently in these chapters and hardly anywhere else in the novel to indicate the difference between his perception and a hardened zek's perception. For instance:

> Four showers were offered for one man!—but Innokenty did not feel any joy (if he had known that in the world of zeks four men usually washed under one shower, he would have appreciated more his sixteen-fold advantage.) He had disgustedly thrown away the repulsive stinking soap issued to him (in thirty years of life he had not held any soap like that in his hand, and had not even known that such soap existed) in the locker room.

The irony appears in other ways as well, such as his "rediscovery" of sewing, and humanizes Innokenty. It also makes us empathize with him and admire his courage as he goes off to his first interrogation.

The near-identity of the narration with Shukhov's perception in *One Day* limits the possibilities of the technique, and we find more variety in the narration of the much longer *First Circle*. Here the narration occasionally makes universal statements about human nature. When Ruska Doronin becomes a double agent, he feels isolated, "and, as always happens, when we lose the good disposition of people, he who continues to love us becomes triply dear." Any reader of Tolstoy recognizes the master's voice in this matching of specifics and universals. When, in *War and Peace*, Mademoiselle Bourienne and Princess Marya grow excited at the arrival of Anatol Kuragin, "as it always happens for lonely women who have lived a long time without male company, all three women in Prince Nikolay Andreyvich's house uniformly felt that their lives had not been life until that time."

Thus, writing (and periodically rewriting) *The First Circle* meant that Solzhenitsyn could begin to come to terms with Tolstoy and the societal meaning of the Tolstoyan heritage. In this novel, whose final version is about half as long as *War and Peace*, he uses a number of his precursor's narrative and stylistic techniques, so that one who knows Tolstoy well feels the master's presence in every scene. Only someone who took the dangerous step of letting Tolstoy permeate his style—in Bloom's terms, "The later poet opens himself"—only someone who has taken this chance of being overpowered by the brute force of Tolstoy's genius in this way can complete the work of tessera, or antithesis.

Solzhenitsyn's tessera with Tolstoy proceeds primarily by showing the dangers of Tolstoy's ubiquitous opposition of innocence and experience. When the innocence of the Rostovs in *War and Peace* reappears as the Makarygins' complacent denial of moral responsibility, it forces us to reinterpret the meaning of the Rostovs. Similarly, we read the Bolkonskys anew after Solzhenitsyn makes Stalin resemble old Bolkonsky, and Innokenty Volodin, Andrey; whereas both Bolkonskys die in *War and Peace*, neither Stalin nor Volodin dies in *The First Circle*. Coming to terms with the precursor and creating an apophrades in this manner meant a great deal for Solzhenitsyn; of course, *The First Circle* was only a partial tessera—all tesserae probably are—and Solzhenitsyn would have to take on Tolstoy ever more explicitly in *August 1914*, his response to *War and Peace*. But in 1963 he was free to open himself to Dostoyevsky in *Cancer Ward*. In the next chapter I will argue that *Cancer Ward* uses primarily Dostoyevskyan techniques (to some extent, the same holds for Tolstoy's second major novel, *Anna Karenina*); still, we will find some of Tolstoy in any of Solzhenitsyn's major works, and *Cancer Ward* is no exception.

Cancer Ward

Like *The First Circle*, *Cancer Ward* takes place in an enclosed, isolated setting, begins with the arrival of new people, and ends with a departure. The *sharashka*, with its guards and prisoners, corresponds in a general way to the hospital, with its doctors and patients. Kostoglotov even thinks, as he leaves the hospital, "This departure from the hospital gates—in what way is it not like a departure from prison gates?" Consequently, one notices a certain continuity between the two novels in that the beginning of *Cancer Ward* resembles some chapters toward the end of *The First Circle*. "The cancer ward would be number thirteen." Thus *Cancer Ward* begins with Rusanov's admission to the hospital; the first and second chapters are narrated for the most part through his perception. The account of Rusanov's indignation at the lack of respect shown him, and his final submission to the rules of the institution, follows, point for point, Volodin's reaction to Lubyanka—even to the fact that neither of them is able to turn out the glaring electric light and go to sleep. An awareness of this similarity gives a comic touch to the frustration of this man who has sent so many people to Lubyanka and other prisons.

Still, substantial differences remain between *The First Circle* and *Cancer Ward*; the characters of *Cancer Ward* are not intense intellectuals, and the government is not holding them against their will. They discuss literature, often uncertainly; they never parody it. If *The First Circle* is not more specific (in dealing with the horrors of Stalinism) and more general (in its discussions of art and the human condition), *Cancer Ward* has greater directness in its treatment of the personal concerns of love and death.

As a result of these differences, the treatment of Tolstoy's life and work in *Cancer Ward* differs considerably from that in *The First Circle*. Here it is not so much *War and Peace* that informs the novel as the later works about love and death: *Anna Karenina*, *The Death of Ivan Ilyich*, and the short story "What Men Live By" (1881). A second major difference is that Tolstoy's presence has become much more explicit. Chapter 20, for instance, deals with Kostoglotov's place of exile, Ush-Terek, where his friend Doctor Kadmin "had taken from his father, a transportation engineer, a thirst for constant activity and love for accuracy and order." These attitudes immediately remind us of old Prince Bolkonsky in *War and Peace*, of course. And, remarkably, the narrative commentary makes the comparison explicit: "Nikolay Ivanovich [Kadmin] sets out the tenth of a hectare of his garden with as much deliberation and energy as old Prince Bolkonsky with all of Bald Hills and his own architect." Solzhenitsyn had never before used Tolstoy so openly in the narrative; paradoxical as it may seem, he could only write like this about Tolstoy after he had proved his mettle against him in *The*

First Circle. Only an artist who believes in his own strength and independence can open his work to the precursor in this way.

In chapter 8, "What People Live By," Yefrem Podduyev, a construction worker, reads Tolstoy's didactic story of the same name (published in 1881), after noting the titles of several others from the same period. Podduyev has never read anything serious before and is very taken with the simplicity and directness of this parable, based on an Old Church Slavonic source. The story concerns one Mikhaylitsa, an angel sent to earth for disobeying God until he learns "what is in people, what is not given to people, and what people live by." At the end of the story, he solves the middle part of the riddle: "I understood that God didn't want people to live separately, and thus did not reveal to them what everyone needs for himself, but wanted them to live as one, and thus revealed to them what they all need for themselves and for everyone." It turns out that "what is in people" is love, and "what people live by" is love for others.

Podduyev asks the other patients how they would answer the question of "what people live by"; some answer haltingly, but Rusanov answers quickly and confidently, "There can be no doubt about it. Remember this. People live: by ideological orientation and the social good." The ambiguity of the relationship between Tolstoy and Lenin appears again when Yefrem thinks that there is a certain similarity between this answer, and the moral of the story, which is that people live by their love of others.

This conversation reverberates throughout the whole novel, especially whenever the topic is the nature of love. For instance, Solzhenitsyn's Asya, a tour de force in characterization who is a twentieth-century version of Turgenev's heroine of the same name, responds as confidently as Rusanov did when Dyomka mentions the discussion of Tolstoy in the men's ward. Asya thinks of the question as a topic for a composition in school; she, too, believes that people live for love, but it soon becomes clear that she really means sex. As she says, "Why put it off—it's the atomic age!"

On the other hand, Yelizaveta Anatolyevna, a woman from Leningrad who was deported during the thirties, wishes she had a chance to live for love.

> Children in schools write compositions: on the unhappy, tragic, ruined, and I don't know what else life of Anna Karenina. But was Anna unhappy? She chose passion—and paid for passion, that's happiness! She was a free and proud person! But if soldiers' overcoats and hats in peacetime come into the house where you were born and have lived since birth, and order your whole family to leave this house and this city with only what your weak arms can carry away?

When Yelizaveta Anatolyevna asks, "Why should I reread *Anna Karenina*?" she is, ironically, turning on Anna the situation in which Anna finds herself during her train ride back to St. Petersburg from Moscow early in the novel. Disturbed by the impression Vronsky has made on her, she seeks distraction in an English novel: "Anna Arkadyevna read and understood, but it was unpleasant for her to read, that is to follow the reflection of the life of other people. She wanted to live too much herself." The need for immediacy destroyed Anna, as it did many Russians who impulsively spoke out after the Revolution. Yelizaveta Anatolyevna knows better than to seek immediate release in life; the situation has come full circle, for she seeks in books other than *Anna Karenina* that which Anna had sought in life.

Recommend *Anna Karenina* contains two prototypes for Rusanov: Aleksey Karenin and Stiva Oblonsky. Feuer calls Rusanov "the Soviet true believer," and says that he "follows each step trod by Ivan Ilyich, yet in his encounter with the unknown he also recalls Tolstoy's other great bureaucrat, Karenin." Feuer perceptively juxtaposes the following quotations from *Anna Karenina* and *Cancer Ward*:

> Aleksey Aleksandrovich [Karenin] was confronted with life . . . and this seemed meaningless and incomprehensible to him, because it was life itself. All his life he had lived and worked in official spheres, which deal only with reflections of life.

> And . . . Rusanov, caught unawares by this stealthy approach of death, not only could not fight it, but he could not in general think or decide or say anything about it in any way. It came illegally, and there was no rule, no set of instructions which would defend Pavel Nikolayevich.

But once we accept that Ivan Ilyich and Rusanov share a common situation—both are bureaucrats who have fallen seriously ill—we realize that they have hardly anything in common. Tolstoy and Solzhenitsyn develop the same situation in radically different ways.

Ivan Ilyich's illness increases his already substantial alienation from his wife and family; Pavel Nikolayevich's illness provides the occasion for his wife and his daughter Avieta to show how they respect him and stand by him. Ivan Ilyich, following the general pattern for Tolstoy's alienated men, meets a peasant (Gerasim, in this case), is purged of his alienation through suffering, and dies. Rusanov, however, fails to encounter anyone in the ward who is sufficiently sympathetic (that is, submissive), suffers little discomfort, and leaves with his cancer in remission. In fact, he feels well enough to tell

his son to pretend to run down Kostoglotov. Whereas in Tolstoy, Ivan
Ilyich's illness forces him to come to terms with himself, Rusanov's illness
inconveniences him more than anything else. (However, Dr. Dontsov hints
that his cancer may still turn out to be terminal.)

But Karenin and Ivan Ilyich are not Tolstoy's only bureaucrats.
Although not a bureaucrat in spirit, Stiva Oblonsky is a bureaucrat in fact,
and he shares a habit with Rusanov, one that has more to do with Russian
ambivalence about literacy than with individual personalities. Early in *Anna
Karenina*, we learn that Stiva reads his paper with the ready intuition that
makes him Anna's brother:

> With the quickness of understanding unique to him, he
> understood the significance of every dig at someone; from whom
> and at whom and on what occasion it was directed; and this, as
> always, gave him a certain satisfaction.

Over three generations later, the Russian newspaper has still not become a
genuinely democratic medium:

> He [Rusanov] experienced nothing else than jealousy if someone
> else before him unfolded a fresh newspaper with uninitiated
> fingers. No one among them could understand what Pavel
> Nikolayevich understood in the newspaper. He understood the
> newspaper as an openly disseminated, but in fact coded set of
> instructions, where it was impossible to say everything directly,
> but where a knowledgeable man, by various little signs, by the
> arrangement of the articles, by what was not pointed out and
> omitted could put together an accurate conception of the latest
> direction.

Since both Oblonsky and Rusanov read the newspaper in similar ways, this
constancy enables us to distinguish between the kinds of innocence which
the two men represent.

In his beguiling way, Oblonsky reacts to the events he reads about in the
newspaper in personal terms: "The liberal party said that everything in Russia
was bad, and, really, Stepan Arkadyevich had many debts, but there was
definitely not enough money." Oblonsky is Tolstoy's greatest innocent, a man
who is completely impervious to the effects of his philandering and profligacy
on others: "He could not now repent of the fact that he, a thirty-four-year-old,
handsome, loving man, was not in love with his wife. . . . He repented only of
the fact that he had not been able to hide it better from his wife."

In a way which characterizes an essential difference between Tolstoy and Solzhenitsyn, Rusanov retains Stiva Oblonsky's attitudes, while applying them to society. Like Tolstoy's characters in general, Rusanov cares passionately about public affairs. Unlike Stiva, he is a perfectly proper bourgeois husband and father who would never think of being unfaithful to his wife and who always has plenty of money. What *he* cannot understand (that is, concern himself with) is the effect of his work on others. He cannot repent of the social injustices that he has committed, any more than Stiva can repent of his infidelity; like Stiva, he repents only that he didn't know how to hide it better. In the chapter "And Shades, Too" he fears that a man will return from the camps to denounce him.

Hence, Rusanov can say to Podduyev with complete sincerity (like Stiva, he is always sincere): "But one must resist evil, fellow, one must struggle with evil." The stroke of genius on Solzhenitsyn's part comes in placing this statement at the conclusion of the discussion of Tolstoy's theory of nonviolence. Solzhenitsyn here pits two of Tolstoy's many varieties of innocence against each other; he opposes Stiva Oblonsky's innocence about the effects of his actions on others, an innocence hardly distinguishable from irresponsibility, to Tolstoy's way of absolving himself of responsibility for the evil in the world by proclaiming nonviolence as a form of withdrawal from the world. Rusanov cites Lenin and Gorky as his authorities for denouncing Tolstoy: "There was a lot, a whole lo-ot that he didn't understand."

No discussion of Tolstoy's importance for *Cancer Ward* would be complete with out some mention of the treatment of medicine. Writing in the tradition of Molière's *The Imaginary Invalid*, Tolstoy consistently makes doctors look like pretentious fools; after the doctor examines Kitty in *Anna Karenina* (to her extreme embarrassment); a "consilium" takes place. "And the famous doctor set forth his plan of treatment with Soden waters, for the prescribing of which the principal purpose, obviously, was that they couldn't do any harm." And the same pretentious, unsympathetic "famous doctor" appears in "The Death of Ivan Ilyich": "Just as he [Ivan Ilyich] put on appearances before defendants, so the famous doctor put on appearances." Tolstoy's ubiquitous system of oppositions distinguishes his treatment of medicine from Molière's; however, Tolstoy opposed folk medicine to Western medicine. The dying woman in "Three Deaths" thinks that perhaps some herbs could be found which would do her more good than a trip to Europe. And in *The Cossacks*, Yeroshka makes the opposition explicit.

> No sir, I would have hanged your Russian doctors long ago if I were tsar. They don't know how to do anything but cut. So they made our Cossack Baklashev a nonperson, they cut his leg off.

They must be fools. What is Baklashev good for now? No sir, there's real doctors in the mountains. So when my nurse Gurchika was wounded in this place, in the chest your doctors wouldn't do a thing for her, but Saib came out of the mountains, and healed her. Yes sir, they know the herbs.

Possibly because Tashkent is close to the Caucasus, the surgeon Yevgeniya Ustinovna recalls Yeroshka's words, regretting that all that she, too, can do is cut.

Kostoglotov, suspicious as always, resembles Yeroshka in that he is interested in two forms of folk medicine even while in the hospital. He brings a mixture of issyk-kul root and vodka to the hospital but pours it out when Vega insists. Far more interesting is the fungus on birch trees that seemed to prevent cancer. Kostoglotov has read about the properties of this fungus, and tells everyone in the ward about it. Like cancer patients everywhere, they are eager to learn about a new remedy, and request the address of one Dr. Maslennikov, who has championed the use of the fungus. But Dyoma asks a discouraging question: How are they to get any of the fungus when birch trees do not grow in Tashkent? At this point, the narrative commentary recasts the issue as one of homesickness, not cancer. "People living at home do not always understand their native land; they want a bright blue sea and bananas, but this is what a man needs: the ugly black fungus on the white birch tree, its disease, its tumor." One senses that Kostoglotov is suffering from the disease of being cut off from Russia, as well as from cancer, and believes that the symbolic birch tree can cure him of both.

In effect, Solzhenitsyn softens Tolstoy's opposition between Western medicine and folk medicine because his doctors are such good, conscientious people. (To this difference corresponds the always crucial difference in narrative technique: we never have insight into the minds of Tolstoy's doctors, but we usually have insight into the minds of Solzhenitsyn's doctors.) To be sure, Solzhenitsyn's doctors have their quirks and individual differences, but they are not quacks, and they certainly are not indifferent to their patient's feelings, as Tolstoy's doctors are. We have here the most distinct case of the change from Tolstoy's fear of science and professionalism (What *would* Tolstoy have thought of women doctors!), and Solzhenitsyn's respect for science.

One can explain Tolstoy's hostility to medicine in purely aesthetic terms. When his men fall ill, they consistently experience a transcendence, which they could not do if a doctor were to alleviate their suffering. After Andrey's dream in which death comes through the door, "He experienced a consciousness of alienation from everything earthly, and a joyous and strange lightness of being." Suffering produces similar effects in Andrey and Pierre, because in Tolstoy suffering always has a teleological character.

Not so in Solzhenitsyn, who sometimes presents suffering as suffering and nothing more. He says nothing at all about the psychic state of Sharaf Sibgatov, whose experience resembles Andrey's:

> It was no longer possible to guess what Sharaf Sibgatov had been like earlier; there was nothing to judge by: his suffering has lasted so long that it was as though nothing remained from his former life. But after three years of continuous disease this young Tartar was the gentlest, most polite person in the whole clinic.

Although there is a certain similarity to Andrey's situation here, the purely external description does not give the slightest hint that Sibgatov has undergone a spiritual transformation as a result of his suffering. In the "more cruel" twentieth century, even greater and more prolonged suffering than Andrey's does not suffice to produce transcendence, only meekness.

Nevertheless, symbols of death and resurrection have a strong appeal for Russian writers. After Prince Andrey has visited the Rostovs' estate, and heard Natasha sing in the night, he sees and old oak tree that had leafed out during his stay.

> Juicy young leaves without twigs had broken through the hard, century-old bark, so that one could not believe that this old fellow had produced them. "That's the same oak," thought Prince Andrey, and a causeless, springlike feeling of joy and renewal descended upon him.

Solzhenitsyn gives us his variant of this symbolic oak tree in the apricot tree which Kostoglotov sees during his day in Tashkent.

> And then from the balcony of the tea-shop he say above a closed hidden courtyard a transparent dandelion, only it was six meters in diameter—a weightless ethereal pink ball. . . . He gave it to himself—for his creation day.

In both cases, the tree represents a state of mind evoked by a woman—Natasha and Vega, respectively—and in both cases the sense of renewal proves illusory. Andrey does not marry Natasha, and Kostoglotov chooses not to stay with Vega. Both trees refer to moods, rather than permanent states.

Cancer Ward thus continues Solzhenitsyn's engagement with Tolstoy and his legacy. He treats Tolstoy's innocents in a wonderfully sly way—by having them enter the government. As the Makarygins offer a comment on the Rostovs of *War and Peace*, so Rusanov offers a comment on Stiva Oblonsky of *Anna Karenina*. In addition to these implicit relationships, Solzhenitsyn opens his work far more to Tolstoy than in *The First Circle* by allowing his characters to discuss Tolstoy and quote him extensively. In this way, *Cancer Ward* leads logically to *August 1914*, which is suffused with references to Tolstoy and even with Tolstoy's presence.

August 1914

One cannot adequately discuss the relationships between *August 1914* and *War and Peace* without some reference to the other novels, both Russian and non-Russian, which have dealt in varying ways with World War I. This topic deserves extensive treatment in its own right, but a few general remarks must suffice here. During the decade 1914–24, time went radically out of joint for Russians, and writers have made numerous attempts to set it right. Russian novels that deal in various ways with the connection between the world before and after 1914 include Aleksey Tolstoy's *The Road to Calvary* (1921), Mikhail Sholokhov's *The Quiet Don* (1928–40), Konstantin Fedin's *Early Joys* (1945–46), and Boris Pasternak's *Doctor Zhivago* (1958). Of these, *The Quiet Don* most resembles *August 1914*; not coincidentally, Solzhenitsyn has attacked the novel as a plagiarism, at least in part, and we may expect fictional reactions to Sholokhov in subsequent volumes.

However, the revolution confused and dissipated the meaning of World War I for Russians. Instead of the despair and disillusionment that followed the Great War in Europe, the revolution evoked enthusiasm and hope for a better future in at least some Russians; the censorship filtered out all but the most muted expressions of pessimism. As a result, the war has had no meaning in and of itself in Russian literature. In treating the war as an ominous harbinger of the future in *August 1914*, Solzhenitsyn is both reversing the usual Soviet treatment and assimilating his novelistic treatment of it to that of Western literature.

It is as though Russians had to go through the cycle of initial enthusiasm and then bitter disenchantment twice—first with World War I and then with Stalinism. As Norman Stone says, "The First World War had not been the short outburst of patriotic sacrifice that men had expected. It became, instead, a first experiment in Stalinist tactics for modernisation." Perhaps Stone overstates the case here, but the survivors of Stalinism certainly felt a disenchantment and a bitterness that resemble the feelings of those who survived the Great War. This resemblance may explain Solzhenitsyn's attraction to the only two foreign writers who have significantly affected his work, Hemingway and Dos Passos: they were among the vehement representatives of the skepticism and disaffection, the distrust of abstract ideals, that characterized so many intellectuals, both American and European, after the Great War. Their responses to the contrast between the senseless, prolonged suffering and the optimism in the press during the war closely anticipated Solzhenitsyn's response to the same contrast during Stalinism.

In fact, a reading of Stanley Cooperman's *World War I and the American Novel* shows that *August 1914* recapitulates many of the themes predominating in American novels about the Great War. Cooperman notes that the merger of nationalism and religion appears again and again in them as an object of derision and scorn, for example. The fourth historical document in *August 1914* does not use the cant phrase that American ministers loved to repeat, "Christ in khaki," but it has the same effect. In announcing the Russian defeat at Tannenberg, it assures the populace that "all necessary measures" are being taken and adds, "The Supreme Commander continues to believe firmly that God will help us to carry them out."

Some of Cooperman's comments apply directly to *August 1914*. After noting the general inadequacy of military strategy, Cooperman continues, "Other factors contributing to postwar mockery of 'the military mind' were inadequate army intelligence and chaotic transport. Officers, indeed, often had no idea where the enemy actually was." As a result of these factors, "lice-ridden, exhausted or nauseated Soldiers of Democracy . . . were frequently demoralized before they had suffered so much as a single casualty in actual combat." Solzhenitsyn makes no mention of lice, but his soldiers are certainly exhausted and demoralized.

Among European works, Emil Ludwig's popular historical account, *July '14* (1929), which has many novelistic features, may have suggested to Solzhenitsyn the possibility of limiting each volume in the series to a single month of a given year. Roger Martin du Gard's *The Summer of 1914* (1936; 1940), one volume of his *roman-fleuve Les Thibault*, offers an especially interesting case in point because he was greatly influenced by Tolstoy, whom he called his "grand Maître." Like Solzhenitsyn, Martin du Gard makes extensive use of contemporary documents and so successfully avoids the overt nationalism of earlier novels about the Great War that hostile critics accused him of pro-German bias.

It may someday prove possible to study Solzhenitsyn's use of sources for *August 1914*, as various scholars have studied Tolstoy's use of sources for

War and Peace. In addition to the memoirs of various Russian generals, he seems also to have read those of von François, as well as *With the Russian Army 1914–1917*, by Alfred Knox, the British general whom he makes into a minor character who constantly annoys Samsonov. He may also, by some miracle or luck and connections, have managed to obtain a copy of Winston Churchill's *The Unknown War: The Eastern Front.* Both Churchill's eloquence and his assessment of the effect of Zhilinsky's tactics anticipate Solzhenitsyn's:

> He [Zhilinsky] has refused all appeals for a halt and in consequence these fourteen divisions—a mass of over 200,000 men—are now about to come into contact with their German foe, reduced by sickness and straggling, wearied by many severe marches, weakened from scanty rations through trying to live on a barren country, with their regimental reserves of food already heavily drawn upon, and their communications so unorganized that no supplies can reach them from the rear. We may picture these brave troops already hungry, worn and footsore, their ardour checked by leaden fatigue, wandering forward through the broad landscape of sombre pine forests, innumerable tawny lakes, infertile stubble fields with squalid hamlets few and far between.

No matter what historians finally decide about Solzhenitsyn's treatment of the Battle of Tannenberg, his intuition told him what Norman Stone concluded in 1975: "August 1914 was . . . an anomalous month. It reflected, not wartime realities, but pre-war illusions."

    With regard to the general similarities between *August 1914* and *War and Peace*, we may begin with the ones in Solzhenitsyn's and Tolstoy's temporal relationships to the events with which they deal. The Battle of Borodino took place in 1812, and the Battle of Tannenberg in 1914, about a hundred years apart; Tolstoy and Solzhenitsyn both wrote about fifty years after the battle in question. (However, Solzhenitsyn did not need to make a special trip to Tannenberg, as Tolstoy went to Borodino; he had fought there in World War II.) They could not therefore use autobiographical material, as Tolstoy was to do in *Anna Karenina*, and as Solzhenitsyn had already done in *The First Circle* and *Cancer Ward*. Both used the personalities of their parents instead; Nikolay Rostov supposedly resembles Tolstoy's father, Nikolay Tolstoy, and Isaaky Lazhenitsyn's name clearly hints at his similarity to Solzhenitsyn's father, Isay Solzhenitsyn. Moreover, Ksenya Tomchak in *August 1914* resembles Solzhenitsyn's mother, Taisya Zakharovna Solzhenitsyn (née Shcherbak), and her father, Zakhar Tomchak, resembles his maternal grandfather, Zakhar Shcherbak. This list makes it clear that Solzhenitsyn changed the names only slightly, following Tolstoy's procedure in changing such well-known names as Obolensky and Volkonsky to Oblonsky and Bolkonsky.

Both novels mix historical characters, relatives, and purely fictional characters. Just as *War and Peace* features two families, the Rostovs and the Bolkonskys, with one character, Pierre Bezukhov, who mediates between them, so in *August 1914*, we find two families, the Kharitonovs in Rostov and the Lenartoviches in St. Petersburg, each of whom has a son in the group Vorotyntsev leads to freedom in the breakout through the German lines.

Of course, one can as yet make only tentative comparisons between *War and Peace* and *August 1914*, since *August 1914* begins a series of an undetermined number of volumes, and is only about half as long as *War and Peace*. Nevertheless, some things seem clear. While Tolstoy divides his novel more or less equally between war and peace, Solzhenitsyn gives war much more emphasis. Of the fifty-eight fictional chapters in *August 1914*, only fifteen deal with peace. And, after all, Solzhenitsyn had read Dos Passos, among other modern authors, and *August 1914* has something of the mosaic quality of *U.S.A.*, as a later chapter will show. It contains two newspaper sections, five film segments, four historical surveys of troop movements, one interpretative historical essay (chapter 40), and six complementary documents—all set off from the fictional chapters. This heady mixture represents a considerable development from Tolstoy's highly polemical essays, which begin to appear only toward the end of *War and Peace*,

Two waves of political exiles returning to central Russia almost exactly a hundred years apart, like the battles of Borodino and Tannenberg, provided a major impetus for the books. The return from exile in Siberia of some Decembrists after the death of Nikolay I in 1855 caused Tolstoy to think seriously about that period in Russian history, and Solzhenitsyn himself returned to Russia from exile in central Asia in 1956, after Stalin's death in 1953. Tolstoy attempted to write a novel about the Decembrists but gradually and involuntarily worked back from 1825 to 1805; strikingly, Solzhenitsyn suggests that the commitment to the public welfare on the part of Vorotyntsev and his fellow graduates of the General Staff Academy may derive from that of the Decembrists. We learn in chapter 12 that these officers were called "YOUNG TURKS (and with a weak, distant nuance perhaps Decembrists as well? . . .)."

Finally, Tolstoy wrote *War and Peace* in part as a response to the materialism of the radical critics of the 1860s, and Solzhenitsyn wrote *August 1914* in order to deal with their twentieth-century admirers. Not surprisingly, then, these groups attacked the two novels. The negative initial response to *War and Peace* caused Tolstoy to shut himself up in Yasnaya Polyana, cancel his subscriptions to the leading journals of the day, and sulk. The Soviet authorities not only attacked *August 1914*; they also commissioned a translation of Barbara Tuchman's *The Guns of August*, in a bumbling attempt to correct what they perceived as Solzhenitsyn's biases. And the publication of *August 1914* in Paris was surely a major factor in their decision to expel him from Russia.

But the battles of Borodino and Tannenberg, and thus *War and Peace* and *August 1914*, differ in two obvious and decisive ways. The Russians won the Battle of Borodino and ultimately repelled an invading army; they lost the Battle of Tannenberg, in which they were the invading army. This reversal appears, both in history and in the novels, with a remarkable symmetry; *War and Peace* pits Kutuzov against Napoleon, while *August 1914* pits Samsonov against von François. However, the outcome is reversed. But an examination of this symmetrical opposition must come after an examination of Tolstoy, and the specific references to him, in *August 1914*.

Bernard Bergonzi remarks, in his book *Heroes' Twilight*, "The dominant movement in the literature of the Great War was, to adapt the terminology of some modern theologians, from a myth-dominated to a demythologized world." In this, as in so much else, *August 1914* corresponds to the conventions of its genre but does so with an additional twist; in Russia, one cannot separate the myth of the spontaneous national uprising which expels the invader from a major source of that myth, *War and Peace*. It is therefore appropriate that *August 1914* seems to mark a culmination in Solzhenitsyn's contest with his precursor; he demythologizes *War and Peace* by showing the Battle of Tannenberg as its logical development. He has progressed from using the structure of Tolstoy's early war stories in *One Day* to tessera and aprophrades with him in *The First Circle*, to quoting him extensively in *Cancer Ward*, to making him a character in *August 1914*.

Since the action takes place in August 1914, Tolstoy necessarily appears in a flashback, when Sanya Lazhenitsyn recalls a visit to Yasnaya Polyana while Tolstoy was still alive. As Chekhov had done on his first visit there, he feels intimidated by the imposing stone gates; but instead of going back, Lazhenitsyn cuts through the park, where he comes upon Tolstoy, who is taking his morning walk. Three features of this encounter seem especially noteworthy here. First, there is the topography of the park itself. The birch-lined path is "long, straight, and narrow, like a corridor" and a part of the park where the trees thin out is "surrounded by a square of linden trees, crossed lengthways, across, and diagonally, with paths." This geometric quality in Tolstoy's estate suggests a certain rigidity in Tolstoy himself. Second, Lazhenitsyn thinks of Tolstoy as "The Great One," "The Gray-

Haired One," and "The Prophet." Both the epithets themselves and the ironic use of capital letters strongly recall the similar references to Stalin as "The Greatest of the Great," and "The Wisest of the Wise," which appear in *The First Circle*, Third, Lazhenitsyn asks Tolstoy, "What is the goal of man's life on earth?" and receives the answer that he expects, "To serve the good." Tolstoy advises Lazhenitsyn to serve the good "only with love," dismisses his objection that such general love does not exist, and tells him not to write poetry. Tolstoy tells him that poetry is "not natural. Words are meant to express thoughts!"

Sanya Lazhenitsyn serves as a surrogate for Solzhenitsyn in more than his name; he is the very image of what Bloom calls the "ephebe" in his oedipal encounter with the precursor. As the precursor, Tolstoy speaks first, and Lazhenitsyn answers hesitantly. Yet, for all his awe and admiration, he cannot follow Tolstoy's precepts; he wants to eat meat, dance with pretty girls, and write poetry. And, worst of all for a Tolstoyan, he is going to war. When he meets Varya in Pyatigorsk early in the novel and tells her that he is volunteering, she asks in amazement, "What would Lev Tolstoy have said about that—have you thought?" In going to war, he makes it clear that he has realized that he must free himself from Tolstoy's adherence to abstract principles and live his own life. He therefore offers a paradigmatic instance of what one must do in order to become what Bloom calls "a strong poet." For Solzhenitsyn the scene states the artistic—as opposed to the psychological—realization that Tolstoy, for all his genius, is inadequate and limiting. (As a fictional character, of course, Lazhenitsyn resembles two previous Solzhenitsyn characters who cannot live in accordance with beliefs—Rubin in *The First Circle* and Kostoglotov in *Cancer Ward*.)

Soviet Tolstoy scholars never tire of telling us that Lenin called Tolstoy "the mirror of the Russian revolution," and the family most in sympathy with Tolstoy's denial of the pleasures of the body and of poetry is the family of St. Petersburg revolutionaries, the Lenartoviches. When Veronya Lenartovich brings home her friend Yelya, an esthete who plays with her shawl à la Akhmatova, and recites Gumilyov's "The Choice," the Lenartoviches are upset. They impatiently dismiss the poem as "symbolist nonsense." Thus these two extremes of "the Protestant spirit in the Russian intelligentsia," the famous pacifist and the obscure revolutionaries, both come together in denouncing pleasure and art.

In all of *August 1914*, only Vorotyntsev dislikes Tolstoy. Over breakfast with Colonel Krymov in Soldau, Vorontyntsev vehemently defends the Duma against Krymov's slurs and condemns the stinginess of the old-fashioned Russian generals: "'And it's thought that the *spirit* of the troops decides everything—Suvorov thought so, and Dragomirov . . . and

Tolstoy. . . . Why spend money on weapons?'" Vorotyntsev is referring, of course, to Tolstoy's fanciful historical equation in *War and Peace*, in which the unknown, x, "is the spirit of the troops"—the factor that historians have neglected in military history. In mentioning "Dragomirov," Vorotyntsev is thinking of Mikhail Dragomirov (1830–1905), the first general who claimed that *War and Peace* had direct applicability to actual military tactics. In "Count Tolstoy's *War and Peace* from a Military Point of View" (1868), he emphasized, in a characteristic passage, "the enormous significance of Count Tolstoy's battle scenes for any soldier who takes his job seriously."

Presumably with Dragomirov's encouragement, virtually all the generals in *August 1914* believe in the relevance of *War and Peace* to the task at hand. Chapter 53, for example, begins like this:

> General Blagoveshchensky had read about Kutuzov in Lev Tolstoy, and he himself at the age of sixty, with gray hair, plumpness, and difficulty of movement, felt himself to be precisely Kutuzov, only with both good eyes. Like Kutuzov, he was cautious, careful, and clever. And, like Tolstoy's Kutuzov, he understood that it is never necessary to carry out any sharp, decisive maneuvers of one's own; that FROM A BATTLE BEGUN AGAINST HIS WILL, NOTHING WILL COME EXCEPT CONFUSION; that MILITARY AFFAIRS NEVERTHELESS GO AS THEY SHOULD, NOT COINCIDING WITH WHAT PEOPLE THINK UP; that THERE IS AN INEVITABLE COURSE OF EVENTS and the best general is he who REPUDIATES PARTICIPATION IN THESE EVENTS. And his whole long military career convinced the general of the correctness of these views of Tolstoy's; there was nothing worse than jumping out with one's own decisions; such people always suffered.

Blagoveshchensky even improves on Tolstoy's theories:

> Even Lev Tolstoy had omitted that in refusing maneuvers a military leader must all the more be able to write correct DISPATCHES. . . . that without such dispatches a general cannot, like Tolstoy's Kutuzov, DIRECT HIS FORCES NOT TO KILLING AND DESTROYING PEOPLE, BUT TO SAVING AND PITYING THEM.

The ironic capital letters recall the false humanitarianism of the official jargon in *The First Circle*, of course.

The remainder of chapter 53 amounts to an object lesson in the effects of this doctrine as carried out by a general who believes himself to be re-enacting the Battle of Borodino, not fighting the Battle of Tannenberg. In order to avoid more decisive action, Blagovshchensky sends a detachment under Nechvolodov "in the direction" of Willenberg. Unfortunately, Nechvolodov proves an able, imaginative commander, and he is about to take the town, when he receives a note from Blagoveshchensky ordering him to return. But what merely frustrates Nechvolodov in Blagoveshchensky affects the whole Russian army in Samsonov.

Samsonov thinks of Kutuzov only once, when his difficulties in communicating with his generals are particularly frustrating him. He realizes that he needs to send a message some forty-six miles, "And at forty-six miles, as under Kutuzov at three, there still remained the same hooves of horses' legs of the same length." He thinks of Kutuzov in terms of logistics, not history, as Blagoveshchensky does, for his relationship to Kutuzov is more complicated than Blagoveshchensky's, and it is one which the reader alone can understand.

First of all, Samsonov resembles Kutuzov, but for perverse reasons and in a perverse way. Early in *August 1914* we read, "And for the first time in thirty-eight years of service, since his half-squadron in the Turkish campaign, Samsonov felt that he was not a doer, but only a representative of events; they were flowing away of themselves." This sounds very much like Tolstoy's reference to Kutuzov as a "representative of a national war" but with a crucial difference. Kutuzov believes that *all* generals are "representatives," while Samsonov believes that he cannot take proper command because of external circumstances. Likewise, neither general can endure formalities: Kutuzov sleeps at strategy meetings and often has his uniform jacket unbuttoned; Samsonov finds the formalities at lunch and dinner with Knox frustrating, for he needs to think things through. When a general tries to explain something to Kutuzov, "Kutuzov seemed to be concerned about something, and didn't hear the general's words." Toward the end of *August 1914*, "It was as though Samsonov had started to pay attention. And not to the hubbub around him. And not to the distant shooting. But beyond." Kutuzov is distracted because his attention is going outward, in his empathy with the troops and the general situation; Samsonov doesn't listen to what people say because he has withdrawn into himself and is preparing for suicide.

When things begin to go badly, Samsonov addresses two battalions, telling them to think of the honor of their regiments.

> But the mighty voice had sailed separately over their heads—and
> with it the strength of his certainty went out of the commander.
> Just a moment ago he had known well what he should say, how

to evoke the miracle of a turn-around of the battalions, and their regiments, and all the central corps—and suddenly his memory broke off, he lost what he should say further.

His problem is that he believes that "the commander's word should be successful, that was the point of military history. In the difficult moment the commander himself addresses the troops, and they, inspired. . . ." His thoughts break off here because he is applying a nineteenth-century solution to a twentieth-century situation. Like the other generals, he remains under the spell of the image of Kutuzov's empathy with the troops in *War and Peace*,

As the French begin their retreat from Moscow, Kutuzov makes a short speech to the troops, whom he calls "boys" (*rebyata*), "brothers" (*brattsy*), and ends with a profanity. The narrative explicates the speech in the following manner.

> The words said by Kutuzov were hardly understood by the troops. No one would have been able to convey the content of the at first formal, and toward the end simple-hearted, old man's speech; but the heartfelt meaning of this speech was not only understood, but the same, the same feeling of magnificent triumph united with pity for the enemies and consciousness of its rightness, expressed by this, precisely this old man's simple-hearted curse—this same feeling lay in the soul of every soldier and was expressed in a joyous cry which did not die out for a long time.

This powerful passage, which is at the heart of the mythic structure of *War and Peace*, holds an obvious appeal for any general. Yet this empathy between the general and the troops is lacking, and, since Samsonov believes so strongly in the need for it, he sinks further into despair. Just before his suicide Samsonov makes one final gesture: he says farewell to the troops. "Thank you for your service! . . . Thank you for your service!" he says. Even here, he cannot escape from Kutuzov, who had said to *his* troops: "I thank everyone for difficult and faithful service. The victory is complete, and Russia will not forget you." Samsonov might have said just the opposite: "The defeat is complete, and Russia will not remember you." This defeated army of invaders therefore finds itself in the plight of the French army toward the end of *War and Peace*, and Solzhenitsyn deliberately used for it some of the images that Tolstoy used for the French army.

Solzhenitsyn uses two images—that of a rolling billiard ball and of melting metal—to describe the retreat, or attempted retreat, of the Russian army; he knows—and expects us to know—that these images appear in the suprapersonal explanation of history in *War and Peace*. Nechvolodov's late-night retreat from Rotfliess begins a more general movement: "The Sixth Corps was rolling back, like a free billiard ball—unattached to anyone, smooth, round, carefree." This simile may seem a bit abrupt unless one recalls Tolstoy's explanation of how the French got as far as Moscow after the Battle of Borodino.

> A collision occurs at Borodino. Neither one nor the other army falls apart, but the Russian army immediately after the collision retreats as necessarily as a ball which has collided with another, bearing down on it with greater force necessarily rolls back.

Solzhenitsyn uses another of the explanations that Tolstoy borrowed from the natural sciences in chapter 39, when the confusion in the Russian army mounts, and no one knows what to do. "The commander refused to go back—nor was he able to point to a way out of this pressed-in condition. The retreat itself began to flow, as hard metal flows without asking anyone, as soon as it reaches its melting point." This second simile derives directly from the one in *War and Peace* which explains why the French army did not surrender all at once.

> One cannot instantaneously melt a lump of snow. There exists a certain limit before which no exertions of heat can melt the snow. On the contrary, the more heat, the more the remaining snow hardens.

Solzhenitsyn can play off these images against their source because Tolstoy is using the analogies from the natural sciences (one indication of his affinities with the radical critics of the 1860s) both to make and to justify the argument that human volition does not decide battles. In *August 1914*, however, human volition—or human incompetence—makes coherent action impossible. When the infantry retreats, cursing, "they exuded that particular soldier's animosity [that occurs] when they didn't do it, but IT WAS MESSED UP FROM ABOVE."

The narrative gives this description of the entrance of the French army into Moscow in *War and Peace*:

> The French soldiers entered Moscow still in regular order. This was a tortured, exhausted, but still martial and frightful army. But it was an army only until that minute when the soldiers of this army dispersed to quarters. Just as soon as the men of these regiments began to disperse among the empty and rich houses,

the army was destroyed forever, and, neither residents nor
soldiers, but something in between, called marauders, was
formed. . . . The goal of each of these men upon leaving Moscow
did not consist, as before, in fighting, but only in taking away
what he had acquired. . . . Ten minutes after the entrance of each
French regiment into any area of Moscow there remained not a
single soldier or officer. In the windows of the houses were
visible men in overcoats and boots walking among the rooms
laughing; in the cellars and basements similar men were making
themselves at home with provisions; in the courtyards similar
men were unlocking or breaking open the gates of sheds and
stables: in the kitchens they were building fires, and with sleeves
rolled up were baking, kneading, and roasting; amusing and
caressing women and children.

Just as a result of pouring water onto dry earth, the water and the
dry earth disappear; so as a result of the hungry army's entering
the abundant city, the army was destroyed, and the abundant city
was destroyed.

I have quoted this passage at length because it served as the model for
chapter 29 of *August 1914*, in which Yaroslav Kharitonov's regiment enters
Hohenstein and promptly falls apart, just as the French army does in *War and
Peace*.

Characteristically, Solzhenitsyn substitutes for Tolstoy's homely mud-
and-water image that of a hero in a fairy tale:

The regiments poured in from the Allenstein highway still with
an impetus to battle, still with a readiness to go right through the
town and go further, where they were ordered to—but, as in the
fairy tale, with the first steps inside the magic circle the forces
flow out of the hero . . . so here the first blocks enveloped the
entering battalions with something—and they went out of step,
heads turned in various sides, the impetus to move toward the
sound of battle softened, broke.

Characteristically again, Solzhenitsyn makes the scene more personal and
specific than Tolstoy does. Kharitonov resists the dissolution of discipline
throughout the chapter, and the looting is given in detail. The simple peasant
boys find German efficiency and abundance amazing: "Here—they're
carrying macaroni, never before seen by peasants! And still odder: veal,

home-roasted in glass jars." Kharitonov takes some maps but nothing else; he enters a clothing store and rebukes a fellow officer for taking warm winter things. The officer, Kozeko, replies: "You and I don't have any warm things, and when will they return to issue them to us? You know the Russian commissary yourself." As in Moscow, fires break out; Kharitonov sees a Russian soldier wheeling off a bicycle for his son (it will reappear in a film segment), and one of his best men gets drunk.

As if all this chaos were not sufficiently disgusting for the idealistic Kharitonov, the scene culminates in a telling parody of one of Tolstoy's favorite situations. Kharitonov sees that his men are drinking something out of heated kettles. Puzzled, he approaches, and a soldier rushes up to him with a cup: "Your excellency, what cocoa!" The soldier who offers him cocoa (which he mispronounced *kakava*—it is a novelty, like macaroni) constitutes a deliberate degradation of all those noble peasants in Tolstoy who offer his alienated male heroes symbolic nourishment in the form of water and food, such as Platon Karatayev, who offers Pierre a baked potato. If the peasants have no wisdom, and the troops no spirit, then only defeat and despair remain.

Like chapter 53, which contrasts the inept General Blagoveshchensky, who justifies his inactivity by his imagined similarities to Kutuzov, and Colonel Nechvolodov, chapter 40 contrasts the completely inexperienced General Klyuyev with the one true hero in *August 1914*, Captain Kabanov. But it does so in a unique way. The chapter forms a golden mean between the extreme artfulness of the film segments and the extreme factualness of the historical surveys, through the only open disagreement with Tolstoy in the whole novel.

> Without allowing ourselves a flourish of imagination, however much we can collect and find out exactly, going closer to the historians, and further from the novelists, we throw out our arms and affirm once and for all: we wouldn't dare to imagine something so totally bad; for verisimilitude we would distribute the light and shade evenly. But from the first battle, generals' insignia flash like signs of ineptness, and the higher you go, the more hopeless it is, and there is hardly anyone on whom the grateful author can rest a grateful glance. (And here we could be comforted by Tolstoy's conviction that it is not generals who lead armies, that it is not captains who lead ships and companies, not presidents and leaders who govern governments and parties—but the twentieth century has shown us too many times that it is precisely they who do so.)

Here we have the most explicit statement of Solzhenitsyn's enduring theme, the difference between the nineteenth and the twentieth centuries; this statement firmly relegates Tolstoy to the nineteenth century. This chapter, and this paragraph in particular, show that neither novelists nor critics can afford to ignore extraliterary matters in dealing with the structure of tradition.

If middle-level officers are the only heroes, then Vorotyntsev epitomizes them. But he has less to do with history than with *War and Peace*, especially Andrey and Pierre, and thus he forms another example of Solzhenitsyn's tessera with Tolstoy. We recall that in a tessera, "a poet antithetically 'completes' his precursor, by so reading the parent-poem as to retain its terms but to mean them in another sense, as though the precursor had failed to go far enough." With regard to Vorotyntsev, this means that Solzhenitsyn treats him with appropriate irony.

Vorotyntsev resembles Andrey in a number of obvious ways: he is a brilliant young officer who can both respect the bravery of his men and criticize the ineptness of the generals; he has a staff appointment that allows him to roam at will; and he welcomes the war because it allows him to get away from his wife, whom he has ceased to love. He first appears in the novel in chapter 11, at Samsonov's headquarters at Ostrolenka, and thus he allows Solzhenitsyn to bring together fiction and history, just as Andrey's relationship to Kutuzov allows Tolstoy to do.

But Vorotyntsev inhabits a different world from Andrey's. Andrey can retire to Bald Hills when he wishes and can take a government position for no pay; he also benefits from his father's name and influence. Kutuzov even says to him at one point, "But remember, friend, that I am a father to you, another father." None of this applies to Vorotyntsev. His family is impoverished; he is a professional soldier who must live on his salary, and he wins Samsonov's respect through his expertise. Vorotyntsev lacks Andrey's absorption in himself, his brittleness, and his fear of ridicule. For Vorotyntsev, "A feeling worthy of a masculine breast could be only civic, or patriotic, or panhuman."

This idealism gives Vorotyntsev an affinity with Pierre, an affinity which—as we now expect—involves a reversal of an incident in *War and Peace*, Just before the Battle of Borodino, Pierre makes an inspection tour with Bennigsen, a German general in the Russian service who believes in the importance of military strategy. As he explains the position, "Pierre listened to Bennigsen's words, exerting all his intellectual powers to understand the essence of the imminent battle, and felt with chagrin that his intellectual capacities were inadequate for that." *Mutatis mutandis*, in chapter 25 of *August 1914* we find Vorotyntsev in Usdau on the night before the big battle, although he has no more reason to be there than Pierre had for being at Borodino. As *Cancer Ward* begins with Rusanov's thoughts, so this chapter begins with Artomonov's thoughts. Both men find much that is annoying in their situation. Rusanov is annoyed at the hospital rules, and Artomonov is annoyed at Vorotyntsev, who has asked about the plan for the next day. Artomonov thinks:

> *Plan!*—the very word was so un-Russian. What plan could there be, and could you talk about it aloud, what a simpleton! The plan was how to hop out of here with the whole corps in good order, and no stain would land on the name of the corps, and you would get an award.

The attitude of the general and the observer have obviously been reversed here. Bennigsen believes in strategy, whereas Pierre, the innocent, cannot comprehend it. Artomonov, who has no doubt read *War and Peace*, does not believe in strategy, and he plays the role of the innocent no less for being a general. Vorotyntsev, a true man of the twentieth century who understands the danger of innocence, is infuriated. And, appropriately, innocence takes its toll: the battle at Usdau is a disaster for the Russians, mostly because of Artomonov.

Another cowardly Russian general, Klyuyev, may or may not be thinking of *War and Peace* in chapter 26, when he fears that through a careless order he will break the fragility of his career, "or that IT itself will suddenly break in from somewhere." He is constantly afraid of IT—when a cart pulls up, or when he hears distant gunfire. Solzhenitsyn's use of the neuter third-person pronoun *ono*, not the more general *eto*, derives from Andrey's famous dream on his deathbed toward the end of *War and Peace*. Andrey dreams that something is trying to come through the door, "and a tormenting fear seizes him. And this fear is the fear of death: *it* [*ono*] is standing behind the door." Try as he might, he cannot keep the door closed: "*It* came in, and it was *death*." Since the word *fear* is masculine in Russian, Tolstoy's use of *ono* startles the reader here. Whereas Tolstoy italicizes the word, Solzhenitsyn capitalizes it. If we are to understand Klyuyev as thinking of this passage in *War and Peace*, the reference has the ironic effect of creating a balance. Russian generals in *August 1914* repeatedly cite *War and Peace* to justify their negligence; as if in compensation, *War and Peace* also instills in them the fear that death will break in on them as it did on Andrey.

To return to Vorotyntsev, his similarities to Pierre continue the next day when he fights with the Vyborg regiment: "Vorotyntsev in the drunken smokiness—loved the Vyborg regiment!" Likewise, Pierre is accepted as a member of the "family" by the soldiers of Rayevsky's Redoubt. And since the Germans do not take Vorotyntsev prisoner, as the French take Pierre, Solzhenitsyn puts Arseny Blagodaryov, his version of Platon Karatayev, in the Vyborg regiment.

Blagodaryov differs from Ivan Denisovich as much as from Karatayev, although all three retain distinct peasant traits while in the army, in the camp, and in captivity respectively. Yet whereas Karatayev is a symbolic figure, and thus a "flat" character in Forster's sense, Shukhov and Blagodaryov are clearly "round" characters. The texts give us narrative insight into the minds of both of Solzhenitsyn's peasants, something that virtually never happens with the peasant in Tolstoy's prose. Blagodaryov thinks of his wife back home in Kamenka in specifically sensual terms: "What she wouldn't think up! She would think up something like that!" Unlike Tolstoy's peasants, Solzhenitsyn's peasants are also on intimate terms with blood and killing; just before Kachkin and Blagodaryov go off to knife the German sentries, Kachkin says, "I slaughter cattle for half the village."

In his perception of the skirmish at the Rutkovich estate, Blagodaryov consistently perceives warfare in rural terms; he dislikes hardtack and thinks, "Funny thing, no one from the road tries to shoot at these ducks." He thus recalls, and nicely contrasts with, the famous instance of estrangement in *War and Peace* in which Nikolay Rostov cannot understand who the French soldiers are and why they would want to kill him. Blagodaryov understands perfectly well who the Germans are and why they want to kill him. He has what Vorotyntsev thinks of as a "preservice, prerank, preclass, pregovernment, ignorantly natural simplicity." No simpleton, Blagodaryov is simply encountering Western material culture for the first time under trying and difficult conditions. No doubt many soldiers all over Europe in 1914 thought, "What kind of oddity is coming: it's like it's on wheels, but you can't see any wheels" at their first sight of an armored car.

Like Ivan Denisovich, Blagodaryov is a complex and fascinating character, but he is complex and fascinating in different ways. First, he can be a delightful comic character, the only one in *August 1914* who provides comic relief in the midst of a national tragedy. For example, he has an absurdly difficult time in remembering not to address Vorotyntsev as "Your Excellency," and at the Rutkovich estate he is puzzled by what he perceives as a "strangely shaped pool table," until someone asks him if he has never seen a grand piano before.

Blagodaryov most clearly provides comic relief in the tense scene in chapter 37, in which Vorotyntsev, Blagodaryov, and some Cossacks unexpectedly come upon General von François and his staff. Vorotyntsev jokingly comments that each should take the other prisoner, thus recalling the scene in *War and Peace* when, during the Battle of Borodino, Pierre and a French officer wrestle: "'Am I taken prisoner, or is he taken prisoner by me?' thought each of them." The confrontation presents a microcosm of differences between the German and the Russian armies in 1914; the Germans are in a car, and an officer pulls out a machine gun, while the Russians are on horseback, and the Cossacks draw their sabers. As in the similar encounter between a Frenchman and a German in Jean Renoir's film *La Grande Illusion*, the officers remain gentlemen; they have a polite conversation in German, and nothing comes of it.

The contrast of peace amid war in this memorable scene often appears in a more general way in *August 1914*. I count no less than nine times when the narrative commentary insists on the persistence of peace. This motif appears, ominously, at the beginning of the first chapter in which Samsonov and his staff appear.

> The army directed by this staff has been advancing toward the enemy for a week—but here there was no anxious dashing back and forth, no arrivals and departures of horsemen, no rumbling of carriages, no noisy preparations, no one catching up with his unit, no changes—everything quieted down toward evening, and was as drowsy as the rest of Ostrolenka.

The drowsy staff headquarters gives us the uneasy feeling that Russian militarism has more to do with words than with guns. Nor is this lack of real preparation confined to the staff. Vorotyntsev rides through a completely quiet northern Prussia on his way to Soldau, the Nevsky regiment finds the people in Allenstein going about their daily business, Sanya and Kostya say goodbye to peaceful, unchanged Moscow, and so forth. The most dramatic example of the motif occurs during the burial of the one genuine Russian hero of the Battle of Tannenberg, Captain Kabanov. "The whole forest was so extensive that the war, raging all around, had not left a trace for the whole week: not a trench, not a shellhole, not a tire track, not even a discarded shell-case. A peaceful morning was warming up. . . . The safe, free feeling embraced the men as well: it was as though there were no encirclement, that they would bury him, and go off to their homes."

While this opposition of war and peace no doubt refers to the opposition of the mountain (transcendent values) and the steppe along which Sanya and his brother Yevstrashka ride (earthly concerns) that occurs on the first page of the novel, it also has an important precedent in Tolstoy. Not just the novel but virtually all of Tolstoy's war stories employ the opposition of war and peace as an essential structural principle. In "Woodcutting" and "The Raid," officers take a break from the action by flirting, in French, with attractive women in carriages. Section 14 of "Sevatopol in May" develops a contrast between a "dewy, flowering valley" and the corpses that litter it. In *War and Peace* itself, descriptions of battle scenes include a church or a peaceful farmhouse, and crowd scenes contrast weary soldiers with frightened civilians.

Clearly, then, *August 1914* and *War and Peace* both use the epic oppositions of war and peace, and it would seem that for once, Solzhenitsyn has taken over something from Tolstoy without changing it. While the opposition of war and peace, as both authors use it, implies a universality of the human condition which transcends petty nationalistic concerns, a comparison of the presentation of Napoleon in *War and Peace* with that of his counterpart in *August 1914*, General von François, shows that Tolstoy denies such transcendence. To use Forster's classic terms again, Napoleon is a flat character, and von François is a round one. The task of creating a foreign general who attacked Mother Russia evoked Tolstoy's jingoistic chauvinism; in ways he probably cannot fully articulate, Solzhenitsyn understands the consequence of chauvinism as Tolstoy could not, and does not allow it into his novels.

We find an analogous shade of difference between Solzhenitsyn and Tolstoy, not in the general presentation of characters, but in the specific manner of introducing them into scenes. One of the great joys of reading *War and Peace* comes from experiencing the major characters both from within and from without. A scene may be narrated through a character's perception, or we may have extensive narrative insight into the character's thoughts, after which he or she may disappear; upon reappearance later, a purely external description may at first not suffice to identify the character. Thus, as Princess Marya goes to see Andrey on his deathbed, she is met by "a red-cheeked girl with a large black braid, who smiled in an unpleasantly false manner, as it seemed to Princess Marya (it was Sonya)." Or, in one of the heart-stopping moments in this great novel, when, after Napoleon's defeat, Pierre goes to see Princess Marya, he does not immediately recognize her "companion." "When she smiled, there could no longer be any doubt: it was Natasha, and he loved her."

The purely external descriptions of characters without identification in Tolstoy often have a psychological motivation, as in the above example. Pierre does not immediately recognize Natasha, because they have both been through a great deal since they last met. I find only one passage in *August 1914* when Solzhenitsyn does this: not long before his suicide, Samsonov in his distraction does not recognize "a colonel and a soldier with long legs hanging down without stirrups," although we do. More frequently, though, the nonidentification of characters serves as a means of surprising the reader, as during the hospital scene at Neidenburg in chapter 34. Here, Vorotyntsev interviews a young officer about the troop movements of the last few days; only as he is about to leave does he voice his concern to the nurse that "Second Lieutenant Kharitonov" not be left in case of evacuation.

More strikingly, though, Solzhenitsyn does something that Tolstoy would never have done—he begins no less than seven chapters (3, 4, 22, 42, 48, 47, and 57) with the thoughts and sensations of an unidentified character. Chapter 47, for example, begins like this: "A feeling of cleanliness flowed stiffly in the resting body. He didn't notice how he woke up, and he hadn't even completely woken up." This revery continues for almost two pages until a reference to one Yegor Vorotyntsev identifies the character as Vorotyntsev, who has fallen asleep in the forest with Blagodaryov. Even more radically, chapters 3 and 4 begin with the sensations of new characters, whom the reader has no possible way of identifying. Thus, the first two sentences of chapter 3 are: "Right at the first break in sleep, before you remember that you are young, and what summer day it is, and how one can live happily—it comes in cold and dull—the quarrel! You've been in a quarrel with your husband again, since yesterday." It turns out, of course, that these are the thoughts of Irina Tomchak, whom Sanya Lazhenitsyn has glimpsed from his train window at the end of chapter 2. But the opening paragraphs of the chapter do not immediately identify either the character or her situation, as Tolstoy or any other nineteenth-century novelist would have done. (Notice, for example, how completely Tolstoy identifies Anna Pavlovna Scherer, whose comments to Prince Vasily Kuragin begin *War and Peace*.) I will argue in a later chapter that only a novelist who has assimilated the effect of film into his prose style would write like this; a chapter that begins in this abrupt manner has the same effect as a scene in a film that begins with a close-up, not an establishing shot.

Throughout this chapter I have suggested that Solzhenitsyn's encounter with his awesome precursor forced him to develop Tolstoy's characters and images in such a way as to counteract the Romantic notions of innocence and simplicity that they imply. One can hardly distinguish Tolstoy's work from its subtle affinities with some of the policies of the Soviet government, which—for example—turned innocence into xenophobia, and simplicity into a justification for censorship. But I would like to conclude this chapter by citing an instance in which the contest between precursor and ephebe involves only style. I believe that Solzhenitsyn wrote the passage in which Ksenya Tomchak returns to Rostov in chapter 59 with a copy of *War and Peace* in front of him, open to the passage in which Nikolay Rostov returns to Moscow after the campaign of 1805.

Before we proceed to the actual quotations, however, the details of Irina's ride (some of which I have omitted here) require some explanation. She starts out on Garden Street (actually, Large Garden Street); presumably, she has come in on the morning train from Moscow and has caught her cab at the train station, which stands at the western terminus of Garden Street, prerevolutionary Rostov's Nevsky Prospect. She rides eastward for a couple of miles; at the public garden, she orders the cabbie to turn right, onto Cathedral Street, for five blocks, until she reaches the Old Bazaar. The Kharitonov *Gymnasium* is located on the bazaar square, in the neighborhood of one A. Ya. Odintsov's bookkeeping school.

> "Will we get there soon? Will we get there soon? Oh, these unbearable streets, shops, signs, street lights, cabbies," thought Rostov, when they had signed their leave papers at the gate and entered Moscow. "Denisov, we're home! He's asleep." he said, moving his whole body forward, as if by this position he hoped to speed up the movement of the sled. Denisov didn't answer.
>
> "There's the corner where Zakhar the cabbie stands, and there's Zakhar, still the same horse! And there's the shop where we used to buy doughnuts. Will we get there soon? Well!"
>
> "To what house?" asked the driver.
>
> "There at the end, to the big house, how can you not see! That's our house," said Rostov, "That's our house!"
>
> "Denisov! Denisov! We'll be there in a minute."
>
> . . . Finally the sled moved to the right toward the porch; Rostov saw over his head the familiar eaves with the broken plaster, the porch, the sidewalk pillar. He jumped out of the sled while it was moving and ran into the foyer. The house also stood immovable, indifferently, as though it didn't care who arrived at it. . . . There was still the same door handle, which angered the countess when it wasn't clean; it opened loosely in the same way.
>
> . . . Someone saw the young master, and before he could run to the living room something flew out of the side door in a rush, like a storm and embraced and started to kiss him. Another and a third such being jumped out of another, and a third door; more embraces, more shouts, tears of joy.

The heart always pounds at the return to Rostov!—especially like this in the early morning when the sharp rise of Garden Street to Dolomanovsky is fresh and clean in the dark green of the trees, and the cabbie races to keep up with the tram on the way up! And the trams are not like the ones in Moscow, they're heavier in motion, not with forks but with rollers, and there are summer cars, open without side walls. There are the Arkhangorodskys' windows on the second floor, the corner balcony off the living room under the cloth awnings, and that might be Zoya Lvovna rearranging the flowers, but you can't tell through the thick trees, all right, I'll go see the Arkhangorodskys tomorrow. The cabbie wants to turn on Taganrog Prospect—no, go further, to Cathedral. . . . The art nouveau building on the corner of Taganrog, you can't find any like that even in Moscow—the upper stories are almost without walls, just glass. . . . There a strong drama at the "Soleil" . . . a strongly funny picture by Max Linder. . . . No, that's the main entrance, take me please, to the other side, to the headmistress's.

The dear staircase. Every dear door! From the first threshold there is that intellectual freedom and ease of relations such as you always find in this family. And—Zhenya, Zhenechka! Embrace me! You came in like a whirlwind, as though you're younger than Ksenya.

These two passages deal with the same situation of returning to a familiar city and house; the returnee notices familiar sights on the street, talks to the cabbie, sees familiar interior details, and is greeted affectionately. But what differences in the presentation, and how clearly they contrast Tolstoy and Solzhenitsyn!

Like all the Rostovs, Nikolay is self-centered in that he cannot distinguish his psyche from the external world. Thus, the features of the city are "unbearable," not in themselves, but because they separate him from his family. Only when he has a personal relationship with something does it not arouse his hostility. He is so impatient that he jumps from the sled while it is still moving; when the intensely awaited moment of reunion finally comes, he is so wrought up that he cannot even recognize the members of the family—he perceives, first, a "something" and then "beings." The whole passage has a curious effect; when read in isolation, it is slightly unsettling because Rostov's solipsism makes it unexpectedly impersonal. In this respect one can think of Rostov's ride as an anticipation of Anna Karenina's fateful last ride, with its justly famous interior monologue.

Perhaps in these passages, at least, we *like* Ksenya Tomchak more than we like Nikolay Rostov, for we can share her delight and interest in everything she sees. She finds the city charming and invigorating, not simply an obstacle separating her from those she loves. When she sees a familiar sight, she sees an apartment, not a bakery. In making this character notice some movement on the Arkhangorodskys' balcony, Solzhenitsyn is using her to anticipate a transition, as Tolstoy never did, and as he had done in making Sanya Lazhenitsyn catch a glimpse of Irina Tomchak at the end of chapter 2. It is indeed Zoya Lvovna who is rearranging flowers on the balcony in preparation for the dinner party of chapter 62.

Unlike the major characters of *War and Peace*, or any of Tolstoy's characters except Vronsky and Mikhaylov, Ksenya is interested in art and notices the movie theater that figures prominently in all of Solzhenitsyn's urban landscapes. Upon her arrival the interior details evoke positive, not negative, associations, and she perceives, and greets, a specific beloved friend, not Rostov's "creatures." The similarity of the image—Zhenya comes in "like a whirlwind" as an unidentified Rostov comes in "like a storm"—may well be Solzhenitsyn's clue to readers who know their Tolstoy as well as he does that he means to play off the two scenes against each other. If so, it is the act of a proud man who has risked as much, psychically, in the process of writing his book as he risked, socially, in the process of publishing it, for only a Russian writer with total confidence in himself would invite comparison with Tolstoy.

"The last truth of the Primal Scene of Instruction," Bloom tells us, "is that purpose or aim—that is to say, meaning—cleaves more closely to origins the more intensely it strives to distance itself from origins." For Solzhenitsyn in his Soviet literary context, this means that the Soviet establishment's relentless praise of Tolstoy, and selection of him as a model for emulation, while insisting on the difference between *his* realism and socialist realism, has helped to keep its literature sterile. By preventing writers from coming to terms with Tolstoy, the Soviet establishment has unwittingly made sure that they have not retrieved the meaning from the master's work.

Bloom's term "apophrades" refers to the change in the structure of the critic's tradition which occurs when it is no longer possible to read a certain passage in the precursor's work without thinking of the corresponding passage in the ephebe's work. Apophrades thus occurs at least twice in Tolstoy: Once, when Natasha's name-day party reminds us of the Makarygin's party—and that the two families share essential values. And again, when Nikolay Rostov's return to Moscow reminds us of Irina Tomchak's return to Rostov—and her sunny disposition contrasts with his emotional instability. As Bloom would put it for the sake of the maximum rhetorical effect, we can occasionally believe that Solzhenitsyn influenced Tolstoy. This does not mean that Solzhenitsyn has won, and that Tolstoy has lost, but rather that Solzhenitsyn is becoming a strong poet in his own right, and that he has done so in the only way possible—by retrieving meaning for his own work in returning to Tolstoy.

Solzhenitsyn begins his public career as a writer very much as Tolstoy did, with a story which followed the events of one day and which draws heavily on Tolstoy's use of authorial commentary set off by parentheses. In *The First Circle*, a much longer and more complicated work, he adapts old Prince Bolkonsky, a petty tyrant, for his large-scale tyrant, Stalin; and the Rostovs, as beneficiaries of the old feudal system. Gleb Nerzhin's prison experience incorporates that of Pierre, and Innokenty Volodin's arrest and imprisonment is played off against Andrey's death.

With Rusanov in *Cancer Ward*, Solzhenitsyn continues his project of forcing us to confront the implications of Tolstoyan innocence and simplicity by playing his *apparatchik* off against Stiva Oblonsky. But in *Cancer Ward*, for the first time, the characters discuss, and find meaning in, Tolstoy's work. When Podduyev reads, and is moved by, "What People Live By," it reminds us that Solzhenitsyn shares with Tolstoy the desire to have a moral effect on his readers.

August 1914 systematically reverses the events and images of *War and Peace*; Kutuzov has empathy with the soldiers, Samsonov does not. Kutuzov triumphs, Samsonov commits suicide, and so forth. Such reversals appear as a culmination of over a decade of intense work. While many of these correspondences and reversals deserve more detailed analysis than I can give them here, the key to all of them is Solzhenitsyn's denial of the oppositions that pervade Tolstoy's work, as they pervade Russian nineteenth-century literature in general. "The Germans are not pagans," Vorotyntsev says in explaining why they must bury Captain Kabanov in Prussia. No patriotic soldier in nineteenth-century Russian literature could have said that, nor could any of the many patriotic soldiers in socialist realism. Russia versus the West, city versus country, intellectual verses peasant, and the rest of the oppositions that became the destructive dichotomies of Stalinism, tend to lose their force in Solzhenitsyn.

As Edgar Lehrman has astutely reminded me, the affinities between Solzhenitsyn and Tolstoy involve more than literature. Solzhenitsyn's absolutism in refusing to have anything to do with the Soviet government; his insistence on the distinction between Russian patriotism and allegiance to the Soviet government; his respect for, and interest in, military life; his role as Jeremiah, a prophet without (official) honor in his own country—all these and more, bespeak an affinity of personality and temperament with Tolstoy, as well as the unchanging elements in the relationship between the writer and the government in Russia.

KENNETH N. BROSTROM

Prussian Nights:
A Poetic Parable for Our Time

Poetry composed by Aleksandr Solzhenitsyn must be, at least initially, an object of curiosity for those who know him as a prosaist of genius. Certainly the special role accorded to verse in his more familiar works would seem to guarantee high aspiration: he often associates poetry and poetic motifs with the most vital movements in his characters' spiritual lives and with their moral dilemmas. For a number of years we have known of the existence of Solzhenitsyn's verse, at least 12,000 lines of which were composed and committed to memory in the camps. (A fascinating and chilling description of the dangers attending this creative labor can be found in *The Gulag Archipelago*.) But only 69 lines, apparently from this corpus, had appeared in print prior to the writer's exile in 1974. Thus, the approximately 1,400 lines of *Prussian Nights* published in that same year were an important addition to his work; together with other short poems and poetic fragments presently in the public domain they provide a rather substantial basis for study of Solzhenitsyn as a poet.

We know nothing and will not speculate about revisions this poem may have undergone after 1950 (the date it bears), nor about possible reasons for its sudden publication soon after its author's exile. Nor will we attempt a definitive judgement of this poetry's ultimate value. Suffice it to say that Solzhenitsyn is an accomplished poet, and that, beyond its verbal artistry, his poetry exhibits

From *Solzhenitsyn in Exile: Critical Essays and Documentary Materials*, eds. John B. Dunlop, Richard S. Haugh, and Michael Nicholson. © 1985 by the Board of Trustees of the Leland Stanford Junior University.

strengths we recognize in his prose. A profound moral awareness informs his powerful depiction of men caught up in events too often terrible and largely beyond their control; the elaboration of their ethical quandaries is accompanied by subtly orchestrated patterns of action, meditation, and imagery which together generate the integrity of an authentic work of art.

The narrative material for *Prussian Nights* is drawn from Solzhenitsyn's own wartime experience, and its narrator is a man much like he presumably then was. A former university student—polite, sensitive, reserved, but exhibiting a youthful lack of moral assurance and marked by a degree of callous indifference born of war's barbarity—the narrator enters East Prussia with the Soviet armies during the winter of 1944-45 in command of the artillery battery. He is swept along in the rapid, unhindered advance and witnesses the orgy of devil-may-care drunkenness, wanton destruction, looting, murder, arson, and rape visited upon German civilians and towns. Unable finally to resist the repellent seductions of this dance of death, he commits a genteel rape and is overcome with self-loathing.

The narrator's irresolute oscillation between the behavior and values of his past and the reckless nihilism of the present determines the general movement of his verse narration, a complex series of shifts between action and meditative withdrawal from action. It also governs Solzhenitsyn's use of extremes in style, from the substandard crudities of rampaging bumpkins to the refined and precise verbal elegance of the intellectual. He is generally successful in fitting either extreme to the trochaic tetrameter line in which the poem is written (with but a single passage in dactyls). But there is no sharp division between the narrator's standard Russian and the substandard reported speech of his troops. Rather the narrator's language encompasses the entire verbal spectrum between these extremes, and his style at any moment registers his dissonant, ambivalent attitude toward himself and his lawless countrymen. For example, rollicking licentiousness, memories of a literary stereotype, and ironic self-mockery conjoin in the following passage addressed to a column of Cossacks and marked by the rhythms and diction of the vernacular:

> V nashei zhizni bespokoinoi—
> Nynche zhiv, gliadi—ubit,—
> Mil mne, bratsy, vash razboinyi
> Ne k dobru veselyi vid.
> Vybirali my ne sami,
> Ne po vole etot put',
> No teper' za poiasami
> Est' chem po nebu pal'nut'! . . .

Our lives don't see much relaxation.
Alive? Watch out or you'll be dead!
By your cheerful brigand faces
—so sinister—I'm comforted.
This road was not our own decision.
No one asked us if or why.
But now under our belts we've something
Worth a salvo in the sky!

And so the narrator celebrates in this discordant song his acquisition of writing materials, gentlemanly plunder removed from an abandoned post office soon to be burned.

These eight lines form two quatrains with alternating feminine and masculine rhymes, but they are printed without stanza breaks. Although *Prussian Nights* is not rigorous stanzaic poetry, its lines nevertheless coalesce into rhymed clusters ranging from couplets and triplets to pentastichs and several hexastichs; two related rhyme patterns predominate in quatrains and pentastichs (aBaB [as in the passage above] and aBaaB). However, the generally irregular rhyme scheme and the unbroken printed text tend to accentuate, not the poetic texture of particular passages, but the developing narrative. That integral narrative is our first concern, for it presents us with more than a young, slightly jaded idealist's pilgrimage into hell. It is a parable for our time, for a century populated more than any before by people of humane predisposition and good intention who have too often stoked the fires of that hell.

We are accustomed to thinking of Nazi Germany in these terms. And no Russian reader of *Prussian Nights* is likely to forget the barbarism which emerged from the world of brick homes and tiled roofs, paved roads, solidly built barns, and well-preserved Gothic churches described in the poem's early pages. But if Nazi atrocities committed in Russia provoke in part the events depicted here, they are not allowed to provide a moral rationalization. Solzhenitsyn refers to past acts of the German army only by implication, while in the present not a single heroic, or even terrible, military engagement is portrayed. He allows no ambiguity to infiltrate his ethical position: Germans, all civilians, women of all ages, the elderly, even an infant, are helpless and pathetic victims of Russian aggression. Repeatedly the narrator echoes Moscow's demand for Old Testament "justice": "Blood for blood! Tooth for tooth!" But replies in kind never rise above the initial wrong. The Russians merely mimic their hated foe by acting upon the barbarous principle that might makes right.

This evocation of Jehovah's wrathful visage figures significantly in Solzhenitsyn's effort to explode all spurious justifications and embellishments of the hideous, the ideological included. In Neidenburg the Russians are met by a longsuffering German Communist, who with solemn joy greets his proletarian brethren with bread and salt, the ancient Russian gesture of humble hospitality. But this "bastard" (*gad*), this "spy," this "vermin" (*chumnoi*), is swiftly arrested and sent off to SMERSH (the police organ for counterespionage), to a certain Solov'ev, who bears, probably ironically, the name of Russia's greatest religious philosopher. Meanwhile, a gang rape has left the German's daughter dead and his dying wife pleading for the deathblow. Similarly, "class allies," an elderly and ill German farmer and his wife, are nonchalantly shot after feeding their guests from the East, while their grandson, perhaps wounded, makes good a hair-raising escape through window and snow into the forest. The "liberation of Eastern Europe," the "inevitable historical collapse of Fascism," the "international brotherhood of the toiling masses," these and other shibboleths grounded in ideology and endlessly propounded in the immense Soviet war literature, collapse here under the accumulating weight of criminal violence.

Despite the callous gaiety, effectively rendered in diction and rhythm, which characteristically attends such crimes, Solzhenitsyn makes of these soldiers something more than obstreperous, vengeful cutthroats. They too are victims of power, first of all the power of ancient fears and prejudices associated with "the German" which are now endorsed by Moscow. Fascist Italians, for example, pass the Russian columns untouched, while Poles, allies but old targets for Russian discrimination, suffer verbal abuse, and their young women are raped while desperately crying out their nationality. Solzhenitsyn's Nobel Speech, his fiction, and his polemical works witness fully to his conviction that values and beliefs impressed by enculturation and individual experience have the power to enslave men's minds. This certainly does not free these Russians from guilt. But their mindless response to old prejudice, their habitual and benighted acquiescence to Moscow's dictates, their brutalization in war, all cause them to view every German categorically as *enemy*, as a noxious, loathsome thing and not a human being. Suddenly they find themselves in a universe where the principle "all is permitted" is a supreme virtue. The enormity of this ethical error is ironically underscored by their ignorance of Dostoevskii, who has at least been read by many of their German victims. (The connotative richness of this reference to Dostoevskii should be apparent, and need not be pursued in detail here.)

The Russian soldiers are victims of power in a more literal sense. They resemble their own leaders, for whom the maxim "all is permitted" has always been a guiding principle of government, especially in dealing with internal "enemies," whom they regard as a species of vermin. The only sustained break in this poem's metrical scheme occurs in a somber description of an endless column of such "enemies," Russian prisoners of war returning to their own "savage land," to its camps for the living dead. The shift from trochees to dactyls, resulting in a longer line, together with the imagery surrounding these men "needed by no one," creates a mood both ominous and funereal. Moscow has termed them *Enemy*! and they have ceased to exist as human beings for their fellows. As it turns out, there *is* one unforgivable sin in this permissive universe: having been a POW.

Solzhenitsyn shares with Dostoevskii a conviction that the human enactment of evil may be conditioned by environment, but that evil itself is rooted more deeply in man's nature. It resides in our impulse to deify the isolated self at the expense of the other, to follow the easy path of self-interest, eschewing the difficult path of self-transcendence on behalf of the other. The gratuitous violence in *Prussian Nights* is reminiscent of a symbolic event described near the conclusion of *Cancer Ward*: an "evil man" blinds a Macaque Rhesus monkey by throwing tobacco into its eyes, "just for the hell of it" (*Prosto tak*!). The principle implicit in this act, in all its infinite permutations and combinations, leads implacably to the law of the jungle between men and between nations—that is, to destruction and chaos.

Creation of a chaotic hell on earth is the perception which shapes the imagery associated with the Russian invasion. A fiery holocaust, an implacable surge of molten "lava," advances over the winter landscape during the first half of the poem; everything falls to the torch. Fire seems to fill the firmament as natural phenomena—dawn, dust, stars, and wind—are transformed into a metaphorical description of this all-consuming inferno: "Chto zh, gori, dymi, pylai, / Trudoliubnyi gordyi krai." Serpentlike flames of "just" punishment engulf entire towns and villages as these Russian surrogates for Satan's demons enact a Last Judgment decreed in Moscow ("Otomshchaem my vragu!"). But certain targets are emphasized: a school, homes and barns, a church. And a piano is destroyed in a street. That is, emblems of a peaceful, ordered existence, of productive labor, culture, the life of the family and of the spirit, are incinerated in an orgy of blasphemous hilarity ("Pir i vlast'! Likuet khaos!").

Especially important here are the interrelated motifs of private life and domestic life: the dignity of the individual is repeatedly violated by rape, while homes, grounded in loving sexuality, are invaded and looted, and an infant is apparently murdered. The ethical nihilism and impulse toward chaos inherent in human evil make war here, not only on persons but on any conviction that life, the life of the individual and of the community in its most fundamental expression, is inherently orderly and valuable. Such nihilism is inevitably life-denying, not life-affirming. So despite their vitality, the Russian troops are agents of hell and hellfire, that is, of death. For them sexuality, perhaps the most basic motif in *Prussian Nights*, is no longer the mysterious source of new life; it is merely a source for nihilistic, aggressive self-pleasure. The victim becomes a thing, and rape becomes the moral equivalent of murder, which transforms the victim into a thing literally. The equation of rape and murder is evident in the sexual undercurrent of the poem's rollicking opening lines; there cannons, death-dealing weapons, acquire their predictable connotations, while Germany is described in feminine terms, as an "evil witch" who now must "open" her "gates."

> Rasstupis', zemlia chuzhaia!
> Rastvoriai svoi vorota!
> Eto nasha udalaia
> Edet russkaia pekhota!
> Kholmik, pad', mostok i kholmik—
> Stoi! Skhodi! Po katre—tut.
> Budet zlaia ved'ma pomnit'
> V nebe zimnem nash saliut!
>
> Open up, you alien country!
> Wide open let your gates be thrown!
> For, approaching, see how boldly
> Russia's battle line rolls on!
> Hillock, dip, small bridge, and hillock—
> Halt! Check on the map—we're there.
> Dismount! The foul witch shall remember
> Our salvo in the wintry air!

This equation has its most powerful expression in the episode preceding the narrator's own rape of a German woman. A magnificent and proud young German woman is stopped by two Russians, one of them, Baturin, a seasoned cutthroat. We anticipate, in company with the narrator, that another rape will ensue. Instead she is shot, riddled by both her captors with automatic weapon fire.

All of this suggests why the narrator's own crime committed in the poem's final episode is the apotheosis of his pilgrimage, a journey of the spirit which takes him from confused and passive, uncertain collaboration in evil (he experiences both revulsion and exhilaration) to active participation in the dance of death. The spiritual pilgrimage is obviously an important structural principle in much of Solzhenitsyn's work, as it often has been in the works of the Russian classics. During the modern period generally, such literary pilgrimages are rather often depicted as unsuccessful. In the present instance, we might compare this narrator to Kostoglotov in *Cancer Ward*, who exits from that novel having failed a critical test but with an anguished awareness of his moral failure. And in that anguish there is some affirmation.

Of course one might view the narrator's crime as the result of his progressive contamination by the world. In a sense he is no stranger to East Prussia, for as a schoolboy he studies Russian military defeats in that area during World War I. The "circles, dots, and arrows" on maps signifying military operations had become familiar and meaningful to him. He begins his own journey-pilgrimage there with preconceptions of a calculated, a *teleological* march toward Berlin. Instead he is swept along in a series of discontinuous, chaotic, disorienting movements which are perfectly in harmony with his troops' aimless violence. His moral sense is eroded by the persistent perception that he moves through a disordered and therefore meaningless world in which morality is irrelevant. His faltering commitment to ethical behavior is reflected in a tawdry refrain from the nineteenth-century Spanish composer and violinist Sarasate, "Oh, what heart could withstand?!" which at intervals haunts and tantalizes him. Like Babel's intellectual protagonist Liutov (*Red Cavalry*), this young man is caught in the moral quagmire which opens up in terrible times between what is and what we dream ought to be. But his dilemma loses every trace of moral heroism or tragedy when he *chooses* to rape. At the very least we can say this: in doing so, he chooses for himself and thus for chaos, and against humanity.

Unlike Babel', however, Solzhenitsyn never allows us to question where the good lies, even as he admits the inevitable impact of events on moral choice. Earlier, when the atrocities in Allenstein culminate in a soldier's intention to murder an infant, a lone voice cries out, "You're King Herod, your priest's a beast!" ("Sam ty Irod, pop tvoi zver',"). The narrator's problem is not so much his uncertain knowledge of the good, but his deftness in rationalizing the bad. An instructive example involves the Sarasate leitmotif noted above. It is linked to another by the same composer, even more tawdry: "This fan of black, a fan so precious. ' The cheap romanticism of these phrases, their philistine vulgarity, is precisely what discredits them: behind their tinsel passion lurks the worm of greedy lust in all its moral insignificance. The fan is certainly related to fire imagery and probably to woman as the object of sensuality; it opens for the first time prior to the final rape, not to cool but to "waft the searing heat of life" toward the narrator. In the same passage he invites the "stings of serpents," and he alludes to the Medusa, who recalls, together with the black fan and the heat, the "evil witch" in the poem's opening lines. Hell is undoubtedly present in his temptation, but he embellishes it with literary, traditional religious, and

musical references to camouflage the ugliness of its spiritual mediocrity—
until it is too late for anything but remorse.

Such "civilized" camouflage is not without parallel elsewhere in
Prussian Nights. Earlier in Allenstein the narrator encounters an old
acquaintance, a former university lecturer specializing in the literature of the
French Enlightenment. They are akin in their literary interests and their war
experiences. Their conversation is excited, even breathless; they recall the
past, they discuss the eighteenth century's pride in man, in reason and
progress, they ponder the questions (Rus', the Mongols, Europe) which have
tormented and entranced generations of Russian intellectuals. But all the
while this "civilized" man forces a German railroad dispatcher at gunpoint to
accept unsuspecting trains into the Allenstein terminal. There they are met
by Cossacks, the passengers are robbed, often raped and sometimes shot,
while most are marched to assembly points for transport to the Russian
camps. Humanity aside, this treacherous ambush serves no rational military
purpose. So this intense discussion of the past and its values, which causes
"living life" ("zhivaia zhizn'") to shine in the previously drunken eyes of this
officer, is nothing more than an escape: those values have no bearing on the
present. As the narrator leaves the terminal, he notices a "civilized," elderly
Russian general limping squeamishly among German corpses, a human
vulture indicating to his aides which valuables he wishes to plunder.
Similarly, the narrator later walks among a group of German wives,
indicating to a master-sergeant which one will share his bed.

Any such escape is illusory here—these actions betray the past and its
values. It will not suffice to say that chaotic, violent events in an alien
German environment sever these Russians psychologically from a dear and
distant, unreachable past. They themselves are eager enough to apply the
past to the present when it suits them: "We won't forget! We won't forgive!"
The narrator's first, venial sin—appropriating writing materials—reflects his
love of repose and reflection, in such contrast to the rape and pillage around.
Still, he hesitates, then justifies his action by referring to his own past
suffering over the wretched quality of pens, pencils, and paper during his
schooldays. There is humor, but also self-mockery in this episode, precisely
because he senses that his moral rationalization is akin to that of his troops
in their policy of revenge through rape.

The narrator plays a third game with the past in order to rationalize
present desires and pleasures: we have been and are helpless pawns in the
paws of fate, of events beyond our control, but now we've had a bit of luck,
so grab it! (See the passage cited above: "V nashei zhizni bespoloinoi . . .") If
the narrator escapes into the comfortable dimensions of the past, he does not
hold the gun pointed at the railroad dispatcher; if he uses the past as moral

rationalization for his appropriation of writing materials, he refuses to play any active role in vengeful destruction by fire. His tendency to be passive is apparent in his gravitation toward this third principle, and it is to it that he appeals during a lengthy tirade on ethics prior to launching his own rape:

> Carpe diem!—gedonisty
> Nas uchili—DEN'LOVI!
> Dni osypiatsia, kak list'ia,
> Zagusteet tok krovi.

> *Carpe diem!* The hedonists, they
> Always taught us—*Seize the day!*
> But the days like leaves are falling,
> The current of the blood runs thicker.

That he is plunged into remorse after the fact is predictable insofar as his passivity reflects his innate moral sense. *Carpe diem* reduces life to the pursuit of hedonistic pleasure, to the flesh alone. If his reason can support this principle in the context of chaos, his conscience knows better.

The source of that final remorse is not betrayal of the past and its values, but calculated betrayal of another human being. In so doing, the cultivated narrator, apparently out of place in a world gone mad, suddenly proves capable of ugly disorder himself. Solzhenitsyn's awareness of man's capacity for moral dereliction is nowhere more clearly expressed; the entire poem moves toward this merger of the passive restrained commander with the active barbarism of his subordinates.

The initial step in this direction is the narrator's appropriation of writing materials; it is important precisely because he is rather ashamed even though no person is betrayed. This episode is bracketed by two others involving rape. The first is the betrayal of the German Communist and murderous rape of his wife and daughter. In the second a woman, dressed and coifed like a German but speaking fluent vernacular Russian, emerges from a house and disdainfully defies the soldier banging at her door with his rifle ("P'ianyi, griaznyi, t'fu kakov!"). But others join him, and this "servant" (so she claims) or Hausfrau suddenly becomes ingratiating, and leads them to a neighboring house filled, she promises, with German virgins ("Nemok-tselok polon dom"). The betrayal of one's neighbor continues in the next episode, in which the German dispatcher sends his fellow countrymen to their doom to save his own skin.

This is an important motive for the narrator's ambivalent passivity as well. He indicates that his restraint is not an unambiguous response to a moral imperative by referring to himself as "Pilate," who collaborated with evil by passively withdrawing, by washing his hands to maintain the appearance of civilized decency. Like Pilate the narrator is a *man in command*, but he issues few orders and none to protect helpless civilians, chiefly women. Is he powerless or fearful of consequences? If primarily the latter, his restrained behavior is less good than evil: it reflects self-interest at the expense of others, it is a betrayal.

Thus, the venial self-interest evident in the seizure of writing materials escalates during the succeeding atrocities, even though the narrator never dirties his own hands. His imitation of Pilate continues in his own assault on a woman, which he arranges to keep secret. He prefaces that episode with the tirade on ethics noted above, in which he criticizes official writers (Shaginian, Surkov, Gorbatov, Erenburg) for "varnishing" reality. But he immediately mimics them by recalling Sarasate and by rejecting the moral relevance of philosophy and religion in a rather arcane reference to the legendary Indian philosopher Charvaki. Having varnished his own greedy, aggressive desire for his share of the women, he embarks upon a refined rape by proclaiming the ethically relativistic, ultimately nihilistic, fatuous slogan, "Everyone acts like this!"

Solzhenitsyn frequently creates multiple thematic resonances through significant juxtaposition of episodes. The moral equivalence of murder and rape is the fundamental bond between the poem's last two episodes, the shooting of the beautiful German and the narrator's rape of Anna. Both episodes begin with the narrator hedonistically preoccupied with his own snug comfort. In the former he is sucking candy and nestled in the soft, upholstered seat of a captured German Opelblitz. So he is rather indifferent to a photograph of a German officer taken from the woman and thrust at him by the vengeful soldier Somin. The officer is her husband, and his insignia *may* be that of the SS. The narrator's almost inadvertent, dismissive wave of the hand seals her fate, and he shouts "Hey, lads!" too late. Initially there is only mild regret: "How fresh" her beauty had been!

But that beauty is not forgotten: after the nihilistic meditation on morality which links these episodes, the narrator enters a lowly room packed with five husbandless German families busy with domestic chores. But "*such a one* I could not find" ("*Takoi* ne nakhozhu"). He arrives from other, far more comfortable quarters nearby, where he has dined and was enjoying an after-dinner smoke and reverie until he learned of the women's presence. For the first time he abandons his passivity. He commits his crime not amid fires nor during the frantic, chaotic advance toward Berlin; his crime arises during repose and from prior moral contemplation.

If premeditation magnifies the narrator's guilt, so does recognition of his victim's humanity—the only instance of such recognition in the poem. Although he enters the room of German women looking for a well-favored female, his first, faltering question of Anna is "Wie heissen Sie?" Certainly he is aware of Anna's lack of flesh, but he also notices her timidity and the almost imperceptible motion which straightens her kerchief as she looks up from a washtub. She is to be brought by a solicitous master-sergeant to a vacant wing of the premises, where he waits in "ambush" (*zasada*, probably an echo of the ambush set earlier for unsuspecting civilian trains in Allenstein). Anna is told she must milk cows for the Russians, and the narrator watches her approach through a window in the wing. He notices she is "somehow touchingly quiet," and that sadness is in her expression, and meekness in her glance, as the sergeant orders her to enter the wing rather than the cowshed. A surprised tremor distorts her mouth as she sees the narrator beyond the door, and he suddenly loses his ability to speak German. He remembers her apologetic smile then, as she realizes her agitation may imply suspicion. Her shawl has slipped from her shoulders in the cold, and the confused narrator, "for some reason," delicately wraps it about her again. This is an exquisite, simple gesture of concern, but he swiftly betrays it and Anna when she backs uncertainly toward the threshold. He slams the door and beckons without looking at her: "Komm!" That gesture ("pomanil") recalls the dismissive one ("makhnul rukoi"), which led to the German bride's murder. Standing with his back to the "beggars' bed" he has prepared, the narrator awaits Anna's word that she is "ready." And we remember that earlier the bride fell to the ground with a scream, then lay motionless in the cold snow, in a curled, fetal ball, ready for the fatal bullets. Anna pleads after the rape, "Doch erschiessen Sie mich nicht!" With anguish the narrator recognizes in the final two lines that the two women are now bound together by his own, personal crimes: "Akh, don't be afraid . . . Ah-h-h / On my soul there's a soul . . ."

Perhaps shame causes the narrator to avoid bringing Anna to his own comfortable quarters. Instead he "squeamishly" tosses a greasy mattress and bedraggled pillow on an old bedstead which he finds in the deserted, cold, trash-filled wing. These hurried "domestic" arrangements recall the violated homes behind the advancing Russian army; they are in harmony with the obsessive lines by Sarasate, which parody genuine feeling. The German women, to the contrary, are performing necessary domestic chores, and Anna's hands still steam slightly from laundry. This is the warmth of genuine life, not the violent fire of destruction. The narrator had expected but did not find in himself the "blaze" of passion or a "molten, joyous ringing in the muscles" (recall the "lava" of the Russian advance). An abandoned home, trash, cold—the chill of moral death—provide an appropriate environment for this criminal parody of private love between a man and a woman.

And this is how civilized, good men can create an immoral parody of genuine life as they act and react amidst the inevitably amoral movements of history. This parable aims to show that they must—we must—rise above the passive distress over barbarism, we must rise to anguish over our passive, and sometimes active, collaboration with it. Morality for Solzhenitsyn resides in what we do and fail to do—not in what we feel.

JOHN B. DUNLOP

The Gulag Archipelago:
Alternative to Ideology

The aim of this paper is to discuss, and if possible to systematize, the "positive" message of *The Gulag Archipelago*. In choosing to focus my attention in this fashion, I am of course aware that the major thrust of *Gulag* is *negative*, that its intention is, in the words of one commentator, to depict "what happens to a man and the world when man and life are *reduced* to ideology." However, while Solzhenitsyn's polemical goals in the book have been elucidated by a number of commentators—to take one example, I might mention Martin Malia's fine essay in the January, 1977 issue of *The Russian Review*—his positive gropings and grapplings have not yet received systematic and sustained attention.

In his seminal *Notes from the Underground*, Dostoevskii examined what the fruits of a logical application of the theories of nineteenth century radical socialists to mankind would be (the work, as is well known, seeks specifically to counter Chernyshevskii's *What Is to Be Done?*). Scrutinizing human nature closely, Dostoevskii showed that Chernyshevskii's "scientific socialism" would result in deforming and tormenting a man and that human nature would inevitably revolt against the logics of this monstrous theory. In *The Gulag Archipelago*, Solzhenitsyn continues Dostoyevskii's work by showing what happened once Chernyshevskii's theories—plus the refinements of his successors and admirers, such as Lenin—became state policy. Both *Notes from*

From *Solzhenitsyn in Exile: Critical Essays and Documentary Materials*, eds. John B. Dunlop, Richard S. Haugh, and Michael Nicholson. © 1985 by the Board of Trustees of the Leland Stanford Junior University.

the Underground and *The Gulag Archipelago* confront human nature with a
materialistic view of man which includes a commitment to determinism,
a flinty ruthlessness toward those who would obstruct "progress," and a
yearning for the social anthill and "Crystal Palace." But there is of course
a crucial difference between the two works. Dostoevskii was combating
theory; Solzhenitsyn is at war with *applied* theory.

In *Gulag*, Solzhenitsyn shows the effect on Russia of the role of
ideology. As he demonstrates, twentieth century totalitarianism presses down
on the individual with awesome force. To survive physically one is frequently
forced to inform on one's neighbors or join the chorus of voices shouting
"death! death! death!" as erstwhile colleagues at work are paraded off to
execution. In the concentration camps—which, in many ways, represent the
purest expression and distillation of ideology—the pressures and incentives to
survive at the *expense* of those around one are overwhelming. Surely all must
capitulate. But not all do. As Solzhenitsyn interjects in one place: "If
corruption was so inevitable, then why did Ol'ga L'vovna Sliozberg not
abandon her freezing friend on the forest trail, but stay behind to face almost
certain death together with her—and save her?"

Like Dostoevskii during his period of Siberian imprisonment,
Solzhenitsyn observed his fellow zeks with the attentive eye of genius. To
his own personal observations he added material derived from the accounts
of others and, after his release, from memoirs sent to him. With wonder he
notes that what is astonishing is not that so many capitulated before a
raging neo-barbarism but that more than a few burst the shackles of
ideology and successfully remained human beings. It is this revolt by the
élite of human nature against the dead hand of ideology that rivets
Solzhenitsyn's attention in *The Gulag Archipelago*; he is keenly interested in
all its manifestations.

On the lowest and least remarkable level, it is the revulsion felt by
Lieutenant Koverchenko, an intrepid parachutist who is simply *bored* with
the vapid proclamations of ideology. His revolt—which is not consciously
motivated—takes the form of wild, drunken adventures which ultimately earn
him a twenty-five-year prison term. (As a footnote, one might observe that
this way of opting out of the system is widely utilized in today's Soviet Russia.
Vladimir Maksimov's uneven but suggestive novel *Seven Days of Creation*
offers insights into this mode of rebellion.)

On a higher level, we are shown the revolt of those who choose
physically to combat the regime. Solzhenitsyn's generally favorable attitude
toward such persons is moderated and, to some extent, undercut by his deep
distrust for what happens to those who take up arms even against unseemly
evils. (At one point in *Gulag*, he asserts his belief that corruption is "probably

inevitable' for those who resort to violence.) Yet, though theoretically he can countenance only "moral revolution," Solzhenitsyn finds it difficult to condemn those who took up arms against an anti-human totalitarianism. Yes, he admits, all the books of the philosophers warn against the consequences of fighting evil with the sword, but what is one to do when one is being crushed and compressed into nothingness? As the popular adage, which Solzhenitsyn cites approvingly, puts it: ". . . evil cannot be cast out by good [*blagusfiu likhost' ne izoimesh'*]."

And in the opening chapter of the first volume of *Gulag* Solzhenitsyn wonders:

> What would things have been like if every Security operative, when he went out at night to make an arrest, had been uncertain whether he would return alive and had to say good-bye to his family? Or if, during periods of mass arrests, as for example in Leningrad, when they arrested a quarter of the entire city, people had not simply sat there in their little burrows, paling with terror at every bang of the downstairs door and at every step on the staircase, but had understood that they had nothing to lose and had boldly set up in the downstairs hall an ambush of half a dozen people with axes, hammers, pokers, or whatever else was at hand? . . . Or what about the Black Maria sitting out there on the street with one lonely chauffeur—what if it had been driven off or had its tires spiked?

He answers his own queries thus:

> The Organs would very quickly have suffered a shortage of officers and transport and, notwithstanding all of Stalin's thirst, the cursed machine would have ground to a halt! . . . We didn't love freedom enough . . . We purely and simply *deserved* everything that happened afterward.

Solzhenitsyn's strictures against physical resistance to tyranny would seem to be balanced or at least held in abeyance in such passages. Similarly, in volume two he cites with obvious approval the "rare and shining example" of a front-line soldier who had not lost his courage in camp. In 1947, this former soldier overpowered and disarmed two convoy guards, shot them both and then informed his shocked fellow prisoners that they were free. When they timorously declined his summons to liberty, he set off on his own and succeeded in killing and wounding several of his pursuers before taking his own life. Solzhenitsyn's comment: "The entire Archipelago might well have collapsed if all former front-liners had behaved as he did."

In volume three, Solzhenitsyn's interest in those who chose to rebel physically occupies a considerable portion of the narrative. He writes with respect and affection concerning a fellow camp graduate, Georgii Tenno, whose plan, once he learned he had contracted a mortal disease, was to dispatch a score of murderers, including the honored pensioner Viacheslav Molotov. Rationalizing and justifying Tenno's thought, Solzhenitsyn writes: "This would not be murder, but judicial execution, given that the law of the state protected murderers." Only the rapid progress of cancer, which sapped his strength more swiftly than he had anticipated, kept Tenno from making the attempt. Solzhenitsyn also describes the rebellion in 1948 of a brigade of zeks, led by a former colonel, who chose to march on the city of Vorkuta. His comment: "The hopelessness of this rising as a military operation is obvious. But would you say that dying quietly by inches was more hopeful?" Volume three also makes more explicit than volume one had done Solzhenitsyn's admiration for the Vlasov movement—a new "Pugachevshcina" supported by the broad masses of the populace. And the last volume extols the great Nevocherkassk uprising of 1962, the first major rebellion in a Soviet city in forty-one years, "a cry from the soul of a people who could no longer live as they had lived."

As I see it, the purpose of this concluding volume of *The Gulag Archipelago* is not to incite the Soviet populace to turn on its masters but rather to show that, with the waning of ideology in the post-war years and Khrushchev era, human nature began to reassert itself in mass actions. A "cry from the soul" occurs, a spontaneous and collective rebellion against institutionalized death.

Another choice for those who refuse to be deformed by ideology is escape, and *Gulag* devotes not a few of its pages to those adventurous spirits who attempted flight. "Escape!" Solzhenitsyn writes, "What desperate courage it took! Without civilian clothes, without food, with empty hands, to cross the fence under fire and run into the bare, waterless, endless open steppe!" Georgii Tenno, with his twin tatoos of "Liberty!" and "Do or die!" seems to represent for Solzhenitsyn the archetypal escaper. (One should perhaps add that the dividing line between escapers and physical rebels becomes somewhat blurred, since those in flight are sometimes called upon to use violence to ward off their pursuers.)

While Solzhenitsyn has great sympathy for the spontaneous rebellion of bold spirits, he is clearly more at ease with purely *moral* rebellion. Here— in a Russian tradition going back to Saints Boris and Gleb—fulfillment is found in self-immolation. In treating instances of moral rebellion, Solzhenitsyn appears to distinguish between those whose reaction to injustice and institutionalized lies is visceral—one simply stands up and says no!—and those whose defiance is grounded in a world-view. An appropriate example of what I have called "visceral" rebellion would be Anna Petrovna Skripnikova, who is discussed at the end of volume two. For her, survival is "nothing in comparison with common justice." And Solzhenitsyn comments: " . . . if everyone were even one-quarter as implacable as Anna Skripnikova— the history of Russia would be different." The costs of moral rebellion, as Solzhenitsyn demonstrates at length, are not significantly different from those of choosing physically to oppose the system. In volume one, for example, we are offered the case of a nonpolitical officer named Smelov who went on a hunger strike in a Leningrad prison. He was visited by a prosecutor who asked him: "Why are you torturing yourself?" Smelov replied: "Justice is more precious to me than life." Smelov was ordered to be taken to an insane asylum, where he was told: "We suspect you may be a schizophrenic." Or there is the case, also reported in volume one, of the dissatisfied prisoner who protested against a suspicious weighing of bread rations: "I demand a reweighing . . ." To the prisoner's visceral objection to injustice the prison authorities have a reflex response:

> 'Which one here spoke out against the Soviet government? . . .
> Aha, you're the bastard? You're the one who doesn't like
> the Soviet government? . . . You stinking scum! You counter-
> revolutionary! You ought to be hanged . . .'

The "rebel" is taken away, and the response to the official's query, "Now who else is dissatisfied?" is, of course, silence.

One mode of protest which might seem almost logical in light of the scale of the suffering is suicide. But this option is vehemently rejected by Solzhenitsyn. ". . . is suicide," he asks, "really resistance? Isn't it really submission?" And elsewhere he adds: "A suicide is always a bankrupt, always a human being in a blind alley . . ."

The next step up the ladder from a spontaneous nonacceptance of injustice and lies is to possess a counter-ideology to the prevailing one. In volume one, we are introduced to a Colonel Konstantin Iasevich, a former White officer who grasped the nature of Bolshevism from the beginning and devoted his life to combating it. Placidly and with a firm spirit the self-disciplined colonel awaits his inevitable execution. ". . . He had evidently," Solzhenitsyn writes, "a clear and exact view of everything around him . . ."

At the highest level are those with a "point of view" (*tochka zreniia*). A point of view is the ultimate and perhaps only enemy of ideology, for not only does it provide a reasoned critique of the ideology and the system it spawns but it offers *an alternative world-view* which prompts its adherents to

do spiritual battle with the ideology. During the infamous Moscow show
trials, Bukharin and his associates, Solzhenitsyn feels, were unable to exhibit
independence because they lacked a point of view and, in fact, remained
slaves to the ideology which was seeking to take their lives. Those with a
point of view possess the necessary artillery to destroy ideology and the
firmness to withstand it by electing *not* to "survive at any price."

Let us examine several examples which Solzhenitsyn offers of persons
who had a point of view:

> They wanted to drag [the philosopher Nikolai Berdiaev] into
> an open trial; they arrested him twice . . . he was subjected to a
> night interrogation by Dzerzhinsky himself. Kamenev was
> there too . . . But Berdiaev did not humiliate himself. He did
> not beg or plead. He set forth firmly those religious and moral
> principles which had led him to refuse to accept the political
> authority established in Russia. And not only did they come to
> the conclusion that he would be useless for a trial, but they
> released him.
>
> The man had a *point of view*!

The second example he gives is that of an old woman and religious believer:

> They kept on interrogating her every night. Two years earlier, a
> former Metropolitan of the Orthodox Church, who had escaped
> from exile, had spent a night at her home on his way through
> Moscow. . . . At first the interrogators took turns, and then they
> went after her in groups. They shook their fists in the little old
> woman's face, and she replied: 'There is nothing you can do with
> me even if you cut me into pieces. . . . you are afraid of each
> other, and you are even afraid of killing me.' (They would lose
> their main lead.) 'But I am not afraid of anything. I would be glad
> to be judged by God right this minute.'

It is not incidental that in these instances Solzhenitsyn finds that "point
of view" related to Christianity. He is not saying, of course, that only
Christians can be courageous—he is even willing to attest the courage of the
SRs and Trotskiites who were ground to bits by the very machine they helped
set in operation. What he appears to be maintaining is that only Christianity
offers an effective antidote to Marxism-Leninism, only it can exorcise the
demons which have been rending Russia since 1917. Solzhenitsyn's views
have understandably not set well with socialists and liberal Marxists. Neo-
Marxist dissenter Roy Medvedev, for example, protests vehemently:

Solzhenitsyn does not even consider it possible for nonreligious people to distinguish between good and bad . . . Solzhenitsyn does not understand that socialist convictions can be the basis for a genuinely humanist set of values and a profoundly human morality. And if up to now the problems of ethics and morals have not yet found satisfactory treatment in Marxist-Leninist theory, this by no means implies that scientific socialism is incapable by its very nature of establishing moral values.

Solzhenitsyn would undoubtedly retort that "scientific socialism" should have pondered "the problems of ethics and morals" a bit more before undertaking to experiment with the lives of millions.

Solzhenitsyn's religious views, which permeate *The Gulag Archipelago* and serve as a bone of contention for many besides Roy Medvedev, seem to have resulted from his close observation of humanity while he was in prison. The analogy to Dostoevskii is again relevant. Their paths to religious belief, however, were different. Dostoevskii, a philosopher and theological anthropologist, deduced laws of human nature which led him to religion; Solzhenitsyn, on the other hand, seems to have concentrated on the question of ethical behavior. A superior ethical stance—rooted in a "point of view"—characterized many of the believers he observed or heard tales of from his fellow zeks. He notes, for example, that during the Kengir camp rebellion the religious believers were "as always the calmest." He frequently lauds Russian women believers for behavior worthy of the Christian martyrs of the first century. And he praises Patriarch Tikhon, first head of the Russian Church after the Revolution, who stated at the Moscow Church Trial of 1922 that he would obey Soviet laws *"to the extent that they do not contradict the rules of piety."* Solzhenitsyn's comment: "Oh, if only everyone had answered just that way! Our whole history would have been different."

An important question which directly relates to Solzhenitsyn's "positive" message in *Gulag* concerns how the past is to be righted. What about the millions who succumbed to the threats and blandishments of ideology? And what about the executioners themselves, the legions of Soviet Eichmanns?

Running like a red thread through the book is Solzhenitsyn's belief that the victims of oppression who gave in should not be judged. "Do not be the first to cast a stone at them," he pleads. And elsewhere he explains that the "basic viewpoint" of the book is that all who suffered "ought rather to be vindicated than accused." The pressures on the victims were, after all, enormous, perhaps unprecedented in human history.

But what about the executioners? At times, Solzhenitsyn gives way to an inconsistent but understandable delight that the terror swallowed up many of its children. Roy Medvedev has lectured the writer on this point: " . . . I was unpleasantly surprised by Solzhenitsyn's words that he had somehow been 'consoled' . . . by the thought of the degradation to which Krylenko was reduced in Butyrki prison before he was shot, the same Krylenko who had condemned others to similar degradation." Medvedev wonders whether this is "decent," let alone Christian, of Solzhenitsyn, though he neglects to mention his own commitment, as a neo-Leninist, to the necessary bloodshed of revolution (see, for example, his book *Let History Judge*).

Solzhenitsyn's wrath against the agents of terror is usually tempered in *Gulag* by an awareness that he himself could easily have become one of the executioners. Besides being an indictment of Marxism-Leninism and all its works, the book is also a confession. Were it not for his own resuscitative passage through the inferno of camps, prison, and exile, Solzhenitsyn could, he admits, have become one of the victimizers. "If only," he writes, "it were all so simple! If only there were evil people somewhere insidiously committing evil deeds, and it were necessary only to separate them from the rest of us and destroy them. But the line dividing good and evil cuts through the heart of every human being . . . Socrates taught us: *Know thyself!*" And in another place he writes:

> 'Know thyself!' There is nothing that so aids and assists the awakening of conscience within us as insistent thoughts about one's own transgressions, errors, mistakes . . . Whenever I mentioned the heartlessness of our highest-ranking bureaucrats, the cruelty of our executioners, I remember myself in my captain's shoulder boards . . . and I say: 'So were *we* any better?'

A knowledge of the dark potentials of one's own nature thus serves to moderate any desire for vengeance. Yet Solzhenitsyn believes that it is possible for a human being to pass beyond the state of moral flux common to all men and to cross over a mystical threshold of evil:

> Physics is aware of phenomena which occur only at *threshold* magnitudes . . . You can cool oxygen to 100 degrees below zero Centigrade and exert as much pressure as you want; it does not yield, but remains a gas. But as soon as minus 183 degrees is reached, it liquefies and begins to flow.
>
> Evidently evildoing also has a threshold magnitude. Yes, a human being hesitates and bobs back and forth between good and evil all his life. He slips, falls back, clambers up, repents, is overtaken once more by darkness. But just so long as the

threshold of evildoing is not crossed, the possibility of returning remains . . .

Solzhenitsyn's strong awareness that he *could* have become a "blue cap" and executioner does not blind him to the depths of evil which can be plumbed by a human being, depths which have been justified and even extolled by twentieth century totalitarianism.

In *Gulag* Solzhenitsyn calls for Nürnberg-type trials of those Soviet citizens guilty of crimes against humanity. Employing the yardstick of the 86,000 Germans brought to trial in their homeland after World War II, he estimates that approximately one-quarter of a million Soviets should be asked to stand in the dock. ". . . For the sake of our country and our children we have the duty to *seek them all out and bring them all to trial!*" Each should be compelled to state clearly: "Yes, I was an executioner and murderer." The country needs these trials as a rite of purgation to prevent its youth from becoming cynical, but above all the executioners themselves are in need of them. Perhaps, Solzhenitsyn seems to feel, such a stark and unavoidable rendezvous with truth may induce at least some of them to cross back over the threshold of evil.

Solzhenitsyn believes that his own arrest and the dramatic reversal of his personal fortunes had a salutary effect on his life. As Dr. Kornfeld, a Jewish convert to Christianity, tells the future writer shortly before being murdered in the camps. ". . . I have become convinced that there is no punishment that comes to us on earth which is undeserved. . . . if you go over your life with a fine-tooth comb and ponder it deeply, you will be able to hunt down that transgression of yours for which you have now received this blow." These words of his murdered mentor remain with Solzhenitsyn as "an inheritance" he comes to realize that "the meaning of earthly existence lies not, as we have grown used to thinking, in prospering, but . . . in the development of the soul." (Incidentally, it was this encounter with Dr. Kornfeld, reported in volume two of *Gulag,* which seems to have been the spark for Solzhenitsyn's conversion to religious belief.)

The Gulag Archipelago is a profoundly *personalistic* book. Respect for the unique value, even sanctity, of the individual is a cornerstone of its message. Where Marxism-Leninism sees individuals as minute particles of larger and more important entities, such as classes—some of whom it may be necessary to exterminate as "insects"—Solzhenitsyn wants to propagate the infinite worth of each individual human being. *Gulag* is a kind of celebration of personality, a personalistic feast. In prison, Solzhenitsyn is "filled to the brim with the joy of being among them [people]." And elsewhere he writes: "I love that moment when a newcomer is admitted to the cell for the first time . . .

And I myself love to enter a new cell . . ." Each human being who perished before a raging totalitarianism was a pearl of great price; each name must be rescued from oblivion.

A final point deserves to be mentioned. The act of writing *Gulag* is itself a "model" of behavior which flies in the face of a materialistic ideology which proclaims physical well-being as the highest good. While at work on volume two, Solzhenitsyn reports: "The dragon emerged for one minute, licked up my novel [the reference is to the seizure of a manuscript of *The First Circle*] with his red tongue . . . and retired behind the curtain for the time. But I can hear his breathing, and I know that his teeth aimed at my neck . . . And with devastated soul I gather my strength to complete this investigation, so that it at least may escape the dragon's teeth." *The Gulag Archipelago* was written in the shadow of death, and that should not be forgotten.

EDWARD J. BROWN

The Calf and the Oak:
Dichtung and Wahrheit

Readers of *The Calf and the Oak* are fascinated and shaken by its account of a lone writer's courageous, unremitting struggle against one of the powers of darkness, with all its police, its armies and navies and its thousands of atomic weapons; though the "Oak" still stands at the end we know that our "Calf," head unbowed and ready to engage the enemy again, is the real victor. David has met Goliath—the comparison is suggested by Solzhenitsyn himself—and while he hasn't killed him, has planted a heavy stone in his stupid forehead and exposed the rude creature to scorn and contempt. Many consider this to be the best thing Solzhenitsyn has yet written, and indeed one is tempted to shout, with the late Vladimir Weidle: "An astonishing, a magnificent book. When reading it you are simply absorbed and cannot tear yourself away. I find no flaws in it. I'm ready to ring out all the bells for it . . ." And Efim Etkind's comment draws attention to its extraordinary linguistic power: "Chaque nouveau livre de cet auteur est une découverte du russe." We shall see that there are some who deny the historical value of *The Calf* and accuse its author of errors, distortions, and worse, but even they offer tribute to it as a work of verbal art.

The *Calf* provides total aesthetic satisfaction simply because it draws upon the primal eldest archetype: the struggle between good and evil, two forces once seen by Milton "in dubious battle" on the plains of heaven. We

From *Solzhenitsyn in Exile: Critical Essays and Documentary Materials*, eds. John B. Dunlop, Richard S. Haugh, and Michael Nicholson. © 1985 by the Board of Trustees of the Leland Stanford Junior University.

follow every turn of that dubious, unequal, and shifting battle in the calf's case from his emergence out of the underground (from the deep water, he will say) to deliver that first magnificent volley *One Day in the Life of Ivan Denisovich*, down to the last but not yet final manoeuvre, his expulsion by the minions of evil from the territory of the Soviet Union itself. And of course that territory is always the ground of contention. The story of the struggle in heaven is exactly reversed: here the forces of evil are in control of Russia, which they have turned into a regimented, infernal paradise, and they expel good angels onto foreign territory which they have designated as Hell.

The genre of such a deeply archetypal work is difficult to fix. It bears the subtitle "sketches of literary life," but what is there literary about the life of a writer who must hide what he writes from the police, protect every source and helper from the threat of incarceration, squirrel away a magnum opus from all eyes until "the proper time," outwit, outflank and defeat the enemies of literature, who happen also in the Soviet Union to be its tutors and publishers? Obviously the subtitle "sketches of literary life" is ironic, and Vladimir Lakshin simply misses the point when he complains that Solzhenitsyn talks only about himself and not about "literary life in the Soviet Union." Literary life indeed. That subtitle suggests a hackneyed Soviet genre under the rubric of which a narrator selects "typical" events from some area of Soviet life to describe and comment upon. But the events set forth here break all patterns of "typicality" and this confused even a good and honest Soviet critic.

Solzhenitsyn's novels all lie on that uncertain border between history and literature, a disputed area occupied by historians but sometimes contested by novelists. *The First Circle* and *August 1914* deal directly with historical matters and, like Tolstoi's *War and Peace*, introduce real historical characters into the artist's plotted action. All of his works, in all genres, investigate, analyze, reflect, and represent the reality of Russian experience in the twentieth century and therefore are historical documents of a special kind. *The Calf* too is located in that border area of which I have spoken, but the historically real personages in it figure as agents in a fateful struggle between God and his enemies, a struggle in which Solzhenitsyn is the chosen instrument of the former. The result is that the people, some of them still living, who take part as actors in this mighty drama play out their parts in a way that transcends the literal and the biographically factual. This has led to some misunderstanding.

The book is aglow with a sense of mission and studded with affirmations of faith in that mission. "Many things in my life I did contrary to my own principal purpose, not understanding the true path, but always something set me straight." "And I think that for the first time in my life I saw, I realized that I was making history." "From December to February, ailing though I was and obliged to tend the fire and cook for myself, I completed the first version of *Gulag* . . . But it was not I that did it. My hand was guided." "*The Cancer Ward* I never dispatched to the West. It was proposed that I do so and there were channels, but for some reason I refused, and without any ulterior plan. But it reached the West anyway (*sam popal*), and—well, that means it had to, God's good time had come." "God saved me from covering myself with shame . . ." And there are of course prayerful acknowledgments of the true source of his more-than-human strength: "How wisely and strongly dost Thou lead me, O Lord!"

Verbal echoes of higher intervention are frequent in *The Calf*. Could it have been an accident that the typing of *Gulag* took place at his retreat far from Moscow, a place of peace and of tender green called Christmas (*Rozhdestvo*), or that Tvardovskii underwent his harrowing experience of truth, the reading of *The First Circle*, during "the three days of Easter"? It is true that military metaphors and analogies are frequent in *The Calf*, but when he speaks of the onward march of those "samizdat battalions" there is no doubt that we have to do here with *Christian* soldiers in a holy struggle.

Indeed it is not easy to pigeon-hole Solzhenitsyn's *Calf* as to genre, and one is inclined to say of it what Lidiia Chukovskaia says of Herzen's *Byloe i dumy* (*My Past and Thoughts*); that it is one of a kind and belongs to no nameable genre except its own: "Memoirs? Autobiography? Novel? Collection of political articles and philosophical statements?" There are elements of them all in *The Calf*, including a kind of profession of faith. I would suggest a close affinity with another great work of literature, the *Life of Avvakum* written by his own hand. Numerous passages in that work parallel the affirmations I've selected from *The Calf*. Avvakum's *Life* glows with faith in the rightness of a cause and as eloquently damns the enemies of that cause. And like the language of *The Calf*, Avvakum's language is simple colloquial Russian, replete with proverbs and sayings and vulgar enough to dispose of an array of sinful and disgusting enemies of truth.

Whatever its value as history, the fact that *The Calf* is a work of literary art becomes abundantly clear if we view it in the context of Solzhenitsyn's novels, since it shares with them essential thematic and stylistic features. A central theme of *One Day*, *The First Circle* and *Cancer Ward* is the transcendence in practical as well as moral reason of the *zek*, the prisoner, and especially the millions unjustly imprisoned. Professor Chelnov in *The First Circle* offers the speculation that "only the prisoner really has an immortal soul, but the free man may be denied it for his vanity." The *zek* is the center of that novel's world and he enjoys fundamental advantages over the free people, most of whom have never escaped the trap of lies and fear. We think of the highly successful novelist Galakhov (probably modelled on the late Konstantin Simonov) who must chose carefully the topics he will treat and exercise adroit circumspection in the selection of "typical" details, or of Iakonov, whose brilliant position has been achieved at the cost of his self-respect. The prisoners on the other hand are free to think, to entertain other than official ideas, to know a part of the truth and to seek the rest. In *One Day* the news that comes to the prisoners from the "outside," from the free world, tells of a life debased and depressed both materially and culturally. In her letter Shukhov's wife describes the tasteless stencilling of cheap carpets, a profitable village "craft," and her account of life and labor on the collective farm chills the honest soul of Ivan Denisovich. Kostoglotov, the former *zek* in *The Cancer Ward*, has a special fund of human strength that grew in him during a long imprisonment, and how can he not feel scorn and contempt for the well-fed and chauffeured Rusanov? A leitmotif of *The Calf* is precisely the unique human quality of the camp experience. Of Soviet literary men who had never shared this experience he says that all of them, "social novelists, solemn dramatists, and of course all the more the journalists and critics, all have agreed in concert not to tell the main truth, whatever they write about." During his years in the underground the Calf had been convinced that there were many more like himself who knew the truth and could tell it: "The truth consists not only of jails, executions, camps, and exile, but if you avoid these things entirely you cannot write the main truth." And the following marvellously moving passage, difficult if not impossible to convey fully in English, reveals the gulf that separated Solzhenitsyn from Tvardovskii, helps to explain the awkward relationship between them, and effectively answers any charge of "ingratitude" to his publisher:

> Of course I was obliged to Tvardovskii, but only for myself. I had no right to consider just my personal interest or what the opinion of me might be on the *Novyi mir* staff, but must take as my main premise that I stand not for myself alone, that my destined career in literature is not just mine but belongs to all those millions who never scratched and clawed their way out, never told in hoarse whispers the story of their fate as prisoners, nor revealed the things they discovered too late in the camps. Just as Troy was not in the least obliged to Schliemann for its existence so also our buried camp culture has left us its own legacy. And so when I returned from a world which never returned its dead I dared not swear an oath of loyalty either to *Novyi mir* or to Tvardovskii, dared not reckon on whether they would see that my head was

not a bit turned by my fame and that I was simply engaged in occupying a *place d'armes* and doing it with cold calculation.

The sense of a prior debt to the unjustly dead of the labor camps permeates *The Calf* and colors every moment of the protagonist's struggle. While writing his Nobel acceptance speech he noted that it had been customary for laureates to speak of the nature of art, of beauty and the structures of literature:

> . . . to discuss the nature of literature or its possibilities would be for me a difficult and boring treatment of what is of secondary importance: what I'm able to do, that I'll do and show; what I can't do I won't attempt. And if I gave such a lecture, just how would former prisoners react to it? Why was he given a voice and a platform? Was he afraid? . . . Has he betrayed the dead?

Solzhenitsyn reports that at one time he believed that there could be nothing worth reading in officially published Soviet literature and that Russian literature existed only among the outlawed and excluded, those like himself who knew the truth but were hiding their works "until the proper time":

> But then I believed a day would come when all of us together would emerge from the depths of the sea like the thirty-three bogatyrs. And then our great literature would be restored, that literature which had been submerged with us on the bottom of the sea since the time of the Great Turning Point, and maybe even before that.

He learned later of course that there were only a few heroes like himself and nothing like the fairy-tale "thirty-three," and he modified his judgment somewhat of the official literary product, admitting that there were a few writers above ground and without camp records who had a vital word to say, yet the conviction remains with him that the ex-prisoner who writes is special and important, and he had no patience with Tvardovskii when the latter rejected the poems of the "camp brother" Shalamov.

Just as in *The First Circle, The Cancer Ward* and *One Day*, the pivot of movement in *The Calf* is contrast and conflict between the *zek* world and the world of those "others" whether camp guards or free and prosperous citizens. It is important to realize, moreover, that the "others" in this work include the editorial staff of *Novyi mir*. The ex-prisoner from the provinces who still lives in a humble shack is repelled by their ample quarters, which one reached by way of a wide and lordly staircase "suitable for filming in a scene of a grand ball." His honest poverty is insulted by the handsome advance they can offer him: "the advance alone was equal to two years of my salary." Tvardovskii loved him "as a feudal lord loves his best vassal." The protagonist (whom I refer to as the Calf), afraid he will not find time in his life to complete his sacred mission, is always in a hurry, but Tvardovskii's tempos are different: "Now, after our great success [says Tvardovskii] why wouldn't we sit a while, sip a bit of tea with rolls, chew the fat (*pokaliakat'*) about big things and little?" And here the Chief offers the example of an establishment writer, Simonov (who might be modelled on Galakhov in *The First Circle*!): "That's what all writers do, take Simonov"—A. T. [Tvardovskii] jokingly offered me him as an example— "They'll sit a bit, have a leisurely smoke. Where are you always hurrying off to?" But the Calf's needs are simple: just to be let alone to do his writing in peace and free of worry about publishers, and to hell with all those unwanted and unasked for laudatory reviews by respectable figures like Simonov, reviews which are like "the threads of a spiderweb" threatening to entangle him and impede him from his true purpose, upon which no Simonov or Tvardovskii could ever look with favor. Nor was he impressed by the "slavishly exaggerated" celebration of his talents that filled the sycophantic press immediately after the appearance, with Khrushchev's blessing, of *One Day*.

The former *zek* is not obliged to treat those others as equals and to be open and honest with them could be a fatal mistake. When Tvardovskii managed to get him an interview with Demichev, the head of Agitation and Propaganda, a man whose face showed not a trace of honest human feeling and whose speech was dull and banal, the Calf managed deftly to pull the wool over the bastard's eyes: "At first he was watchful and suspicious, but in the course of our two-hour interview he warmed up to me and believed everything I said." Similarly in his informal chat with the secretaries of the Writers' Union he quite frankly lied (*vru*) about the writing of his famous letter to the Congress of the Writers' Union, and they believed and nodded. Not even with Tvardovskii could he be open about his plans and strategies: "I hadn't opened myself to him, the full network of my plans, moves, and calculations had been concealed from him . . ."

Among them all the Calf does make an exception of Tvardovskii, who figures in the book as a kind of tragic hero, his fatal flaw symbolized by the red party booklet he carried in his coat pocket ("next to his heart"); whose conscience is crippled by his commitment to the vile system that rewarded him so well. The Calf tried with some success to reeducate the Chief of *Novyi mir*, and if he never fully succeeded the reason probably was that Tvardovskii had never walked through the purifying fire of the camps:

> My own head had been straightened out by my first years in jail and a similar process had begun with Tvardovskii after Khrushchev's speech at the Twentieth Congress. But, just as in the Party as a whole, the process soon slowed down, then was choked off and even reversed itself. Tvardovskii, like Khrushchev, was in a trancelike (*zabliatom*) state of lifelong captivity to the accepted ideology . . .

And if Tvardovskii lacked the fortitude to fight when *Novyi mir* was slowly being strangled, the reason was that "[for such a struggle] Tvardovskii needed that fire-resistant hardness which is cultivated only in the Archipelago of the *zeks*."

What separated him from Tvardovskii and from all successful Soviet figures, then, was the camp experience. Only the camp, only isolation and suffering bestowed upon a human being the mark of authenticity. In one of many great scenes the Calf, with an uncanny sense of novelistic structure, reduces the Chief of *Novyi mir* to a drunken stupor in the course of which, visiting upon himself an exquisite poetic justice, he demands to be treated as a *zek*, and asks the Calf to abuse and tongue-lash him like a camp officer. It happened in Solzhenitsyn's house in Riazan' during a visit there of Tvardovskii for the purpose of reading *The First Circle*. The Chief was mesmerized by the book as he read it over a three-day period, swilling the while heroic quantities of cognac and vodka. Friends of Tvardovskii have expressed understandable outrage at this scene and at Solzhenitsyn for invading the privacy of an embarrassing alcoholic episode, but he has replied that no one has a right to withhold the truth, and he might have added that in the artistic economy of the book as a whole the scene could not be spared. Here is the scene. Tvardovskii had been joking drunkenly about the possibility of being sent to jail himself:

> He kept on joking, but the air of the prison penetrated him more and more as he read, and it infected his lungs . . .
>
> The feeling he had that maybe he himself would not escape a sentence (or, more likely, a melancholy stirring within him, just as in Tolstoi when he was an old man: it's too bad I wasn't jailed, I'm the one who really should have been . . .) showed itself a number of times during that visit . . . He was especially interested in life behind bars and he'd question me curiously: "But why do

they shave the heads?" or "Why don't they allow any glass dishes in?" Apropos of one line in the novel he said "If you're going to the stake, then go, but it has to be for something." Several times, without any air or feeling of amusement, he reiterated his promise to take packages to me in jail, but only on condition that I bring things to him if I stayed out.

And toward the evening of the second day when it became clear as he read that the jailing of Innokentii was inevitable . . . —and also after three tumblers of well-aged vodka—he got terribly drunk and insisted that I "play" with him at being an "MGB lieutenant," in fact that I shout at him and accuse him of things while he stood at stiff attention . . .

I had to help him undress and get to bed. But in a little while we were all awakened by a loud noise: A. T. was shouting and carrying on a conversation with himself, in a number of different voices, taking the part of several speakers. He'd lit all the lamps that there were in his room (in fact he liked to have all the lights on he could in a room—"it's jollier that way") and he was sitting at the table, no bottle now, in just his undershorts. He was saying pathetically: "I'll soon go away and die." Then he'd give out a roar: "Silence! On your feet!" and he'd leap up at his own command and stand at attention before himself. Then again he'd feel very grieved: "Well, no matter, I can do no other." (Meaning that he'd made up his mind to go to the stake for my fearsome novel.)

Thus the Chief who claimed to have "discovered" Solzhenitsyn and who treated him as a "vassal," who had prospered under Stalin and even given his talent to a poetic justification of collectivization, is so shattered by *The First Circle* that he catches at last a momentary glimpse of the prison truth, and is ready, even if only for an alcoholic moment, to accept the stake itself for the sake of that truth. Truly a moving and a pregnant scene, the product of a consummate artist who has himself suffered through to the truth and spares no one in his pursuit of it.

The portrait of Tvardovskii in *The Calf*, though it has offended his friends and family, is in fact a brilliant literary achievement. The Calf brings to life an immensely attractive and able human being, a good poet and in his deep Russian heart an honest man, who suffers from the afflictions of intellect and conscience that have resulted, as the Calf sees it, from a long compromise with evil. But Tvardovskii is not totally lost, and the account of his dealings with the Calf is also the story of his gradual evolution toward enlightenment. At first he is shown as a typical bloated, brutish Soviet bureaucrat, alien to the streets of Moscow and unable to move about in them except by chauffeured limousine—and he had to have a large limousine, his bulk was uncomfortable in a modest Moskvich; often absorbed in familial creature comforts, the purchase of a new dacha, for instance; a lordly *barin* who hardly spoke to his subordinate editors on the lower floor, and who regarded the *Novyi mir* operation as his own "fief"; an eminence of power who when he took a train never had to stand in line with other people to get his ticket; a typical Soviet contradiction in terms: a poet decorated with a Stalin prize. In his social position and in his style of life with all its power and privilege that Tvardovskii is hardly distinct from the Party bureaucrats, literary hacks and successful writers we meet both in *The Calf* and in the novels. But Tvardovskii is radically different from all of them because he had once allowed himself, as we've seen, a breath of the prison air.

It was Tvardovskii's fatal flaw that he was devoted both to the Party and to Russian literature, and it was impossible to serve at one time those two masters. He served Russian literature well by publishing Solzhenitsyn's works, but only at the cost of persuading himself that "there was nothing in them incompatible with the idea of communism," that, in fact, they were not anti-Soviet works. He even maintained that Solzhenitsyn "took a party position":

> "A party position"—that's my novel he was talking about! Very interesting. Nor was that the cynical formulation of an editor determined to "push the novel through." That confusion of my novel with the "party position" was honestly and sincerely the only possible method, otherwise Tvardovskii, a poet and a communist, could not have set himself the goal of publishing my novel.

Clearly the Calf could never open himself fully to his benefactor: "Our orbits were so far apart that we could never meet." He is aware, moreover, that Tvardovskii's false position accounted for his many weaknesses, not least the weakness for alcohol. As he himself is drawn deeper and deeper into the sickening and frustrating struggle with the literary bureaucrats he grows in understanding of Tvardovskii and even sympathizes with that worst fault:

> . . . As I prepared to break a lance again [with the various "secretaries"] I felt weary and needed to shed that useless, sterile, and totally unnecessary nervous tension that I felt. But how? Take medicine? But there is one simple remedy: a little vodka early in the evening. Right away all edges softened and I wasn't

harassed for an answer or a snappish retort, and I slept soundly. And then I understood another thing about Tvardovskii: for thirty years what had he had except vodka to help him shed that vexing, scalding, shameful and bootless tension? Just cast a stone at him after that!

One of the chief themes of *The Calf* is Tvardovskii's suffering, hesitant movement toward resolution of the inner conflict. Gradually the Calf came to recognize that the Chief possessed qualities he hadn't expected and that did not fit the image of a Soviet bureaucrat. To the Calf's astonishment he warmly approved the famous letter to the Writers' Union on censorship and other things. "No. I hadn't really figured that man out" is his comment. And evidence begins to accumulate that Tvardovskii is changing. After circulating copies of a second letter of complaint to the "secretaries" the Calf, for a moment doubting and disheartened about the course he had taken, shared his doubts with Tvardovskii, but to his great surprise the Chief said he'd done just the right thing: if you start something you should finish it. "Once more he astonished me. What had become of his timidity and all his weary evasions?" And a further reflection in the same context: "How long we'd known one another—and we didn't know one another at all." The deeper into the "plot" we go the more attractive Tvardovskii becomes. The Calf, with his perfect eye for a scene, pictures Tvardovskii as he saw his visitors off from the dacha on a snowy evening:

> A. T. thought he'd like to take a walk and he put on a kind of rough half-length jacket and a cap, took a stick for support—not a very thick one—and in the quiet snow he walked with us to the gate. He looked very like a peasant, maybe a just barely literate one. He took off his cap and snow fell on his bright, huge, balding head, the head of a peasant. But his face was pale and haggard. He was heartsick. I gave him a farewell kiss . . . The car moved off and he just stood there in the snow, a peasant leaning on a staff.

As Tvardovskii's evolution proceeds and he moves closer to his downfall and death, he not only excites our sympathy as a human being but we see him more and more in his true native context as a peasant from Smolensk, out of place in the lordly quarters of *Novyi mir* among his sycophantic staff, one whose party booklet had been an honest aberration.

Throughout the year 1968 his evolution proceeded apace and we hear of the rapid "broadening and deepening" of views and principles that had

seemed fixed forever: "And he was going on fifty-eight! Neither straight nor
eary was the path of his growth . . . but he was moving!" He even got to be
interested in western broadcasts: "And what do you know! We were sitting
and chatting and suddenly he jumped up, very gracefully considering his bulk,
and caught himself up, quite openly: 'Why we've missed three minutes of it.
Come on and listen to the BBC!' *Him*?! The BBC?!" Soon we find
Tvardovskii being called by his patronymic alone, Trifonych, a measure of
rapid progress toward enlightenment, the simple life, and intimacy with the
Calf. That "Trifonych" has come a long way from the power-conscious
literary bureaucrat we met in the early pages of *The Calf*. I would suggest
without any attempt at irony that modern literature offers few examples of
"character development" more poignant than this account of Tvardovskii
during the last years of his life, and the poignance is sharpened unbearably by
the fact that the events of the story are intimately involved with our own
history and heavy with our hopes and fears. With overtones of agony and grief
the Calf unfolds the story of Trifonych's gradual reduction to impotence as
editor of *Novyi mir*, his forced resignation and his death. In a scene which
Solzhenitsyn tells us in a footnote is reminiscent of the defeated and hopeless
General Samsonov's farewell to his troops in the novel *August 1914*, we
witness Tvardovskii's last words to his editorial staff, even including those on
the lower floors who had worked faithfully but with little recognition from
Tvardovskii or anyone else. And after the Chief's departure:

> . . . the members of the editorial board had some drinks in
> Lakshin's capacious office, sat together for a while, then left.
> But the small fry couldn't bring themselves to break up on that
> last day They ante'd up a ruble apiece—even some of the
> authors, the more modest ones, contributed—got some wine
> and refreshments, and it occurred to them: why not go up to
> Tvardovskii's office! It was already dark but they lit the lights,
> set the plates and glasses around and sat down in quarters to
> which they'd seldom been admitted and never all together.
> "We're abandoned now!"
>
> No one sat at Tvardovskii's desk but they poured a glass for
> him and set it down there: "We forgive him his persecution!"

One thing the Calf could not forgive, that he had surrendered spinelessly,
not even a whimper: "There are many ways of dying. *Novyi mir* died ignobly,
as I see it, with its head bowed."

The Calf's judgment of the *Novyi mir* editorial board, apart from
Tvardovskii, is severe, and his opinion of the journal itself quite low. "The

devotees of *Novyi mir*," he says, "had no standard for judging it except comparison with the utterly worthless company of the other Soviet journals, dull and even nauseating as they are in their content and sickening in their lack of any literary standards." The fatal flaw in the character of *Novyi mir* itself was its concept of its own role as a loyal opposition. That made it necessary for them to induce in themselves the belief, before they could publish him, that Solzhenitsyn too was loyal, in fact one of their own (*nash*). At times the Calf's wrath against *Novyi mir* seems stronger than against all those miserable Soviet rags that nobody read because *Novyi mir* provided a flickering and really false light in the dark and gave many people hope where there was no hope. Anything that ameliorates or improves the situation of the enemy impedes the ultimate aim: to destroy the system itself. And here Solzhenitsyn's position seems to parallel that of extremist revolutionaries in our own times who believe that action to relieve the people's lot under capitalism is a betrayal of the cause. The Calf reveals his deep contempt for *Novyi mir*, perhaps inadvertently, when he tells us that he never read it until after it published *One Day*, and then only at the urging of Tvardovskii he got out back numbers and read them from cover to cover. He emerged from the reading with a modicum of respect for the journal, though it still fell far short of the standards he would have set. It could hardly have published a single number had it met them—but then, so be it!

Tvardovskii is a tragic figure, but his associates on the editorial board seem a company of evil grotesques. And it is precisely as a *company*, a band of weaklings and compromisers that they appear in *The Calf*. Several pages are devoted to Lakshin individually but as a rule he is coupled with the others and we are invited to feel distaste for the spinelessness or dishonesty of Lakshin-Kondratovich, or Lakshin-Khitrov-Kondratovich, or Zaks-Kondratovich. (Three other members of the board at that time, Mar'iamov, Dorosh, and Vinogradov, are mentioned only occasionally, and with no particular venom.) They are the ones who counsel caution: "Let's not rock the boat," "There's just so far we can go," "Let's not take a chance on wrecking the journal!" and so forth. Their evil effect on Tvardovskii is clearly related to the fact that they are members of the Party. Lakshim forfeited all respect by joining the Party in 1966, the year of Siniavskii and Daniel'(!), an action not forgivable and beyond understanding. Party members they may be, yet their motives for base actions are also base. The Calf blames them for the failure to capitalize on that golden moment right after the twenty-second Congress when Khrushchev's campaign against Stalin reached its apogee and radical departures on the part of *Novyi mir* might have succeeded. And why weren't any undertaken? "Only because the vital forces on the journal were crushed and the camouflaged puppet-show at the top (Zaks-Kondratovich) were quick to sacrifice anything you like just as long as nobody made any waves or rocked their comfortable boats."

Solzhenitsyn has contrived an aesthetically satisfying structure for the editorial operations of *Novyi mir*, one that fits well the overall design of the book. Presiding on the very top floor is a heroic but flawed figure who has been granted a glimpse of the truth but still serves the devil and lies. On the lower floors the work of producing the journal proceeds under the guidance of honest people like Berzer, head of the prose section, and others devoted to literature and to the truth. It is they who welcome the *zek* when he brings them a manuscript and through their crafty intercession succeed in bypassing the editorial board to bring *One Day* directly to the Chief, who immediately understands its virtues and knows he must publish it. Between the people on the lower floor with whom the *zek* identifies and the Chief sits the editorial board, Lakshin-Zaks-Kondratovich-Dement'ev-Khitrov, whose function it is to maintain the journal's comfortable compromise and see to it that the Chief does nothing "foolish." The pattern faintly suggests an old Russian political archetype: the Little Father Tsar' is a benevolent force if you can just get to him; but his officials are deceivers and oppressors.

Lakshin in his answer to *The Calf* contends that this picture is a primitive distortion of the facts, then promptly wrecks his case by ascribing Solzhenitsyn's "mistaken" picture to the lies and gossip of Berzer; a curious lapse on the part of a frequently perceptive literary critic.

So far I have attended to *The Calf* as a structure of basic archetypal themes, but the artistic power of the book is an effect also of its carefully fashioned language, a style that perfectly suits the theme of truth in conflict with lies and evil. In this too *The Calf* invites comparison with Solzhenitsyn's work as a whole. What stunned and delighted readers of *Novyi mir* when they found *One Day* in 1962 was precisely its language, and Tvardovskii in his Introduction was at pains to explain and justify such a radical departure from "normal" publishing practice. To a generation raised on the controlled and labored pursaic banality of the Soviet literary journals Solzhenitsyn offered a prose saturated with the reality of a language free from all official norms: the idiom of the *zeks* themselves, who are thus superior to the clean world even in the way they speak. Read against the background of Soviet socialist realism, the uninhibited conversational style of *The Calf* is a sudden free torrent of truth, a speech full of honest scorn at the faces of evil the ex-prisoner sees all around him. In a wonderfully revealing passage the Calf tells us how he "dreamed of a photo album":

. . . some photographer should do an album to be entitled: "Dictatorship of the Proletariat." No commentary, no text at all, just *faces*, two or three hundred self-important, over-fed, sleepy but also violent mugs—getting into their limousines, mounting the speakers' platform, looming over their desks—and no commentary at all, just "Dictatorship of the Proletariat."

That passage is a key to *The Calf*, which invites us to contemplate just such a collection of faces, caught at ugly work of various kinds. These pictures are of course created out of language and supplied with a commentary where the dominant linguistic figure is the epithet, in the use of which the Calf exhibits impressive range and resources. B. G. Zaks of the editorial board seldom appears without an epithet: "sterile, somewhat boring," "cowardly," "the circumspect Zaks." Adzhubei, the editor of *Izvestiia*, is "red-faced and supercilious" and Satiukov, the editor of *Pravda*, is "worthless and insinuating." And the Calf meets with three secretaries of the Writers' Union to discuss his famous letter: "K. Voronkov (a jawbone!), G. Markov (a fox fresh from a meal), S. Sartakov (an ugly mug but kind of funny)." And when the Calf entered the room: "Voronkov deferentially swung himself out of his armchair—he had the build of a heavyset bouncer— and draped a smile over the jawbone. For all you knew it could have been one of his happiest days." And when all the "secretaries" and their companion lackeys gather at a meeting to discuss your latest novel they are like an assemblage of dogs and they bite at your heels. There's the "poisonous" Chakovskii, editor of the *Literary Gazette*, and the "fierce" Gribachev, a poet who writes lyrics about the unity of party and people. "Cheats and swindlers" (*zhigany*), all of them. The repugnant gallery of grotesques includes the face of the venerable and long established novelist, Fedin, member of the editorial board of *Novyi mir*, and Chairman, no less, of the Union of Writers. His long life has left the ugly marks of all his baseness and many betrayals (Siniavskii and Daniel', Pasternak): "In the case of Dorian Gray all of it accumulated on the picture, but Fedin managed to show it all on his face." Pozdniaev, editor of *Literaturnaia Rossiia*, is "bald, shameless, slippery, and cautious." Not only their faces, but their names also, by some happy poetic accident, are grotesque. At the Sheremet'evo customs office he meets one "Zhizhin" and he asks, "But what has become of the Russian people? We know where they went—they were sucked down into the Gulag. And look what's come up to the surface: these Zhizhins, Chechevs, Shkaevs." The name of Ovcharenko appropriately suggests a police dog. And the whole crew collectively are nothing but "*pliugavtsy*," a vulgar epithet of contempt palely translated by some such English paraphrase as "scummy bastards."

The Calf is loaded with vulgar epithets, studded with popular proverbs and sayings (in fact the Calf refers explicitly to the proverbial riches upon which he draws) and colloquial in its syntax and sentence structure. Its sentences, though not short, tend to be loosely structured. Syntactical inversion, occasional anacoluthon and casual ellipsis are elements in the structure of an oral discourse so charged with emotion that sometimes it forgets the "rules" of syntactic clarity. A better vehicle could hardly have been contrived for conveying the Calf's high anger at the very sight of the moral lepers, who, he maintains, dominate Soviet society. In fact that photo album he visualized is this book itself, *The Calf*.

Epilogue: "Who Steals My Purse Steals Trash"

There is already a formidable set of essays that sharply challenge the historical value of *The Calf* and even call into question the honesty and humanity of its author. Nor is it surprising that some of the living people who figure among the gargoyles displayed in it have spoken up in their own defense. The historian Roy Medvedev, who receives brief but harsh treatment for his mistaken views, has answered with an essay in defense of Tvardovskii accusing Solzhenitsyn of ingratitude to a number of people "who in fact contributed a great deal to his literary career." Medvedev enters a number of corrections into the picture of Tvardovskii and presents convincing evidence both of character and courage in the editor of *Novyi mir*. He touches the nub of the matter in trying to make a distinction between Tvardovskii and other card-carrying characters such as Sofronov and Kochetov:

> . . . Yes, Tvardovskii was a member of the party. But the main lines in the struggle of the 1960's ran precisely between various currents of *socialist* thought and between different tendencies within the party . . .

Da ist der Hund begraben! As I've suggested above, the Calf viewed all those card-carriers from a galactic distance; in his perspective they merge into a single mass whose disputes over the correct "socialist" path are pointless quibbling far astray from the principal business of humanity. I've also tried to show that he singles out Tvardovskii alone and presents him as a beautiful human being torn by a tragic contradiction between "ideology" and his best impulses. In my opinion Solzhenitsyn in that portrait does not break faith with essential historical truth. The friends of Tvardovskii who object to the dark colors in the portrait betray, I think, an expectation that someone they admired and revered will be presented to history as a kind of saint, an icon worthy to hang on wall beside Belinskii, Tolstoi, the "sainted" Pushkin, and even, perhaps, Lenin. In other words, the shape taken by this dispute betrays its Soviet provenance, as I will try to show.

Tvadrovskii's daughter, Valentina Aleksandrovna, composed an outraged open letter to Solzhenitsyn which bitterly accuses him of injustice to the memory of her father, who was responsible for his, Solzhenitsyn's, literary career. She makes in a briefer compass some of the same points made by Lakshin: 1) that Tvardovskii did indeed discover and push through his works to publication against heavy odds, and that the treatment of him in *The Calf* is evidence of base ingratitude; 2) that Solzhenitsyn arrogates to himself a special, privileged knowledge of what's true and right; 3) that he rejects absolutely Soviet life and any "democratic" organization in favor of a return to some earlier "patriarchal" form of social organization. The latter two charges are undoubtedly just, as Solzhenitsyn's later writings make perfectly clear, but what about the Calf's ingratitude? Both Lakshin and Valentina Aleksandrovna insist on standards of "gratitude" more suitable to a feudal society or a modern analogue of feudalism than to a society based on intercourse between free and equal men. Solzhenitsyn acknowledges no fealty to Tvardovskii as his lord, master and protector, and why should he? He was obligated only to give Tvardovskii works of high literary quality and to treat him with respect; having done that his debt is fully discharged. Nor did "fealty" oblige him to soften the contours or touch up the rough spots (of which there are many) in his portrait of Tvardovskii. As a matter of fact the reactions to *The Calf* of Lakshin, Medvedev, V. A. Tvardovskaia and many others betray in the most innocent and unsuspecting manner the effect of Soviet conditioning, of the attitude that the lone individual, having no assured rights in law or custom, has a special need for and owes a sacred debt to his patron and benefactor. It is an attitude not unknown outside the Soviet Union, in the Mafia for instance, or in certain modern American political or business organizations where the one thing you must have is "loyalty to the man who put you in your job." But obviously the accusation of ingratitude contributes nothing to an understanding of *The Calf*, or of Tvardovskii, though one must sympathize with Valentina Aleksandrovna's feeling that her father has not been presented in the most favorable light, and with Lakshin's urge to defend the staff of *Novyi mir*, a journal which published, after all, some of the most important contemporary writers: Vladimov, Nekrasov, Siniavskii, Belov, Bondarev, Erenburg (his memoirs), and of course Solzhenitsyn.

There is one important piece of evidence that the Calf does less than justice to Lakshin. We recall the many pages given to Tvardovskii's alcoholic episodes and the Calf's final judgment that the strain of his false position in dealing every day with brutish apparatchiks was responsible for his excesses and "who should cast a stone at him?" But there is no suggestion anywhere that Lakshin or other members of the staff ever felt disgust or strain or sought relief from them in vodka, an omission which I think falsifies history in the interest of literary effect. In the structure of *The Calf* there could be only one tragic hero, Tvardovskii, supported by humble editors on the lower floor—and one lone *zek*.

The Calf itself, together with the polemical literature which has grown up around it, is, as I have suggested, a peculiarly Russian and Soviet cultural phenomenon. I have already mentioned Avvakum's *Life* as an early example of a literary work having certain stylistic features in common with *The Calf*. A striking historical precedent not only for *The Calf* but also for Solzhenitsyn's views as to the weakness and worthlessness of the West is provided by Aleksandr Herzen. In his *My Past and Thoughts* Herzen creates a great literary work out of the materials in his own life, a literary work, moreover, deeply involved with the fate of Russia and her suffering under a dreary and immoral gendarmerie. Herzen, like the Calf, often adopts a system of emphasis and omission that lends to real events an artistic form. Figures on the side of evil, beginning with Nicholas himself and including officers, landowners, noblemen, gendarmes, and even some of Herzen's comrades at the University, are stigmatized and belabored with great verbal skill and without fear of action for libel.

Some commentators have noted a resemblance to Lenin in Solzhenitsyn's dogmatic style of thought, his scornful intolerance of opposition, and his inability to see nuances in the spectrum of that opposition: who can forget Lenin on "the *renegade* Kautsky"? And the Calf attacks such western left-wing activists as Bertrand Russell and Jean-Paul Sartre with about equal venom. Devoted and religious in serving his own concept of the world, he needs simplification, and certainty that the struggle of good with evil is between a sharply defined evil and a clear good. And when Valentina Aleksandrovna mockingly quotes to the Calf: "I know better. I see farther. I decided," and then adds, "These words from your book sum you up totally for me, Aleksandr Isaevich," she is using, apparently unconsciously, a description often applied to Lenin himself by former collaborators. And the style of Lenin's thinking and writing as Solzhenitsyn brilliantly mimics it in *Lenin in Zurich* bears a distinct resemblance to the style of *The Calf*, as witness many passages from the former, taken at random:

> Piss-poor, slobbering pseudo-socialists with the petit bourgeois worm in them would try to capture the masses by jabbering away "for peace" and even "against annexations." And

everybody would find it quite natural: against war means "for peace," doesn't it? . . . They must be hit first and hit hard.

Talk peace with the menshevik scum!

There were so many of them everywhere, these pseudo-socialist muddlers . . . Was Trotskii any better though, with his pious fatuities—"neither victors nor vanquished"? What nonsense.

It would be misleading to suggest that these similarities are any more than superficial; certainly Lenin could never have fashioned great works of art such as *Lenin in Zurich* and *The Calf.*

And the mark of contemporary Soviet ways of life is also upon the polemic which at the present writing is in full swing. *The Calf* impugns the motives and the behavior of a number of people still living in the Soviet Union and exposes them to obloquy and also ridicule, but because those people live in the Soviet Union they cannot enter an adequate defense, and the attacks would therefore seem unfair by our standards. Yet such a procedure is normal Soviet practice: those attacked in the Soviet press never have a chance to reply. The pattern was broken when Lakshin, who suffered grievously at the hands of the Calf, found an outlet for an answer in an émigré journal *The Twentieth Century* (*Dvadtsatyi vek*) edited in London by Roy Medvedev. His answer when it appeared in Russian impugned the motives of Solzhenitsyn, questioned his character and his veracity, and, while granting him the title "great writer" exposed him otherwise to obloquy. Up to that point nothing had happened that went beyond the usual bounds of a Soviet polemic, but when Lakshin's article was translated into English and submitted for publication (along with two others intended to set the *Novyi mir* record straight) to the Cambridge University Press in London, problems arose, and the Press withdrew the book from its publication list until changes could be considered. Soon after that *The Calf* was translated into English and published by Harper and Row in New York, and Lakshin's answer has appeared in book form under the imprint of the MIT Press. The polemic has thus been removed from its original Soviet ambience and set down within the jurisdiction of a democratic legal system. It will be interesting to observe what follows.

MIKHAIL S. BERNSTAM

Solzhenitsyn: The Russian Liberal

When an influential group of American intellectuals, liberals and neoconservatives alike, unites against one man, a Russian scribbler at refuge in a New England town, there ought to be something big at stake. Their own explanation is that Aleksandr I. Solzhenitsyn is a reactionary, a social conservative, an antidemocrat, a 19th-century romantic or paternalist, a strong statist, a nationalist, and whatever else.

There is an irony about this case, because true social conservatives like Patrick Buchanan, paternalistic statists like George Will, religious romantics like Malcolm Muggeridge, and extreme political right-wingers like James Burnham are not similarly ostracized by the entire intellectual community. Perhaps a simple example can hint at the reason. Jeane Kirkpatrick argued for the comparative advantage of an authoritarian state in some lesser developed, overpopulated countries of Latin America in the 1980's. Solzhenitsyn argued for the comparative advantage of an authoritarian state in Russia in the 1900's–1910's and in the hypothetical transitory period after communism. Yet Kirkpatrick is acceptable, at least to neoconservatives, and Solzhenitsyn is not. The only explanation I can see is that a corporate body of American intellectuals identifies itself with the power-sharing aspirations of Russian intellectuals of the 1900's–1910's and 1980's–1990's, while most Latin American intellectuals are integrated into their authoritarian political systems.

From *Chronicles* 12 (10 October 1988). © 1988 by The Rockford Institute.

Solzhenitsyn hit where it hurts most: he explored the costs of ideas—the ideologies and social arrangements of intellectuals—to ordinary people.

From an economic perspective, Solzhenitsyn is, contrary to conventional wisdom, an original and distinctive libertarian. He is the only important libertarian who ever published in the Russian language. Libertarianism is, after all, alien to Russian intellectual tradition. Solzhenitsyn noted that the Russian intellectual community was very special in never having understood true classical liberalism. The proof of this is in the modern Russian language itself. With the emergence of the term *intelligentsia* in the mid-19th century, Russian terms for urban homeowner and petty-bourgeois, *obyvatel'* and *meshchanin*—terms of the same cultural milieu as burgher, citizen, and businessman in English, *citoyen* and *bourgeois* in French, *Burger* in German—changed their connotation in the press, literature, and subsequently in the common usage. For over a hundred years these terms have meant stupid, greedy, narrow-minded, anti-intellectual; the modern dictionary translates both terms into English as *Philistines*. To achieve such remarkable changes in language, the entire Russian intellectual community worked hard for several decades.

A key insight into Solzhenitsyn can be discerned from his comment on his friend, Grigori Samoilovich M-z, in *The Gulag Archipelago*. M-z was a former powerful Communist official who, during World War II, was sent by his superior to convey an order to a Soviet regiment to retreat. This order, if delivered, could have saved the lives of many soldiers and officers. But M-z was so afraid of being killed on the way to the regiment that he stopped and said a prayer and gave a pledge to Yahweh that if he will just survive he will be a religious follower for the rest of his life. The regiment perished or was captured by the Germans; M-z survived, spent 10 years in the Soviet prison camps, and then years in internal exile. From all conceivable standpoints, says Solzhenitsyn, M-z was guilty of selfishness, of the sacrifice of hundreds of lives for his own survival, and, last but not least, of insufficient hatred for the most deadly enemy of the Jews that had ever existed. But, Solzhenitsyn goes on, there are higher principles than simple cold logic. By these principles nobody has any right to oblige an individual to do anything involuntarily, much less risk his life for the survival of others. By the very fact of his birth, an individual does not belong to any institution or group, but to himself alone, despite all the ideologies that claim otherwise. Ideologies may make a claim for the collective on the individual, but, says Solzhenitsyn, it is not the state that gives birth to man; it is his mother. The man's transactions with the world outside himself are, therefore, either voluntary transactions and contracts in accordance with his own preferences and decisions—or slavery.

This extreme antistatism led an insightful Israeli author, Emil Cogan, to conclude that Solzhenitsyn is actually an anarchist. Yet I would argue that for Solzhenitsyn the difference between his libertarianism and true anarchism is no less significant than for another Russian anomaly, Ayn Rand. Anarchism discounts the costs of one's actions for other individuals. Anarchism implies the imposition of one's preferences over others regardless of their consent; that is, it implies involuntary transactions. In practice, what anarchism would achieve would be another instance of the power of special interests, usually intellectuals. Therefore, anarchism is an anticapitalistic as any other socialist design; it is a nonstate totalitarianism of another breed of intellectuals.

In an essay included in *From Under the Rubble*, Solzhenitsyn rejects two symmetric concepts of freedom: the collectivist concept of freedom as submission of the individual to group or state preferences, and the anarchist concept of freedom as a free ride at the expense of others. For Solzhenitsyn, as well as for classical liberals, freedom from restrictions on individual transactions is complemented by freedom from imposition of involuntary costs. The latter condition is, of course, the very foundation for the rule of law and for the functioning of the state.

Yet Solzhenitsyn would like to see the state and the courts not only as secondary, but as redundant social contrivances. In voluntary transactions, one party tends to impose additional costs on the other by means of such general contracts as the rule of law or of the majority. But, as Solzhenitsyn suggests, the same things can be accomplished by self-restraint. His concept of self-restraint (roughly translated into English as "self-limitation") is not, as some critics have misunderstood it, an attack on selfish capitalist profiteering. Rather, it is an attempt to circumvent the multipersonal and impersonal contracts that may require an active involvement of the state and of the courts. In addition to Adam Smith's Invisible Hand of the market, there is, in the words of Arthur Okun, an Invisible Handshake of human participants. What is important here is that implicit contracts and self-restraint do not abuse individual preferences, while institutional protection of interests of the third parties may clash with individual freedom.

Solzhenitsyn is neither a statist nor a social conservative. If we check public records, we find that he never spoke on or for any issue on the social conservative agenda, except the role of religion in the family. He always strongly opposed state involvement in private and family affairs. He spoke in favor of voluntary school prayer in public schools in his 1983 Templeton speech, but from a perspective quite different from that of social conservatives. He considers the prohibition of school prayer to be a state-imposed and ideologically motivated violation of the rights of individuals forming the family. (The natural desire of parents to reproduce their own preferences in their children is a basic economic notion associated with Gary S. Becker.) Solzhenitsyn believes that state-guided intellectual development deprives the family of its basic rights and imposes the collective preferences of ideologues on the next generation. For him, this is a fundamental assault not only on human freedom but also on human nature.

Solzhenitsyn is a firm believer in the separation between church and state, believing that the destruction of this separation under Peter the Great spelled disaster for Russia. Judging by his writings on these matters in Russian journals, unfortunately unavailable in English, the Russian Church Schism of the mid-17th century was in reality the Russian Counterreformation. The spirit of Russian Orthodoxy before the schism was, unlike that of Catholicism, the spirit of enterprise, hard work, thrift, and market relations. It was the schism and then the domination of the state over the Church under Peter that converted Orthodoxy to the spirit of communitarianism and ubiquitous statism. (Peter practically abolished private property rights in Russia in 1714; they were restored years after his death, in 1731.) About two million nonconformist Old Orthodox adherents, the so-called Old Believers, were brutally punished, and their faithful descendants were persecuted for over two centuries. Religion was turned into ideology and the Church into a state institution. Yet, as Solzhenitsyn observes, most Russian industrialists, merchants, and entrepreneurial peasants were Old Believers (see, especially, *The Oak and the Calf*). Solzhenitsyn went so far as to declare that in a Russia of Old Believers the communist revolution would have been impossible.

Solzhenitsyn must have surprised both liberals and conservatives when he candidly admitted to Japanese journalists and academics in Tokyo (September 1982) that he is not a Slavophile nor has he ever been one. Moreover, he said, he was never influenced by the writings of Slavophiles. As a matter of fact, these notorious 19th-century Russian Slavophiles were the only Russian followers of Adam Smith on the issues of free trade and state nonintervention in the economy and private life. This is, of course, fine with Solzhenitsyn, but the Slavophiles also embrace the Russian rural commune— and this Solzhenitsyn passionately rejects.

Solzhenitsyn interprets the commune as a more significant form of serfdom than feudal serfdom itself. The commune meant the predominant economic power of the state, not just of landlords, over the peasantry by means of taxes imposed on rural settlements collectively and the abolition of private land. The collectivist system of the commune constrained peasants' incentives and economic development.

On many dozens of pages of the new two-volume version of *August 1914*, Solzhenitsyn describes how the Tsarist government, under the premiership of Peter A. Stolypin, worked hard in the period 1906–1910 to create a new class of farmers by abolishing the rural commune as an institution and by establishing private land property for peasants. Solzhenitsyn also describes how most of the parties of the newly emerged Russian parliament, both left and right, and most of the intellectual community resisted this capitalist reform of Russian history.

The truth of the matter is that the alleged Russian liberals were not liberal at all in the sense of classical liberalism. Solzhenitsyn endorsed, in his preface to Victor Leontowitch's *The History of Liberalism in Russia, 1762–1914*, the author's argument that the only liberal force, however inconsistent, in modern Russian history was the Tsarist government; the most antiliberal, anticapitalist force was the Russian intelligentsia.

Here, of course, is one of the painful points for Western critics of Solzhenitsyn, who have a natural affinity with Russian intellectuals and their fight against Tsarism. When in February 1917 Tsarism was finally overthrown, one of the first acts of the liberals who came to power was the abolition of the Russian parliament, whose rights they had ostensibly championed against the Tsarist government for years. The long-sought dictatorship of liberal intellectuals is known in Western literature as the short-lived Russian democracy. At that time one could really speak out, without fear of pejorative associations, and the first postrevolutionary issue of the *Journal of the Constitutional-Democratic Party* (*Vestnik Partii Narodnoi Svobody*) acknowledged in an article by the most sophisticated ideologue of Russian liberals, A. S. Izgoev, that the Russian liberal movement was in effect, in all of its objectives, a socialist movement. Victor Leontowitch noted that the program of the Constitutional-Democratic Party did not mention the right to own private property on its long list of basic rights.

On the laundry list of proofs of Solzhenitsyn's antidemocratism, a major item is his critique of the February 1917 revolution and of that short-lived Russian democracy. As a matter of fact, this was not a freedom-oriented government, but a system that provided a high degree of freedom exclusively for intellectuals. Socialism with a human face can and did exist; several cases are available, and Russia of 1917 was a textbook example. There was little economic freedom; land property rights were suspended for good; most prices were imposed by the government; grain was virtually confiscated from producers; the country was run by arbitrary committees of competing intellectuals; there was unlimited political freedom for anybody on the left of the center and a tolerable sliding scale of freedom for those on the right of the center; there were political prisoners, though mostly former Tsarist officials, and some were kept in solitary confinement (former Prime Minister

Boris V. Shturmer happened to die in jail a few days before the Communists took over: his main offense was that he was of German origin).

The most significant act of the liberal-socialist Provisional government was that of June 28, 1917. On that day, the government suspended the Stolypin agrarian reforms, prohibited all land deals and transactions and canceled all previous land contracts. In effect, the government abolished property rights and private land ownership by peasants throughout the nation. The great socialist experiment began months before the Communists seized power. It is no wonder that Solzhenitsyn is less than enthusiastic about this pseudodemocracy.

If Solzhenitsyn is willing to defend Tsarist Russia, that alone does not make him a nationalist. Indeed, he denied the charge in his open letter to President Ronald Reagan in 1983. As George J. Stigler recently suggested, we are in want of a good economic theory of nationalism. While we will have to wait for its development, a few points will summarize the existing literature and my own thinking on the subject.

Nationalism is a modern reaction to capitalism, which destroyed feudal walls between classes and opened equal opportunities for every individual to compete in the market for social and economic mobility. Many individuals, especially intellectuals, would like to avoid too much competition. Those individuals who do not expect or, in fact, do not successfully cope with the opportune but also tough conditions of the market, prefer to circumvent them. This is also true in the case of those who initially succeed in the market but need to turn their success into feudal-type tenure in order to avoid being ousted by new market entrants. In a multiethnic or multiracial country, nationalism establishes a mutual social welfare consensus and network among the members of a homogenous group on the basis of ethnic origin. Nationalism is the movement which switches arrangements from individual competition to competition between groups and communities.

A few implications follow. First, the most effective arrangement for nationalists is reliance on the state against the market. Secondly, the procedure employed by nationalists through the state is special treatment in terms of vertical mobility, privileges, direct and indirect subsidies, quotas, and, last but not least, restrictions imposed on other groups. That is why nationalism sees the best opportunities not in the private sector but in the bureaucracy and works especially hard at monopolizing the state apparatus. And that is why nationalism is especially attractive for intellectuals and is, in fact, their movement par excellence.

Within the bureaucracy, nationalism establishes a network for a protracted arrangement which would guarantee collective privileges and insure collective success. To put it plainly, nationalism is a protection racket and insurance against market failure, insurance for which other groups pay the price of restrictions imposed on them.

While nationalistic arrangements allow individual success to be secured as part of the group's success, nationalistic sentiments allow the individual to blame his failure on the real or imaginary privileges and communal network of the other group. Both tendencies feed further expansion of nationalism, which is, therefore—in Tsarist Russia, in the Soviet Union, in Africa, in the United States, and everywhere else—a platform for self-generating distribution and redistribution of socioeconomic mobility.

Anti-Semitism in Tsarist Russia, as elsewhere in Europe, including the notorious pogroms of the 1880s-1900's, was a typical manifestation of the desire of the Gentile business communities to monopolize rapidly developing markets. Businessmen found assistance in the nationalistic groups in the administration on the local and central level in their attempt to eliminate tough competitors by physical means. On the Russian political scene of that period, pogroms were ideologically instigated by the two extreme parties. The precedent was established by the left-wing terrorists of the socialist underground, "The People's Will," who murdered Tsar Alexander II in 1881 and circulated leaflets in which they blamed the Jews, as a capitalist minority, for various Russian economic problems. The line was followed by the ostensibly right-wing "Union of the Russian People," better known as the Black Hundreds, who carried on general propaganda for Russian blue-collar workers to strike against exploitation by Russian and Jewish capitalists. In the Tsarist government there was a long struggle between nationalistic bureaucrats, who functioned as protection racketeers on the growing Russian markets, and laissez-faire groups who worked hard to eliminate nationalistic restrictions and to curb the anticapitalist lobbies of the right.

For 80 years, historians of pogroms did not pay attention to the fact that the most active in the pogroms were retail and city-market traders, shopkeepers, salesmen, fishwives, street hawkers, and the like. Was it an irrational outburst of Russian spiritual traditions, as some sophisticates would tell you at Ivy League seminars? Rubbish. The times of the pogroms were the periods of the highest degree of civil rights rhetoric in Russian history. What was lacking was a sufficiently rooted laissez-faire consciousness in the local population and effective, nonnationalistic police committed to the preservation of the market. When Solzhenitsyn's main hero, Peter A. Stolypin, took over the Russian government in 1906 and reorganized the police, pogroms in Russia stopped for good. They reemerged in the summer of 1917 when, under the Provisional government, the police disappeared and anticapitalist propaganda flourished.

Solzhenitsyn in *August 1914* developed a key insight that, in his own words, the Black Hundreds and the Red Hundreds shouldered Russian economic development from the free-market path and worked hard to smash it. There is an abundant literature on the feudal right. Less explored is the derivation of the anticapitalist right from the business community, on various stages of economic development, which worked to restrict market access for alien economic forces.

I want to emphasize here that we are dealing with a universal socioeconomic phenomenon. Anti-Semitism did and will exist wherever members of various ethnic groups could employ the institutions to restrict the markets for Jews and monopolize markets for themselves. Pogroms did and will exist wherever these members could secure the protection of the state and of the local administration to beat the Jews out of the market. It takes decades of capitalistic development before people recognize that they are interested in security, equality, and prosperity of the middlemen minorities not so much because pogroms are abominable, but because people will get better prices on the markets with broader competition. Unfortunately, it takes even more decades before educated members of the Jewish community recognize that the security, equality, and prosperity of the Jews derive not from good intentions of the elites of the host countries, but from the developed market instincts of the host populations and from an environment in which the only function of the state is to protect the freedom of the market.

The various kinds of nationalism in the Soviet Union—as well as Soviet anti-Semitism—are obviously not Russian aberrations of socialism, nor the continuity of specific Russian traditions. Soviet nationalisms and anti-Semitism represent logical socialist reactions of more numerous and more powerful interest groups who employ the state in order to compete with each other and with Jews for education, positions, and rewards. This nationalism is, of course, more embittered and aggressive in a country where all well-paid, prestigious jobs and promotions are concentrated in the state bureaucracy.

For Solzhenitsyn, preferential social mobility, ethnic subsidies and privileges, restrictions and quotas, protection rackets and hooligans at the market gates, are detestable and intolerable to the highest degree, not only because they violate the rights of minorities, but also and no less because they corrupt and doom to protracted failure those nationalities who practice them. Such is also the position of Thomas Sowell, who argues that persecution of the Chinese in Malaysia and preferential mobility for the Malaysians actually, in terms of economic development, hurt the Malaysians; and the same argument applies to the Jews and the Russians in prerevolutionary Russia.

A simple and unequivocal test of Russian nationalism is given by the attitude towards promotions within, and monopolization of, the Soviet political system. Real Russian nationalists call for Russian intellectuals and youth to penetrate and overwhelm the state bureaucracy, thus taking the lion's share of the power market. Solzhenitsyn in his essay, "The Smatterings," in *From Under the Rubble*, calls the intellectuals and the youth, the Russian first and foremost, to withdraw from the system, take simple jobs, give up any participation in communist institutions, even at the expense of not receiving any formal education. One can say many things about Solzhenitsyn, but a Russian nationalist he is not.

Even his obvious Russian patriotism has an extreme libertarian coloration. In *The Gulag Archipelago* he makes an unprecedented statement that it is governments who need military victories, while people need military defeats. Solzhenitsyn argues that prosperity and freedom are preferable to military victories and territorial expansion, and moreover, that defeats and territorial losses are beneficial for national prosperity and development toward freedom. He says that the Russian victory over Sweden in the early 18th century was a catastrophe for Russia and an unmitigated boon for Sweden. For Russia, that victory led to two centuries of expansion, new wars, inefficient allocation of resources, poverty, and restrictions on freedom. Solzhenitsyn rejects Russian national pride in the victory over Napoleonic France: as a result of that victory the abolition of serfdom was delayed for another half-century. He makes a challenging remark that he would have rather settled with the French occupation. He reminds the reader that Russian defeat in the Crimean War in 1855 at the hands of the British and the French led to the abolition of serfdom and to liberal legal reforms. Russian defeat in the war with Japan in 1904 led to liberation of peasants from the collectivist power of the commune and of the state to the spread of private land property and to the establishment of the Russian parliament. From this perspective, for Solzhenitsyn, the Soviet victory in World War II was a devastating defeat for Russian freedom.

Evidently, Solzhenitsyn makes a distinction between the country and the state. His patriotism, based on the criterion of freedom, is antitsarist and populist. His patriotism is measured by what is good for the country and for the people, and what is best for the country, in his view, is not the expansion of the country, but the reduction of the state. As far as I know, we do not have a good economic theory of patriotism either, and it seems to me that Solzhenitsyn gives us quite valuable insights for its conception.

So far we have dealt with the issues on which Solzhenitsyn's theoretical contribution was to some extent marginal. There is, however, a special niche for Solzhenitsyn in modern social theory. It deals with the costs of ideas and the primacy of ideologies in the truncating of freedom and dehumanization of man.

Economists long recognized the crucial role that ideas and intellectuals, as producers and transmitters of ideas, play in establishing restrictions on freedom. The Austrian School economists Ludwig von Mises and Friedrich A. Hayek wrote extensively on the subject. Thomas Sowell said in *Knowledge and Decisions*:

> The despotisms . . . were seen as vehicles for the imposition of intellectuals' designs on society at large. . . . Freedom is not simply the right of intellectuals to circulate their merchandise. It is, above all, the right of ordinary people to find elbow room for themselves and a refuge from the rampaging presumptions of their "betters."

John Maynard Keynes wrote in his celebrated dictum:

> The ideas of economists and political philosophers, both when they are right and when they are wrong, are more powerful than is commonly understood. Indeed, the world is ruled by very little else. Practical men who believe themselves to be quite exempt from any intellectual influences, are usually the slaves of some defunct economist. Madmen in authority, who hear voices in the air, are distilling their frenzy from academic scribblers of a few years back.

From this perspective, most economists of different schools will be on the side of Solzhenitsyn in his dispute with the majority of Soviet experts on the origins of communist terror and Gulag.

Solzhenitsyn went on at length to elaborate and document his basic proposition: the main source of terror and forced labor on the mass scale is the imposition of ideas on people by ideological states. Solzhenitsyn's books, and *The Gulag Archipelago* in particular, are all about the price of ideologies to people. Unlike various precapitalistic economic systems and despotic states in the past, the modern socialist economy is built on the base of ideology. Older systems of a socialist cast, dubbed by the Marxists as the Asiatic mode of production and better known in Western literature as Oriental despotism, regulated already existing economies and life-styles; they did not invent new ones. But on the second day of revolution, Lenin summoned an amateur economist, Yuri Larin, an expert on the German economic model of War Socialism, and ordered him to establish and expand that model in Russia. Within three years, 1917–1920, the system of collective transactions known as War Communism was built. Gross national product declined to the range of 4 percent to 20 percent of the prewar level (estimates vary). Famine began in 1918 and continued through 1921–22, although the system had to be suspended in early 1921. The official Soviet data reported the famine-related death toll in 1921–22 in the range of 4.9 to 5.1 million. My calculations of the human losses during the War Communism period between the censuses of 1917 and 1920 amount to 15.6 million.

The process of socioeconomic implementation of the ideological model requires not only oppression of individual political opponents but, first and foremost, the mass destruction of whole social classes and ethnic groups who do not fit the new system. The older despotisms imposed additional constraints on human activities, but they did not try to impose a new model that would require fundamental changes in behavior itself. Behavior is determined by individual preferences rooted in human nature. Lenin's error, corrected later by an unappreciated economic whiz of the century, Joseph Stalin, lay in the fact that one cannot change basic modes of human behavior without making a so-called Cultural Revolution that would change human minds and human nature. Until this is done, ideological experiments on human guinea pigs are limited to negative selection, to the mass slaughter of the unfit groups of human raw material. From Lenin's and Pol Pot's experience we know that the more ideologues hurry, the more they kill. The era of détente, when the USSR, Romania, Poland, and East Germany began to exchange their undesirable subjects for Western subsidies (instead of murdering them), resulted in an implicit consensus that the slave-trade is a progressive improvement upon uncorrupted, idealistic communism.

That is why a conventional method of historical analogies between communism and various despotic regimes in the past, whether in Russia or elsewhere, yields shallow results. Communists or Nazis may seem to be not much different from past tyrants, or even from Chicago gangsters of the 1930's for that matter, but this does not explain a crucial difference neglected by all theoreticians of continuity with the past: the old despots' business was robbery, not murder. Violence was only the means of securing submission from the next in line to be robbed. Institutionalized robbery is an extreme form of taxation. As good businessmen, despots make sure that their benefits exceed their costs, and thus they do not want to waste their taxpayers. Ideologues in a hurry to build a new economic system opt for mass murder even if they destroy their sources of robbery. They allow the costs to exceed the benefits and forgo future gains because their main benefits are nontangible and nonmonetary ones. Their business is imposition of ideologies, not taxes. Unlike even most conservatives, let alone liberals, Solzhenitsyn insists that communism is not about power. Power for communists is only a means of imposing ideologies on people.

Intellectuals habitually blame communist massacres on despotic precedents that they can easily find in the historical records of any country. But Solzhenitsyn points out that Russia makes an especially difficult case for these theoreticians of historical continuity. Russia was for all practical purposes a capitalist country, although most peasants did not own their land until the Stolypin agrarian reform of 1906–1910. However, most economic and social relations were based on laissez-faire individual transactions, and the general trend of the development of the country was toward universal freedom.

Like leading neoclassical liberal economists, Solzhenitsyn argued for the preeminence of economic freedom and economic development over the political freedoms of interested groups (compare Solzhenitsyn's preface to Leontowitch with George J. Stigler's "Wealth, and Possibly Liberty," in *The Journal of Legal Studies*, June 1978). Exactly this approach is at the center of Solzhenitsyn's analysis of the economic and social policies of the Tsarist government versus those of the liberal-socialist Provisional government of 1917.

Solzhenitsyn suggests that scholars who ignore facts of the history of Russian free market economy, including its destruction under the liberal-socialist government, and derive communism from Tsarism and oppressive Russian institutions, are actually searching for a scapegoat. They want to salvage the general right of well-meaning intellectuals to impose their preferences on ordinary people—the right they confuse with the freedom of expression. In this, intellectuals ignore the costs of ideologies to ordinary people on whom social designs are imposed. Here we are at the heart of the matter. Intellectuals perceive Solzhenitsyn's case against ideology, socialism, and Marxism as a general assault on intellectual freedom. It is a horrifying idea, as Richard Pipes puts it, to take a German scribbler to task for what happened in Russia many years after his death.

Professions have become increasingly risky. Doctors are afraid of the epidemics of malpractice suits. Journalists are frightened by the wave of libel suits. We hire lawyers to sue lawyers for legal malpractice. And if this were not enough, here comes Aleksandr Solzhenitsyn with what many perceive as the case against wordsmiths for instigating mass murder. Naturally, the entire corporation, regardless of political persuasions, feels endangered. Although many intellectuals as individuals continue to admire Solzhenitsyn, the recent hostility, which cuts across ideological borders, is a corporate response. This is a correct response because Solzhenitsyn is indeed after the corporate power of ideas, that is, after ideologies.

Solzhenitsyn has raised the issue, as yet unexplored by economists, of the hidden costs of ideas to people. Ideas are goods with two unique properties. First, they are both private goods, for they can in a sense be licensed, and public goods, for they can be used by others at no cost. Therefore, individual ideas may have tremendous hidden benefits for many generations. But ideas can also be abused by others at no cost to them and at real costs to the third parties. Therefore, individual ideas may also have tremendous hidden costs to the public. Ideas are as much public bads as they are public goods, and one cannot be sure what the eventual effect of an idea may be. Ideas are thus time-bombs.

Secondly, those who produce and transmit ideas enjoy doing their work. They circulate their merchandise even without real market demand for it. Naturally, they would like to generate demand for their goods. At the same time, their dealers are aware of the hidden costs for the public. There always is a danger that the costs of public goods or bads can be applied to the dealers of ideas. Historical precedents are abundant.

Some writers, myself included, can live with these sad facts of the market, namely low demand and potential bills. Others tend to circumvent the market. In order to do so, they incorporate ideas into loose or not-so-loose arrangements. These arrangements are ideologies.

One has to emphasize that ideologies are not the only type of socialized arrangements derived from ideas. Paul A. Samuelson in his classic paper, "An Exact Consumption-Loan Model of Interest with or without the Social Contrivance of Money" (*Journal of Political Economy*, December 1958), discussed how individual transactions may not be sufficient for human survival. Many goods are perishable, and people cannot store goods for their old age. Many goods lose their value on distant markets and people cannot operate efficiently. Therefore, people invented various arrangements, which Samuelson calls social contrivances. The most conspicuous of these is money. Another one is an implicit contract between children and parents for old age security in exchange for previous support of the young. Those arrangements create social norms and customs which people take for granted. Although Samuelson says that these arrangements compensate for the failure of the markets, I would rather suggest that they are complementary to the markets. Social contrivances are voluntary private arrangements, they still operate through mutually beneficial individual transactions according to human preferences. Not so ideologies.

Ideologies, or Ideas Incorporated, substitute collective transactions between groups, classes, or nationalities for individual transactions. Ideologies work as collective arrangements, both when they remain within the network of intellectuals and when they are imposed on the public at large. Ideologies create collective behavior according to collective ideas and values which, in turn, should replace individual preferences. Here is the crux for Solzhenitsyn: despotisms impose constraints, ideological systems impose changes on individual preferences, on human nature.

Precisely in order to impose themselves on people, incorporated ideas and corporate networks of intellectuals need to employ institutions and institutionalize themselves in the state. Ironically, intellectuals, who as individuals need freedom more than anything else, impose servitude upon the world when they work as a corporate entity.

When collective behavior is substituted for individual behavior, the value of human life declines correspondingly. There are no limits in terms of human costs for ideological states. Once ideologies work as collective arrangements and constitute collective behavior, they take upon themselves the price an individual would otherwise pay for his actions. An individual has a constraint: he may refrain from a crime because he cannot afford the price, be it capital punishment, monetary penalty, revenge, or just expulsion from the market. Ideologies relax individual constraints, replace them with collective constraints. Ideologies, insists Solzhenitsyn, provide an environment for mass slaughter and for any crime against humanity. People turn into either guinea pigs or henchmen. Ideologies provide for their corporate members the very justification for enslavement and unlimited brutality. This applies, according to Solzhenitsyn, to all ideologies, to all ideas which opted for incorporation into ideologies, not to Marxism alone: Christianity, the superiority of Western civilization, patriotism, Nazism, etc.

Solzhenitsyn concludes that the main source of evil in the world is the very existence of ideological arrangements. This is a disquieting conclusion for all intellectuals, much more disconcerting than an economic philosophy that only related various assaults on freedom with ideas and ideologues, without making a cost-benefit analysis. The dealers of ideas do not want to bear individual responsibility for their unpredictable and precarious goods, nor risk their goods stored without use on dusty shelves. They complain that Solzhenitsyn wants to bring them to task. Actually, what Solzhenitsyn wants is to bring them back on the market.

This is what he proposed in his widely misunderstood *Letter to the Leaders of the Soviet Union:* separation between ideology and state. The dealers of ideas complain that Solzhenitsyn is after intellectual freedom and against freedom as such, but Solzhenitsyn is only out to get the collective free riders off people's backs.

Q. D. LEAVIS

Solzhenitsyn, the Creative Artist, and the Totalitarian State

Aleksandr Solzhenitsyn's work presents for the reader this side of the Iron Curtain a particular difficulty. We who as of right and unthinkingly breathe the air of a democratic society, with our ancient traditions of freedom of thought and speech and publication, must make a great imaginative effort to realize the peculiar conditions in which Solzhenitsyn's works were written and disseminated. Fortunately he has provided us with documentation of these conditions in his open letters to public figures, his debates on his difficulties with his political critics and the Soviet Writers' Union, and his Nobel Prize lecture. All of these are now conveniently accessible in his volume where they are collected, *The Oak and the Calf* (1980), and the necessary background is presented in the three volumes of his great work, *The Gulag Archipelago* (1973).

We can check that these are not the products of monomania nor even exaggerations of the facts of his life and times by comparing his non-fictional writings with obviously reliable, unheated if embittered, books available in print—and God knows how many more have perished unpublished—such as the great composer Dmitri Shostakovitch's autobiography, *Testimony* (1979), with the invaluable notes appended by his pupil and confidant Solomon Volkov; the two volumes of Nadezhda Mandelstam's autobiography, *Hope Against Hope* (1970) and *Hope Abandoned* (1972); Anatoly Marchenko's

From *Modern Age* 32, no. 4 (Fall 1989). © 1989 by the Intercollegiate Studies Institute, Inc.

account of his life in prison and labor camps under both Joseph Stalin and Nikita Khrushchev, *My Testimony* (1969) (he, a Siberian child of Stalin's Russia, achieved moral and intellectual freedom from communism in Khrushchev's Russia and after two bouts of imprisonment has disappeared into a death camp); *People, Years, Life* (1961), the memoirs of Ilya Ehrenburg, a novelist and critic who wrote the well-known novel *The Thaw* (1954) and who survived all changes of régime; and novels by other writers anatomizing the system and structure of the Soviet machine and the ethical problems its theory and workings pose, such as Victor Serge's *The Case of Comrade Tulayev* (1950), Arthur Koestler's *Darkness at Noon* (1940), and Vladimir Dudintsev's *Not By Bread Alone* (1956).

The Serge and the Koestler books, it should be noted, preceded any of Solzhenitsyn's works, and it is certain that he never read them, as they have never been published in the Soviet Union and were not in fact written in Russian, so they are particularly useful in being independent of him and each other and he of them. Shostakovitch's autobiography gives a detailed history of music and the struggles of musicians in post-Revolutionary Russia which is parallel and comparable to, though independent of, other accounts of the situation as regards literature and the effects of communism in practice on the life of the mind generally and on men of letters in particular. There can therefore, I take it, be no argument as to the facts of what we are going to consider. Nor is it sound to argue that these conditions apply only to Stalin's régime, for Manchenko and Shostakovitch show that conditions were even worse under his successor, and in 1973 Andrei Sakharov had the courage to tell the outside world through a press conference that "the USSR is one great concentration camp," while Nadezha Mandelstam declared that the only difference between Stalin's age and the present is that "they don't take you away in the night any more." In 1973 the typist of *The Gulag Archipelago* was tortured by the State Security police until she revealed where she had hidden a copy and was then murdered by them. The situation of the writer in Soviet Russia is to be considered unchanged.

A striking deduction from all these books I've mentioned is that though written by people living in Soviet Russia or in the case of Serge and Koestler by subscribers originally to European communist theory, they could only have proceeded from a critical attitude, passionately detached from the ethos they shared. They are surely witnesses to an indestructible source of integrity and intuitive knowledge of the difference between good and evil that these writers have somehow tapped in spite of their original conditioning by Marxist-Leninist ideology. Some of them of course, like Mandelstam and his wife, Boris Pasternak and Anna Akhmatova and their circle, had the advantage of having in their youth inherited from parents and teachers the liberal ideas of the intelligentsia of Tsarist Russia, and also imbibed the values and principles of that ethos through the works of the great Russian poets and novelists of the past, and the opera, drama, and music of the nineteenth-century Russian geniuses, as well as through the works current in Russia till the Revolution of the great thinkers and writers of England, France, and Germany that equally formed part of Russian culture under the Tsars. But this still leaves us with the cases of those like the composer Shostakovitch, the proletarian worker Marchenko, and the scientist dissidents like Sakharov, who were all born after the Revolution and exposed to a Soviet education and conditioning from infancy. Such also are the literary dissidents like the poet Andrei Sinyavsky and his friend, the writer Yuli Daniel, both born in 1925 and imprisoned for publishing their banned works abroad; Yuri Galanskov, the poet, prose writer, and editor born in 1939, imprisoned repeatedly in psychiatric institutions and finally moved to a strict-régime camp which killed him off; and Aleksandr Ginzburg, born in 1937, who was repeatedly arrested and imprisoned for demanding human rights and finally deported in 1974.

II

The older Russian writers—Akhmatova, Mandelstam, and Pasternak—were figures who, grown up before the slave-state came into operation, were writers from outside it and could never be assimilated into it morally or intellectually. Solzhenitsyn, born in 1918, unlike Shostakovitch (1906) was literally a child of the Revolution and knew no previous freedom. But they both had to work out for themselves the position in ethics which, as creative artists and intellectuals, they could adopt as their own, without help from outside. Shostakovitch did this by means of the rule of *yurodivy*. Solzhenitsyn, with the help of Leo Tolstoy's and Fyodor M. Dostoevsky's writings and in the light of his own experience of prisons and prisoners, became the interpreter of the Soviet world and its moralist. His awakening to what communism and Stalin had made of Russia was due to his experience of the Second World War and his arrest and imprisonment for criticism in a letter of the leader's conduct of the war, and his release ten years later into a monstrous society. His indictment of it parallels that of Nadezhda Mandelstam. Her husband, Osip Mandelstam, tried to survive as a poet who, though not allowed to be published, carried on privately in freedom of spirit; yet he felt obliged at some point to register his criticism of the régime by writing a poem on Stalin's crimes ("the devourer of peasants," etc.) and reading it to friends, from whom it inevitably leaked, leading to his imprisonment and death.

In *Hope Against Hope* Mrs. Mandelstam considers the consequences of the developing official hostility towards independent writing from the 1920s onwards. Stalin ordered that all literature must be "natural in form and socialist in content." Mandelstam attacked his call. Form and content are indivisible, he pointed out; otherwise writers are only "translators of ready-made meaning."

> People were always saying how impossible M. was. In fact, it was simply that he was uncompromising: what a pity this was not a quality that could be doled out to others—he had enough of it for a dozen writers. He was particularly uncompromising in his attitude towards our academic intelligentsia. "They've all sold out."

> People were generally presented with such [Party] "statements," and asked to put their signature to them. "He probably only signed it," I suggested. "That makes it even worse," said M. But what, objectively, could the academician have done? Could he have revised the text? I doubt it. Or could he have thrown out the person who came to collect his signature? Can one expect people to behave like this, knowing what the consequences will be? I do not think so, and I do not know how to answer these questions. But a question one may ask now is: was there a moment in our life when the intelligentsia could have held out for its independence? There probably was, but, already badly shaken and disunited before the Revolution, it was unable to defend itself during the period when it was made to surrender and change its values. . . . People talked much more freely and openly in working-class homes than in intellectual ones in those savage times [outside Moscow, that is]—"hereditary proletarians" were scathing about the show trials. . . . They clung firmly to their proletarian conscience.

A woman told Mrs. Mandelstam that in the forced labor camps she and her companions in misfortune always found comfort in the poetry which, luckily, she knew by heart and was able to recite to them.

The second part of Mrs. Mandelstam's memoirs, *Hope Abandoned*, confirms how stark was the choice demanded by tyranny:

> A poet is a private person who works "for himself" and has nothing whatsoever to do with literature as such. In the Union of Writers the poet is always a foreign body, subject to expulsion like Pasternak or Solzhenitsyn. There is no point in making a

great fuss when this happens, and I have little faith in the well-meaning youngsters who do: they also eat their oats from the feed racks of the Writers' Union.

All of us, M. and Pasternak included, were never able to develop some of our ideas. . . . The mind was captive. To some extent the mind is always captive to our times, but these can either enlarge or limit its horizon; in ours it was reduced to the most beggarly dimensions. We were so weighed down by the cruel realities of our epoch and the prevailing philosophy of life that we were incapable of real thought—only of idle talk. The times favoured those who had really nothing to say. Three poets [Akhmatova, Pasternak, and Mandelstam] who had something to say also had to pay their price: for a time they were stricken dumb. This was by no means the highest price one could pay. Prose writers, whose work by its nature depends vitally on ideas, paid even more dearly.

Typical of the empty work of the Marxist-Leninist ethos is that of Ilya Ehrenburg as a novelist the lackey of Stalin obediently toeing the party line. *The Thaw* duly delivers the message that all the troubles of the Stalinist economy and all the apparent wrongs were due to the managerial level and the bosses in the Party didn't know about them, but now they did, all would be put right; the thaw had begun including that of the censorship of the arts. No matter that nothing had really changed and another freeze soon followed.

Ehrenburg was an ambiguous figure, explained to some extent by Mrs. Mandelstam, who was able to observe his changing attitudes to her husband's poetry and the work of other writers of their Russia. Under the influence of Hitler's conquest of France he became a changed person and told her, "There is only poetry left," but when Russia entered the war his despair disappeared; he was again indifferent to the countless victims of Stalin except for Mandelstam, who, he finally argued, had brought his arrest on himself by writing a poem against Stalin. But he did what he could for writers as long as it did not endanger himself, and in *People, Years, Life* (his memoirs published a few years before his death in 1967) he gives a powerful account of the fate of the Russia intelligentsia under Soviet rule, salvaging many lost names for history and the younger generation, who, Mrs. Mandelstam thought, profited by this work of recovery. She sums it up thus:

He was as helpless as everybody else, but at least he tried to do something for others. It may well have been he who first roused people into reading *samizdat*.

Yet Ehrenburg, a pre-Revolutionary intellectual, ran a periodical advocating a Marxist utilitarian view of art, and always paid lip-service to the régime and so managed to be extremely productive as a novelist and journalist, though after Stalin's death he felt safe enough to advocate freedom for writers and artists and to support the cultural values that the Soviet system had attempted to do away with. He was an opportunist who thought integrity demanded too high a price as things were, but he was not really base; he seriously cared for the artist and, though unfeeling personally, gave advice and help to some writers. His sardonic tone and irony were the inevitable accompaniments of his basic ambiguity; Mrs. Mandelstam noted that he had developed this in his earlier days as a writer. She says he "took refuge in a kind of ironical knowingness. He had already understood that irony is the only weapon of the defenceless."

The Revolutionary period and the civil wars and aftermath—as may be seen in the poet Pasternak's novel *Doctor Zhivago*—gave rise to the problem of keeping civilized values in being for a future Russian society after the transitional phase was over, to keep in touch with Russia's spiritual past in an officially determined atheistic society: of keeping a way of life somewhere that can support creative minds. (Many poets and artists committed suicide from disappointment and moral shock at what had happened to the Revolution: more were killed by hunger, disease, unjust imprisonment, or execution.)

With Pasternak and Solzhenitsyn the great Russian tradition was picked up again. In *Doctor Zhivago* Pasternak takes his doctor-poet through the Revolution and the Civil War that followed, by means of the family life, loves, and career of the protagonist, thus making use of Tolstoy's model *War and Peace*. Instead, however, of a nation defending its fatherland from a foreign invader, a purely physical conflict, Pasternak's Russia is at war within and there are no clear-cut divisions of who are the enemy and who the patriots— as political and ideological groups temporarily get the upper hand, right and wrong, good and bad, patriot and traitor constantly change their meaning, and the moral bewilderment in political chaos is the worst feature of the wars that destroyed not only the cities, animals, crops, and populace, but also even more the certainties and values of innocent people. Yet amidst these horrors, both physical and spiritual, the human values—love, responsibility and home, the love of nature and the life of the spirit—are salvaged and kept alive however fragmentarily, like a flickering flame that is never quite extinguished in a storm. This is symbolized, but also exemplified in convincing detail, by the chapters in which the fugitive poet Yuri (Pasternak), shut up in the deserted village with his second wife (his inspiration, Larisa) and her child, can recapture the happiness of family life in spite of the horrors of the civil war now outside and the privations of cold and hunger in the depths of the forest in the Russian winter. Outside he is threatened by the wolves (hungry animals; human beings waging a relentless war) or by nature (the Russian winter) and by fate; but he finds that these conditions are the challenge and the stimulus he needs to compose—he writes through the nights poems related to his position and that of humanity, at peace in the midst of war because he is fulfilling his function, by day cutting wood and carrying out other domestic duties to enable the family to survive, by night working "for the race." He is (symbolically) a doctor and has functioned as such with the partisans but—at the risk of his own life from the partisans—carrying out the doctor's ethic of treating wounded enemies as well.

Both as poet and doctor Zhivago is a dedicated man, though unlike his creator he finally decides to emigrate with his family. This dual role means that the creative writer lives a personal life as a man *and* a professional life as a poet and writer, which together commit him absolutely to serve society in his vocation. In *Doctor Zhivago* Pasternak even takes us into the poet's workshop and shows the tremendous effort of concentration and the devotion it demands. But society also has its obligations to the artist—it must allow of conditions which will support genius. In the last stage of the novel, Zhivago has given up writing poetry and has married a girl of the people, supporting his family by menial work and gradually dying of heart trouble: He has lost his vocation as doctor and as poet. The dictatorship of the proletariat and the physical conditions brought about by the civil wars have robbed him of it. Society is the poorer. And the child of Lara and Zhivago's passionate love is a waif, abandoned of necessity during the flight to the East as a baby and now one of the wretched hordes of such children who struggled to survive by whatever means in Soviet Russia. But unlike Zhivago, Pasternak refused to emigrate with his family, showing by implication his own courage and outspokenness.

III

My concern is with the particular case of the creative writer or musician. There is no need to describe the effects on higher journalists, literary critics, and historians, who are exposed to direct censorship on unmistakable lines laid down by state authorities and who only risk losing their integrity if they bow to current directives in their subjects.

Solzhenitsyn points out that "a literary critic is even more vulnerable to any rap over the knuckles from politicians than a creative artist." The critic had hurdles to surmount: An extensive course in Marxism-Leninism at the university was needed to get a good degree: to study for a higher degree it was necessary to be a member of the Konsomol. A genuine creative elite, Solzhenitsyn says, is always very small in number and individualist through and through. But in contemporary Russia a shoddily educated rabble has usurped the title of the intelligentsia.

The dilemma of the creative writer in a Communist society is illustrated by the case-history of Alexander Tvardovsky, a peasant-poet and would-be innovating chief editor of *Novy Mir*. Frustrated by the state censorship and, even worse, torn between the dictates of his conscience as a writer and his loyalty to his Soviet principles, he took refuge in huge drinking-bouts which eventually destroyed him. Fortunately he was a peasant by origin (and so was Khrushchev); thus, *One Day in the Life of Ivan Denisovitch* (1963), the peasant's eye view of a prison camp, got permission to be published. Solzhenitsyn says: "It was not poetry or politics that decided the fate of my story, but that unchanging peasant nature. . . ." That was in 1962 and no other novel of Solzhenitsyn's was ever allowed to be published in Russia.

Tvardovsky was "a famous poet, the editor of the best magazine in the country, an important figure in the Writers' Union, and not unimportant in the Communist Party."

> A true artist himself, he could not reproach me with not telling the truth. But to admit that it was the whole truth would have undermined his political and social beliefs at their foundations. . . . It was not of course the first time that he experienced a destructive collision within his soul. . . . His first "loyalty" was to Russian literature, with its devout belief in the moral duty of a writer. . . . He had wanted only to be like them—like Pushkin and those who came after him. But this was another age and another, more powerful truth had been implanted in all of us, especially in chief editors, and had been everywhere acknowledged: the Party's truth. In our time he could not set the course of Russian literature, could be of no help to it, without a Party card. It was vitally important to him that these two truths should not diverge but merge. . . . Whenever Tvardovsky's first [poetic] self felt strongly attracted to a manuscript, he had to test the feelings of his second [political] self before he could publish it as a work of *Soviet* literature.

Tvardovsky was removed in 1954 for publishing an article "On Sincerity" but reinstated in 1959; he was dismissed in 1970. He and his staff had learned their lesson, so that when *Cancer Ward* (1968) came in to be considered for publication they all knew that "writing *about sincerity* was wrong." They insisted that Solzhenitsyn should amputate the chapter with Aviette and the discussion of sincerity in literature, though Solzhenitsyn pointed out that actually the subject of sincerity had come up in the hospital in which he was being treated for cancer, and that everything Aviette says about literature was taken from Party utterances or the official comments by Party critics. Hence this chapter is as much a necessity in the novel's structure (because an essential part of the theme) as the section of Tolstoy's *Anna Karenina* where the role of the artist and relation of the painter to the world of the Russian aristocracy are investigated by the drama enacted between Vronsky as amateur artist and the true artist.

The head of the KGB at this time (1966) saw the writer as the main danger to the régime. Solzhenitsyn says, "A poet cannot be a Party member for so many years without paying the price," but 100 writers supported him in 1967, amounting to "a writers' rebellion."

Creative writers—novelists, playwrights, and especially poets, if major talents, are bound to be recalcitrant to the coarse party-line directives of the dictatorship. The difficulty for the instruments of the Party machine is determining what in fact is the message of any given work and whether its technical means are objectionable to the authorities. It is easier for the artist to make these tasks impossible in music and poetry, whose language is obscure, than in novels or drama. The problem of the *creative* mind is how to survive spiritually and intellectually in a totalitarian climate, that is, how to go on writing or composing under at worst the fear of death and at best knowing the book could not be allowed to be published or the music performed. Opera and songs were more vulnerable, because more easily understood, than music without words. It was his successful opera, *Lady Macbeth of Mtsensk* that brought about Shostakovitch's original downfall.

To circumvent censorship, Shostakovitch reorchestrated and made a new edition, for performance, of Modest Moussorgsky's opera *Boris Godunov*, which powerfully appealed to him as the recurrent Russian tragedy of the people oppressed by a tyrant. It was a way of expressing allegorically what he had dared not utter in any other form. "Music," he said, "is man's last hope and final refuge," and "I always felt that the ethical basis of *Boris* was my own." Again: "I sometimes got so carried away that I considered the music mine, particularly since it came from within, like something I composed." The *yurodivy* plays an important part in *Boris*. (Shostakovitch says that the *yurodivy*'s utterances at that time seemed like news from the papers—"not the official brazen lies that were packed in to fill pages but the news that we read between the lines.")

Shostakovitch contrasts Moussorgsky with Igor Stravinsky. He says that the latter and Sergei Prokofiev, with their love of publicity, show "the loss of some very important moral principles . . . Stravinsky . . . always spoke only for himself while Moussorgsky spoke for himself and his country." Stravinsky and Prokofiev were not thoroughly Russian composers therefore, because of the "flaw in their personalities." And Shostakovitch says that he admired another Russian composer, Alexander Dargomyzsky, along with Moussorgsky: " . . . both men brought bent backs and trampled lives into music, and that's why they are dearer to me than so many other brilliant composers."

Shostakovitch's revival of *Boris Godunov* may be compared with the situation during the last war in German occupied Paris, when playwrights wrote plays on classical myths that were easily seen to apply to their present situation and its ethical problems. These plays were performed and applauded in the public theaters because German military censorship did not see that the dramas had a contemporary application. But the writers in occupied France had the French nation (except for those top-level traitors who sympathized with the Nazis) with them to give moral support and eagerly buy dissident poetry or attend deviously critical drama and opera—the French dramatists had recourse to the same "underground" art-forms as Shostakovitch. In Russia the dissident intellectuals were unsupported by the workers or the middle class of bureaucrats and managers.

Shostakovitch was bitter towards Western journalists and visiting politicians because they could not possibly understand or even believe in the all-embracing power of the state in Soviet Russia or the pressures under which its citizens lived. Except for the brief period of the Terror after the French Revolution, the inhabitants of Western Europe in the past few centuries have had no experience of anything of the sort. At the beginning of the eighteenth century when the poet John Gay's satiric work *The Beggar's Opera* was performed (a deadly satire on the Prime Minister, Sir Robert Walpole, and his government), Walpole sat in a box at the first performance and made a point of applauding, sending for Gay at its end to praise the piece, and following this up with a handsome present of money to him. When the absolute monarch Frederick the Great noticed and read a satire against himself pasted on a wall he merely remarked that "they have fixed it too high up," and passed on. In short, until the rise of the Fascist, Nazi, and Soviet states, artists in Europe had a fair chance. Even in Russia in Pushkin's time, a phase of revolutionary movements when the poet was subject to literary censorship, the Tsar himself took over the censoring of what Pushkin wrote and the poet's voice was not silenced. The disconnectedness of Stavrogin's character and actions in Dostoevsky's *The Possessed* is said to be due to Russian censorship; but only the chapter recording a piece of

Stavrogin's depravity and the history of his offences against decency seems to have been deleted in order to satisfy the censor at the time of publication, and Dostoevsky's finest novel was not impaired by this excision.

But under the Soviet régime artists, prose writers, poets, and musicians could not escape compulsory subservience to the state. Shostakovitch illustrates this in his autobiography with his anecdote about the monstrous White Sea canal, which was made over the bodies of millions of slave laborers. (For the conditions of making this, see *The Gulag Archipelago*.)

> An entire brigade of respected Russian dullards wrote a collective
> book praising that canal. If they have any excuse at all, it is that
> they were taken to the canal one day and the next day any one of
> them could have been shovelling dirt there. Then again, Ilf and
> Petrov [well-known Russian satirical writers] got out of
> participation in that shameful "literary camp" anthology by
> saying that they "knew little" about the life of the inmates. Ilf and
> Petrov were lucky and they never did find out about that life, like
> many hundreds of other writers and poets did.

Thus the difference between Soviet censorship and that of any previous régime in history is that formerly censorship only suppressed heretical opinion, whereas Soviet censorship, as a Russian scholar has pointed out, "not only censors a writer, it *dictates* what he shall say." Russian literary classics, when restored after the censorship they had endured, are seen to be not substantially different, whereas post-Revolutionary works would not be altered because the Soviet censorship transformed manuscripts into the opposite of the authors' intentions.

Shostakovitch justifies his own ambiguous position when he argues that the "famous humanists" of the West (represented by delegates and journalists visiting Russia for information), gullible, biased, and unable to realize that if any Russian questioned spoke the truth to them he would be shot, have no moral right to question or lecture *him*. He admits he is "not happy, lest my students have adopted my suspiciousness." His system was not to implicate himself, but never to help the tyrants by reporting anyone else and protecting musicians and music where he could. He avoided moral degeneration but his life foundered in bitterness and resentment. Others, even musicians, degraded themselves morally, but he stood up to Stalin sometimes and admired Maria Yudina, a pianist of great stature professionally and fearless in religious faith, who, when Stalin sent her a large sum of money to thank her for a recording of Mozart she had made at his request wrote back that she had given the money "to our church" and would pray for all his sins against God and man to be forgiven him. The horrified authorities who read this letter had her death-warrant all ready for the Leader to sign, but he did nothing against her, and the Mozart recording she had made was on Stalin's record player when he died, the last music he had heard in life. Shostakovitch said of Yudina's moral courage: "The ocean was only knee-deep for that one." But Yudina's case was unique; all other dissidents, who hadn't the advantage of being great pianists admired by Stalin, went to prison, labor camp, or execution: Sinyavsky, Daniel, Sakharov, Solzhenitsyn, *et al.*

The war years had been better for artists because they had more freedom—in peacetime unclouded optimism was required of art. As soon as the war was over, repression and mass terror began again. From 1946 onwards books, films, painting, music, and plays were attacked by Party resolutions. The "historical resolution" of 1948 attacked all the leading composers as "formalist" and anti-democratic. Andrei Zhdanov, instructed by Stalin, "gathered the composers, and they began hanging one another. Of course, almost nothing surprises me, but this is one thing that's too repugnant to think about." "Formalism" was used as a weapon to attack any disinterested creative mind or serious critic of art and exterminate them, e.g., a promising young and original analyst of the structure of Russian folk-tales was charged with "formalism" and disappeared forever, his valuable work cut off entirely. Formalism was defined generally as "the expression of bourgeois 'ideology' in the arts." The works of "Formalists" were suppressed and even their names removed from all Soviet reference books, so that no knowledge of them should remain for posterity. There were two main anti-formalist campaigns, in 1936 and 1948.

Shostakovitch, evidently as a relief for his feelings, wrote for private consumption "a satirical vocal work mocking the anti-formalist campaign of 1948 and its main organisers"—but it isn't available. He could never forgive the musicologist Boris Asafiev for allowing his name to be used to support the attack on the alleged "formalist" composers.

The Party views on "formalism" were supported by Khrushchev and are still in force. As Mrs. Mandelstam said to a journalist before she died, "the only difference now is that they don't come and take people away in the night, but the same trash still write the books," that is, the submissive, whom her husband had described as "translators of ready-made meaning."

After 1948, Shostakovitch's works disappeared from the repertory and he was constantly made to appear in public bitterly reading confessions which he had not written. In order to survive he withdrew into private composition. He had to earn his living and his right to survival by composing music for at least forty films mostly praising Stalin, about which he was bitter. The changes of régime after Stalin's death didn't do him much good; his *Thirteenth Symphony* (1962), which used Yevgeny Yevtushenko's poem *Babi Yar* and was directed against anti-Semitism (a cause Shostakovitch always felt strongly about), dissatisfied the authorities and was banned by them after its premiere in Moscow. In 1966 Shostakovitch developed his last illness and signs of general strain which were reflected in his works. He died in 1975 worn out and embittered. It was remarked that the only time anyone had seen him smile was as he lay dead, not yet sixty-nine.

Solzhenitsyn was a Christian and found in religion a support for his inner life and conscience. Shostakovitch resented this, though he himself had an uncomfortable conscience, the result of his creative genius that made him feel responsible and have a sense of duty and an obligation to protest—and that were all frustrated by his instinct for self-preservation, society being what it was after the Revolution. Characters in Solzhenitsyn's novels are revolted by the servile behavior of Soviet men of letters to Stalin, the murderer of their fellows.

The novelist is a special, the extreme, instance of the impossibility of the creative genius exploring the totalitarian tyranny—because, as Solzhenitsyn points out, the novelist must be a *critic* of society, a prophetic voice visualizing its future from forces inherent in its past, a rival government. This is the novelist's function and he is indispensable to the health of society.

Most great novelists have been acutely conscious of the importance of art and of the artist's responsibility to society, and have explored these topics in their work, for example Charles Dickens in *Bleak House*, where Skimpole, the aesthete and amateur, suggests the developing *fin de siècle* attitudes of hostility towards real artistic values. In *Little Dorrit* Henry Gowan fulfills a similar role and another kind of enemy is presented in the form of Mrs. Clennam and her Calvinism.

Later, in *Daniel Deronda*, George Eliot contrasts the amateur musical enthusiasm of Gwendolen Harleth with the dignified devotion to his art of the European musician Klesmer. In *Middlemarch* the dead scholarship of Casaubon is set against Will Ladislaw, descended from an actress and a violinist, a radical in politics, educated in a German university, and at home with the artists in Rome. With his sunny nature, his singing and painting, he initiates Dorothea into the necessity of art.

From his early novel *Roderick Hudson*, via innumerable tales, Henry James examines the relationship of the artist to society and the values of art itself, the last and best consideration begin that in *The Tragic Muse*. Likewise D. H. Lawrence constantly explores, in his mature novels and tales, the role of the artist and the nature of art, for example in *Women in Love*, where

Ursula's passionate rejection of the German sculptor Loerke's views may fairly be taken to represent Lawrence's own position.

The classic instance in pre-Revolutionary Russian literature may perhaps be found in *Anna Karenina*, where we see Tolstoy's concern with the real artist as against the dilettante in Vronsky's attempts to "be an artist" in Venice and his condescending lack of true understanding of the genuine paintings produced by the professional Mikhaylov. We have already noted that the Aviette chapter of *Cancer Ward* which Tvardovsky was so frightened of is no less essential to the structure of the novel than the Mikhaylov episode is to Tolstoy's: and there are comparable scenes in *The First Circle*. For example, Clara, the privileged daughter of a high official, had found that at school

> [t]heir teacher had advised them not to read Tolstoy's novels, because they were very long and would only confuse the clear ideas which they had learned from reading critical studies about them. . . . The teaching of literature in school had consisted entirely of forcible instruction in the meaning of these writers' works, their political attitudes and the ways in which they had responded to the pressure of the laws of class struggle; then when the pre-revolutionary writers had been exhausted, it was the turn of Soviet Russian literature and the writings of the non-Russian fraternal peoples of the USSR who were ground through the mill of Marxist analysis. To the very end of it all Clara and her school friends never did manage to discover just why so much attention had to be paid to these writers. Was it surprising that young people left school with nothing but loathing for these monstrous taskmasters?

At the university the study of literature was what you would expect from such a preparation and attitude to it.

Inevitably Solzhenitsyn gets to the artist and his function as well as his position in the new society in chapter 42 with the artist Kondrashev-Ivanov, implying the question: What place has the new communist culture for the artist? Either like Clara's brothers-in-law he is a subservient hack whose talents have been nullified by this necessity to conform and take instructions, or he is in trouble with the authorities and loses his license to publish at all. The painter Kondrashev is a prisoner in the special prison, "kept there rather as landowners once kept talented serfs because the walls of the officials' apartments needed adorning with pictures that were large, beautiful and free of cost." He is a necessary figure in the novel to supplement the histories of the scientists with whom he shares the prison, the outer circle of hell in which, we are shown, its creator Stalin is himself the greatest victim in his degraded self-imprisonment in fear and madness.

The *sharashka* is Dante's Limbo. But the good—that is, those who reject evil to obey their consciences—are shown at the end to be turned out into the depths of hell represented by the transit camps and finally the forced labor camps. At the center of Solzhenitsyn's hell is Stalin, as is Satan in Dante's, and he is both tormentor and tormented, following his immediate instincts. Lavrenti Beria and the other heads of departments, themselves always on the edge of downfall, exercise their power while they have it by torturing and terrifying their subordinates. This system, invented and promulgated by Lenin, had been extended by Stalin in Solzhenitsyn's youth and he only awakened to its wickedness when he lost his rank and was confined to prison.

The Stalin episode in *The First Circle* and the description of him were criticized, especially by Western communists and sympathizers with the Soviet system, as false, a caricature, a lapse in the stylistic unity and tone of the novel. But it is not false; it is true, and corresponds exactly to the accounts of Stalin and his actions and character given by others, especially Shostakovitch, who, by understanding how Stalin's mind worked and what his weaknesses were, was sometimes able to deflect him from the characteristic impulse to torture or destroy people. That amounted to heroism in Shostakovitch, seeing the risk he ran of activating the tyrant's vindictive impulses against himself. And Stalin's last years, and his last days, now that they are known (a nightmare for Russia), bear out the portrait of this deified madman that Solzhenitsyn created through imaginative insight.

A former communist, Dr. David Craig of Lancaster University, has argued that the (to him more satisfactory) picture of Stalin in Victor Serge's novel of 1943, *The Case of Comrade Tulayev*, shows the falsity of Solzhenitsyn's. But Serge's Stalin is the Stalin of his prime, and because Serge was an anarchist, is a comparatively anodyne one, which explains why it leaves no impression. Victor Erlich, a professor of Slavic languages at Yale, says that these Stalin chapters in *The First Circle* are an organic and indispensable element in the novel's structure, where the Soviet system is shown as a bureaucratic spiral of fear from top to bottom. This "pyramid or terror" is capped by the Leader who is pathologically terrified himself and extends his terror downwards.

Solzhenitsyn makes us recognize the radical reductiveness of Soviet ideology and the systematic degradation of the individual by the Soviet system: He shows us what happens to man when so reduced and what to the state whose ideology justifies murder, injustice, torture, starvation, and every conceivable oppression of mind and soul. "Where else can you argue

if not in prison? You'd soon be put inside if you tried anywhere else"—
a theme constantly echoed throughout *The First Circle* till its final page.
Sologdin says: "Prison is the only place in Soviet Russia where there is
freedom . . . free to say what you like, free to find out about yourself . . .
time to sort yourself out, to understand the part of Good and Evil in human
life. Where could you do this better than in prison? . . . Where else . . .
could one get to know people so well, where else could one reflect so well
on oneself?"

Innokenty, at the end of chapter 84, finds that he has learned the folly
of Epicurus' philosophy: " . . . for Innokenty good and evil were now absolute
and distinct, by the experience of his first night in prison." He also achieves
inner freedom. Clara learns the truth about the society in which she has lived
her life of the privileged when she gets a post in the prison and talks to the
prisoners. Kondrashev-Ivanov is unchanged by prison because as an artist of
complete integrity and unworldliness he already is free and, being "inside,"
leads the same life as when outside, a life devoted to painting. Solzhenitsyn
says he was virtually invulnerable: " . . . for [him] art was a way of life, the
only possible one." He had lived in exactly the same way as a free man as he
does as an imprisoned artist commandeered to provide pictures for the walls
of the governing class at the rate of at least one a month.

We see also the dishonesty in the discussion in chapter 57 between "the
well-known writer and Stalin Prize-winner Galakhov" and Innokenty the
diplomat; also the aesthete and critic Lansky. Literature in the USSR has to
be written in obedience to the dictates of the régime—"but then why have
literature at all?" asks Innokenty. He concludes that "for a country to have a
great writer is like having another government." That is why the Soviet
system can't allow great writers, only safe writers. The safe writers also are
"scared stiff of losing their jobs" and so they conform, in dread of being
hounded as "anti-social" characters, as Tolstoy and Dostoevsky would have
been if they had lived after the Revolution.

Indeed, when we turn to *Cancer Ward*, the affinity with the Tolstoy of
The Death of Ivan Ilych is undeniable, as Erlich points out, and the parallel
between the two works inescapable. Yet there is a significant difference, as
Erlich says: Whereas Tolstoy's tale is an exhibition of an average
bureaucratic man realizing in the face of death the ultimate futility of his
whole existence, Solzhenitsyn uses a comparable situation to elicit in a wide
range of people of both sexes and of all ages condemned to the cancer ward
a variety of responses not all of which are depressing, for some are
encouraging.

One of these people, Shulubin, about to die of cancer, is chosen to
voice what seems to be the novelist's own social ideals—"ethical socialism."

Shulubin is an ex-academician who has been driven to take refuge in librarianship, where for twenty-five years he outwardly acquiesced in everything, even dutifully burnt all the library books condemned by Soviet authority and apparently renounced all his beliefs. Dying in pain he whispers, 'Not all of me shall die"—a quotation from Pushkin, and reminiscent of Tolstoy's tale. Nevertheless he has kept inner freedom—that is, he resembles Shostakovitch.

It is only when we have grasped the literary and ideological situation in the Russian world Solzhenitsyn had to live with that we can appreciate the connection between the parts of the novel, particularly why the characters of Rusov and his daughter are there; why there are the discussions on sincerity and on the world of literary journalism; the choice of personae to voice attitudes about life and Marxist views; and the evolving feelings of Kostoglotov. The form presented itself to Solzhenitsyn in life, a phase of his own experience as a cancer patient, just as *The First Circle* was the obvious form for his experience in the superior-grade prison for scientific research; *The Gulag Archipelago* enshrines his tremendous experiences in labor camps and transit prisons and his remembrance—guilty in that he survived them— of his dead companions there. Father Alexander Schmemann, writing on *Gulag*, argues that it is not for the facts that the work is so valuable, since others had revealed such data before, but for "the spiritual perspective" in which they are seen and described—"the reality behind" the prisoners' experiences. (Marchenko's *My Testimony* [1969] deals with the later phase of post-Stalin prisons. Marchenko was a heroic dissident and stoic character like Solzhenitsyn, similarly forged by suffering and an inflexible resistance, and tempered by compassion for his fellow-victims of Soviet oppression.)

It is understandable therefore that Solzhenitsyn chose as the form of his novels a prison situation (literal or symbolic) in which moral choice or a similar challenge faces each character in it. His play *The Love-Girl and the Innocent* (I used to think *Woyzeck* the most depressing in existence until I read this) links with *Ivan Denisovitch*; it supplements the novel to give a complete picture of the running of a labor camp (mixed sexes) and its part in the destruction of both the innocents and those of good intention by the authorities and the corrupt system on which they run the camp. Though interesting and obviously dramatic it could hardly by staged because of the very large cast needed and, still more, on account of the complicated and very demanding setting stipulated by the dramatist, which is designed to make the audience feel they are inside the prison camp. The play was actually rehearsed by a Russian theater but the authorities stopped it after the dress rehearsal (1962). The authorities felt that Solzhenitsyn's works "are more dangerous to us than those of Pasternak" and that they are "ideologically incorrect." He was turned out of the Writers' Union, which meant he could not be published and had no salary, no privileges of working in buildings appointed for members, and no translation jobs to keep him going. One of his fellow writers said, "I always strive to write only about joyful things. Why does he see only the dark side?"

But as Solzhenitsyn says in *One Word of Truth*, his Nobel Prize speech, "Literature becomes the living memory of a nation." Along with the Russian proverb which provided that title—"One word of truth outweighs the whole world"—Solzhenitsyn believes as his creed that "Violence can only be conceded by the lie and then be maintained by violence." Violence, he says, demands from its subjects that they become accomplices in the lie. (This is what Shostakovitch's contemporaries felt he was doing in rubber-stamping with his public approval the party line, though in fact he read aloud to audiences the statements prepared for him as fast and unimpressively as possible.)

"The lie can withstand a great deal in this world but it cannot withstand Art." But unless the Russian writer had had Western publishers (and brave men prepared to risk smuggling out the typescripts of literature) and *samizdat* distribution in Russia, his art could not have survived. Composers, painters, and sculptors had no such resources. And how many countless hundreds of poets and creative writers and other artists, great actors like Solomon Mikoels, innovatory producers like Vsevolod Meyerhold (both friends of Shostakovitch's who were murdered) were cut off prematurely in the terrors or, if surviving, were silenced by being forbidden publication, like Pasternak and Akhmatova, or performance, like Shostakovitch?

Few creative minds had the physical stamina and the moral courage of Solzhenitsyn and the dedication to fulfill what he felt to be the writer's obligation to bear witness to the fate of his fellows in prison. "A whole national literature has been left there, buried without a coffin. . . . Should Art and the artist go their own way or should they constantly bear in mind their duty to society?"

One sees what Solzhenitsyn got by recovering the Russian tradition through Tolstoy and Dostoevsky. He added Dante and Shakespeare to this tradition and ultimately fell back upon the Christian tradition inherited through the Russian Orthodox Church of Russia. An extract from one of his letters to Tvardovsky provides a fitting conclusion:

> I can say without affectation that I belong to the Russian convict world no less, and owe no less to it, than I do to Russian literature. I got my education there and it will last for ever.

APPENDIX I
Andrei Sinyavsky

Imprisoned as a dissident who had committed the crime of sending his poetry and prose work to be published abroad (though under a pseudonym), Andrei Sinyavsky was sentenced to seven years' servitude in labor-camps. The letters he wrote to his wife during the five-year period he served before his release and exile were kept by her, and it was out of these notes recording his experiences as a prisoner that he constructed his book *A Voice from the Chorus* (1973). The voice is his; the chorus is that of the various categories of prisoners: old men suffering for their religious faith who were the repositories of Russian traditions; the criminals and thieves; non-Russian nationalists imprisoned for demanding freedom for their countries or displaced tribes' return to their homeland; and also genuine dissidents like himself; lastly, he was in a hospital zone with a prisoners' cemetery, which obliged him to listen to the voices of the dying too.

This book represents a departure from Sinyavsky's previous literary work, and critics consider it an advance, for it registers the changes the experiences of the labor camp made in his life, thought, feeling, and attitudes to his fellows, whose lively conversation in all kinds of idioms and directness of thought refreshed the language for him. It represents the discovery of himself too, a discovery of what literature can mean. For it was his literary resources that kept him going—like Pasternak's *alter ego* in *Doctor Zhivago*, he sustained himself because he was a poet and writer. He remembered *Gulliver's Travels* and *Robinson Crusoe* from his childhood and thought himself into them, realizing their utility for a prisoner; *Crusoe* as an invaluable model of how to make an enforced solitary life tolerable and *Gulliver* because it shows that "there are no uninteresting objects" so long as the artist looks at them with fresh eyes. The books' narrators are, like himself, thrown out of their own world and become necessarily self-dependent, "teaching survival where there can be no escape." He realized that prison was the "living model" he needed through which to examine his society and come to terms with himself by means of the Voice and the Chorus in their changing relationship as the book progresses through the years in prison.

Sinyavsky, writing on Pasternak, said "art is an attribute of the personality, the nation, the age and of all mankind, like the instinct of self-preservation." In *A Voice from the Chorus* he starts by declaring that an artist must discover his "living world"—"When, by the will of chance or the force of fate he comes upon a life that corresponds to his thoughts, he is happy. He looks at this country and he says 'rise.'" And he saw the prison life was the "living model" he needed. It was the same with Solzhenitsyn, but *he* saw all

Soviet Russia as the prison or the cancer ward. And intellectuals who could toughen themselves to endure the prison camps had direct access to all Russia instead of, like Jean-Paul Sartre, knowing only other intellectuals. They can thus tell the truth about Russian life as an *avant-garde* writer can't.

Professor Henry Gifford sees *A Voice from the Chorus* as one of "a series of modern classics in the literature of endurance" and adds that "only in this class does the literature of the Soviet Union tell the truth about Russian life." And the Russian language in which they are written had to be revitalized to be a language of truth instead of falsehood and deceit.

Hence we see that the suffering of *some* creative writers of Soviet society has resulted in the revival of Russian literature even if the writers have been prematurely killed (like Mandelstam) or for long silenced (like Akhmatova and Pasternak) or their works only circulated surreptitiously.

APPENDIX II

The Case of the Marxist Critic Georg Lukács

Whether Georg Lukács would ever have been a good literary critic if he had lived in a free country is arguable, but by examining his history we can certainly see what happened to a man of letters who wished to be a literary critic in a communist state. An excellent essay by the American critic and professor Irving Howe, "Lukács and Solzhenitsyn," which he wrote in 1971, is reprinted in the Collier-Macmillan volume on Solzhenitsyn. Howe says of Lukács:

> He had always to keep looking over his shoulder, sometimes literally and more often figuratively, so as to measure the latitude allowed him by the Party. Long ago he had chosen the role of the (at times) semi-dissident Communist, but never an openly oppositionist Communist and certainly not a public opponent of the party-state dictatorship.

But the consequent deviousness, defensive tactics, and sense of precariousness in trying to keep at all costs on the right side throughout the changes in Party line, as well as the changes in the successive régimes in Hungary, made Lukács a time-server and a mere manipulator of dialectics, with a consequent self-defeating opacity of style. These compulsions, Howe thinks, explain Lukács's fascination with Solzhenitsyn, whom he kept praising for the virtues of independence and courage which he himself dared not practice. (The more usual reaction to Solzhenitsyn of Soviet-state writers was fear and hared, so Lukács was a comparatively decent man of letters.) One sees that Lukács was at least ashamed of himself, and though generally abject was not wholly so.

In a free environment he could and would have abandoned the compulsory Marxist dialectics and the prescribed attitudes of a "Soviet person" and, for instance, in writing his book on *The Historical Novel* would not have been driven to conclude, as a good Marxist, that Scott's *Ivanhoe* (that historically ridiculous romance) is a good model for writers in that *genre*. And a more serious result of Lukács's cowardice, in addition to his uselessness as a critic, is that his surrender to Marxist jargon and literary fallacies produced a foggy medium which West European left-wing intellectuals have foisted on our world and its young as important literary criticism and a proof of the value of the Marxist-Leninist procedure.

APPENDIX III
Solzhenitsyn's Language

One of the results of the falsity in the Soviet system was that words no longer had true meanings. They easily lent themselves to ironic use, and the Russian satirists got into trouble for thus exposing the absurdity of the Party slogans and clichés.

Russian writers and journalists and many critics have complained that the written and spoken language is a mess of foreign words, shabby communist jargon, prison and camp slang (such a high proportion of its citizens having been through one or both of these institutions, very often for a large part of their lives)—an impoverished, contaminated, and unloved idiom. But how to revitalize language and restore the connection between words and reality, without which there can be no literature worth reading? Solzhenitsyn with his creative interest in language has made it the expression of human truths, and so revived the medium of literature: purified it of worn-out words and mechanical phrases (which he often invokes for ironic purposes) and enriched it from traditional folk-words and lively native idiom. He began this movement of regeneration of the Russian tongue in *Ivan Denisovitch*, which is told in the first person by an uneducated peasant.

Victor Erlich says: "Solzhenitsyn's immediate targets are not literary conventions grown stale, but externally imposed and enforced taboos and clichés. . . . To establish a reliable connection between words and things, between language and the facts of experience, is to recreate the essential conditions of a genuine literary enterprise . . . its natural function, that of search, exploration, and above all testimony." Another competent critic, Alexander Schmemann (a theologian and specialist in Slav thought), wrote that Solzhenitsyn *exorcised* the Russian language, making a language of truth where the Soviet system had altered and subverted all meanings to produce a language corrupted by lies and deceit.

It is important for us who can't read him in the original that we realize what Solzhenitsyn did for the Russian language and how bad are the translations, hastily and incompetently done into English or American. We have his works, but they are marred not only by errors but by paraphrases, omissions, and revisions, which we are told denature his work by changing the narrative structure and ignoring the metaphor, wit, and subtle irony. Thus we are likely to fail to appreciate Solzhenitsyn's original handling of the Russian language, which he regenerated by rejecting the new idiom created by the dishonesty of the bureaucratic régime and the parrot-language of Marxist-Leninism, working instead in a direct speech-based idiom of creative truth. Alexis Klimoff says that in spite of the disservice his English and American translators have done Solzhenitsyn, "his work is so rich in thought, imagery and texture that even in an imperfect or partial rendering the prose of this verbal master still produces a powerful and sometimes overwhelming effect." But we lose the parody and irony, the numerous literary and historical allusions, and the sudden changes of tone in his writings, as well as the nuances on which the reader's grasp of the meaning sometimes depends. *The Gulag Archipelago* by the nature of its material merely as brutal fact makes an unforgettable impact in any language. But its subtitle is *Essays in Artistic Investigation* and it is the literary *art* that has been obscured by the translator.

Solzhenitsyn himself has complained about the "stylistic levelling" of his works, something that English translators had done with Dostoevsky too—*both* novelists are original stylists.

APPENDIX IV
Practical Difficulties in
Preserving Literature

Many of Solzhenitsyn's writings were first composed cerebrally and memorized and only put down on paper after a lapse of years, *The First Circle* taking about nine years to write. This was due to his being in camp or prison without facilities for writing, or to fear that the police would search his room or flat and find incriminating pieces of prose or verse. (Compare this with the practice of Akhmatova and Mrs. Mandelstam, who preserved poems by memorizing them and constantly repeating them.)

The so-called "thaw" after Khrushchev had "exposed" Stalin, which enabled Solzhenitsyn to publish *Ivan Denisovitch*, lasted only a brief while and the authorities soon closed up again, dashing the hopes of the writers and of editors of literary journals like *Novy Mir*. Neither *Cancer Ward*, *The First Circle*, nor *The Gulag Archipelago* were allowed publication in the Soviet Union. Russians could read them only in *samizdat* (clandestinely circulated typescript). This is the first fact that differentiates Solzhenitsyn from any modern creative writer in Western Europe or North America. And though denied publication in his own country he has been nevertheless vilified and exiled for writing his books and for first trying to get them published in Russia and then, on failing to do so, smuggling copies for publication abroad. This and his general attitude of uncompromising and intransigent dissidence ended in his summary deportation to West Germany—only the pressure of world opinion prevented his immediate execution or ultimate extinction in a labor camp.

ANNA DIEGEL

Human Rights and Literature:
Solzhenitsyn and Pasternak

Violations of human rights in the Soviet Union reached an unprecedented
peak during the Stalin era from 1929 to 1953, and particularly during the
great purge years between 1934 and 1939. For millions of Soviet citizens, the
concrete meaning of human rights abuses is expressed in the mechanism of
imprisonment in jails and concentration camps. Though Stalin had been
publicly declared an enemy of the people, abuses continued up to the
present. Yet in the first decades after Stalin's death and during the years of
cold war the question of violation of individual rights received little
international attention. A turning point was the 1966 trial and condemnation
to labour camps of the writers Sinyavsky and Daniel, which raised a storm of
protest abroad, as it did in Russia. In 1975 Amnesty International prepared a
150 page document with evidence on the treatment and conditions of
prisoners of conscience in Russia. During the last two decades the question
of human rights in the Soviet Union has become the subject of relentless
investigation and commentary abroad and the focus of the dissent movement
among the *intelligentsia* at home.

One of the most important voices of protest since the late Sixties has
been that of the Soviet humanitarian and scientist, Andrei Sakharov. He was
a *glasnost*-oriented activist very much in the manner and spirit of the
nineteenth century 'Westernizers' (as opposed to Slavophiles, the patriotic,

From *Theoria* 75 (May 1990). © 1990 by the University of Natal Press.

religious-minded idealists who called for a return to the values of Russia's past) and he denounced the abuses in numerous letters and petitions and spelled out for the government the reforms necessary to achieve 'Progress, Peaceful Coexistence and Intellectual Freedom.' Sakharov was subjected to years of persecution and exile. Since *perestroika* he was rehabilitated and even elected to the new People's Congress shortly before his death.

However, the concern about human rights abuses, and particularly about the arbitrariness and cruelty of the punishment of dissenters, was first voiced in the Soviet Union and abroad chiefly by literature: since the late Fifties personal accounts, novels, stories and poems have been read by Russians in *samizdat* (the underground press consisting of typewritten and carbon-copied scripts circulated among friends) and some of these texts have found their way abroad and been published there. Most of the dissident writers have met with harsh punishment, ranging from internment in psychiatric hospitals or labour camps to banishment. The reason for writers being so abominably treated in Russia is paradoxical and has historical roots: in Russia writers, to a far greater extent than in the West, are *important*. They have traditionally been regarded as a source of knowledge and as moral educators, exposing social injustice or providing instruction for a better life. But more importantly, many Russian writers have been concerned not only with 'what is to be done,' but with the ultimate question of 'what men live by.' Their subject is *pravda*, truth in an idealistic sense. They ask basic questions about the meaning of life and about man's function in the universe and thus remind readers that thinking about politics is inseparable from thinking about ultimate values. This is why they are considered dangerous and why their role, which is still taken seriously in Russia, is essential in the battle against the violations of human rights.

Less then ten years after the death of Stalin, during the first 'thaw' in the official attitude to literature instituted by Khrushchev, two works were published which were to have a major influence on the dissent movement. Both of them are the works of passionate 'Slavophiles'—or at least, admirers of Russia's spiritual past. The first book was Pasternak's *Doctor Zhivago*, published in Italy in 1957, to tremendous praise abroad. It is at first difficult to see why the novel was rejected by the journal *Novy Mir*, to which Pasternak first ingenuously submitted it for publication. *Doctor Zhivago* does not make any sensational revelations. It is not even a systematic attack on the regime in the style of the works of 'denunciation literature' in vogue during the 'thaw.' It seems to be a somewhat haphazard and fragmentary chronicle of events and situations which every Russian citizen who had lived between the revolutions of 1905 and 1917 and the Second World War would have experienced: for example, the first decrees of the Bolshevik government, the

New Economic Policy, fighting in the Carpathians during the second year of the Second World War. It describes the well-known experiences of economic hardship and rationing, or common sights such as charred fields and untended villages. Curiously, it contains hardly any mention of the Stalinist terror. Why then the uproar? *Doctor Zhivago* soon became one of the hottest *samizdat* properties in the Soviet Union, particularly after the famous 'Pasternak Affair' in 1958, when Pasternak rejected the Nobel Prize under threat of exile, a year before his death. Even though he was a 'cosmopolitan' writer steeped in European culture, he could not face the prospect of leaving his beloved Russia. *Doctor Zhivago* was published for the first time in the Soviet Union in 1988.

The second literary event was Solzhenitsyn's short novel, *One Day in the Life of Ivan Denisovich*, which received immediate success at home. In this case the work was published in the Soviet Union by *Novy Mir* in 1962 and its appearance was sanctioned by Khrushchev. The problem-free publication of Solzhenitsyn's novel is explained by the fact that it deals specifically with the inhuman conditions in a camp under *Stalin*, whose image Khrushchev was interested in blackening at the time. Solzhenitsyn, however, soon fell out with the government with his subsequent works denouncing the system, and was eventually expelled from the Writers' Union. After accepting the Nobel Prize in 1970 and publishing *The Gulag Archipelago* in Paris in 1974, he was finally arrested and banished from the Soviet Union, the harshest punishment that could be meted out to such an ardent patriot. Recently Solzhenitsyn's works were published almost integrally in the Soviet Union and newspapers are calling for his return from exile.

Beyond their love for Mother Russia, Solzhenitsyn and Pasternak seem to have little in common. Solzhenitsyn, the younger writer and unknown until the publication of *One Day in the Life of Ivan Denisovich*, is the more prolific of the two and wrote unceasingly, under the most appalling circumstances. He survived twelve years of prison, labour camp and exile (not to mention cancer) and remains an outspoken activist, having in the last decade joined Sakharov's Human Rights Committee, donated his royalties to the families of prisoners and written petitions and letters of protest to the government. His writing, even at the most artistic level, is explicitly political and like Tolstoy he distributes prescriptions for the righteous life. Pasternak, on the other hand, led a relatively untroubled life. He was a well known and respected poet before Stalin's access to power. During the years of terror he was mysteriously spared and wrote almost nothing. Even though he did occasionally act to help his friends (for instance once in a telephone call he pleaded with Stalin for the release of the poet Osip Mandelstam), his political behaviour, particularly in the case of his rejection of the Nobel Prize, was criticized by some dissidents and by Solzhenitsyn in particular for its lack of firmness. Pasternak's only concern seemed to be with art and nature, and he had no wish of being a 'guru' of any kind.

Yet in spite of their different personalities and approaches to political problems both writers are considered giants in the protest movement that has advanced the cause of human rights in the Soviet Union during the last decades. Solzhenitsyn and Pasternak are not merely representatives of a political position. They are *'artists* of the written word,' as even the authorities in Russia respectfully call writers. As such, both fulfill the messianic task Russian readers traditionally expect from literature. Not only, like Sakharov, do they offer firm practical or moral guidelines for solving problems, but by using art as their medium and showing the effect that history has on private lives, they provide readers with a larger, more complex framework and lead them to ask themselves essential questions about the meaning of life and about man's position in the universe.

Solzhenitsyn's concern with the violation of human rights is present throughout his work. A good part of his work is dedicated to the description of prisons and prison life during and after the Stalin era: *The First Circle, One Day in the Life of Ivan Denisovich*, and especially *The Gulag Archipelago* all depict the inhumanity of incarceration, where privations and torture rob most men of their dignity and integrity. Solzhenitsyn stresses the arbitrariness of prison sentences and conditions and raises the questions of why people are imprisoned. Again and again, he makes the point that prisons are an instrument of absolute power and have nothing to do with justice or the nature of the crime committed.

Solzhenitsyn furthermore suggests that the iniquitous prison conditions are a reflection of life in Soviet society in general, where the arbitrary use of power frequently crushes people's spirit and makes them into puppets of the state. One example of a man broken by the system outside the prisons is Shulubin in *Cancer Ward*, who has abdicated all human dignity in order to preserve his life and that of his family.

But the chief impact of Solzhenitsyn's writing is not so much as 'denunciation literature,' important as this aspect of his work may be. What his readers best remember is not the lies and tortures, the hypocrites and the broken wretches, but those individuals who *survive* the outrages of arrest and captivity, morally and spiritually: Ivan Denisovich, the simple man whose incorruptible moral sense and love of work gets him through 'one day'; Kostoglotov in *Cancer Ward*, and his proud, independent and questioning spirit, unbroken by his years in labour camps; the numerous prisoners in the Gulag who refuse to submit to the moral degradation that the system tries to impose on them; Gleb Nerzhin in *The First Circle*, whose passion for truth makes him voluntarily leave the relative safety of the *sharashka* for one of the terrible camps of the Gulag. These survivors embody Solzhenitsyn's conception of human dignity and provide part of his answer to the Tolstoyan question of 'what men live by,' formulated in *Cancer Ward*.

To these people, whom Kostoglotov recognized as brothers because they would 'smile while others were serious or while others laughed,' suffering has taught wisdom about the value of life: slowly savouring food, seeing an apricot tree in bloom, being able to stretch out one's legs in a crowded cell, these are pleasures which only those who have known the experience of the closeness of death can appreciate. Privations have given them the power to restrict and control their desires. The moral survivors also know the joy of work, which, like Tolstoy, Solzhenitsyn regards as a purifying discipline. Most of all, they value human fellowship and understand that there is no place for envy or anger in a world where every day 'great-souled people are being dragged out to be shot.' Solzhenitsyn's 'survivors' are able to celebrate life and have achieved inner serenity because they have not allowed the integrity of their personality to be reduced by the inhuman system under which they live. All of them, to a greater or lesser extent, are aware of a spiritual dimension to life. Shukhov, the illiterate peasant who has known nothing but godless Marxist ideology, senses a mysterious force emanating from the believer, Alyosha the Baptist, one of his fellow prisoners. Gleb Nerzhin's choice is the expression of his growing spiritual awareness. The protagonist of *The Gulag Archipelago* who never tires of affirming the victory of the spirit over the body exclaims: 'My name? I am the Interstellar Wanderer! They have tightly bound my body, but my soul is beyond their power.' (Even the broken Shulubin in *Cancer Ward* dimly senses within himself 'something else, sublime, quite indestructible, some tiny fragment of the universal Spirit.')

Solzhenitsyn urges his fellow men to look inward for the solution to the problems of the violation of human rights. In his 1970 Nobel Prize speech he stresses the existence of an absolute, universal and divinely inspired concept of justice which, according to him, the Marxist regime has violated. In the same speech, he equates Marxist revolutionaries with Dostoevsky's *Devils* and appoints the artist as guardian of divine truth. 'In Russian literature,' he says, 'there has long been the inborn idea that a writer can do much for his people, and that it is his duty.' The writer must follow this calling and not 'depart into a world of his own creation or into the wide spaces of subjective capriciousness, leaving the real world to mercenaries, or even madmen.'

Whether or not one agrees with this dogmatic conception of art as the vehicle for ideas is irrelevant. The irritation the Westerner may feel at the self-righteous disdain with which Solzhenitsyn sometimes treats foreigners who have not suffered the soul-purifying experience of imprisonment or terror, at his nationalist bigotry or at the inconsistencies contained in some of his more recent public pronouncements is also beside the point. Essential is that Solzhenitsyn, in putting art at the service of the human rights cause, shows his readers that to right the wrong it is necessary to ask the basic question of 'what men live by.' This is a question which Westerners also might well ponder.

The case of Pasternak as champion of human rights is more complex. Unlike Solzhenitsyn he seems to feel no urge to enlighten his fellow men. In fact, at first sight he seems to be one of these writers who delve into 'the wide spaces of subjective capriciousness' and appears strangely lacking in social conscience. A widely read, well-informed intellectual, he witnessed the revolution and Stalinist period, having written little more than poems about love and nature. However, the fact that in his youth he had once been (like most cultured liberals of his time and like his hero Zhivago) *in favour* of the new regime, having published a eulogy of Lenin in his 1923 poem 'The Lofty Illness' and an epic poem about the revolution (*Nineteen Five*, published 1927), indicates that he was not as politically innocent as he has sometimes been made out to be.

Even though he was a mere observer in the tragedy of his time, a man of Pasternak's calibre could not have been unaware of the abuses perpetrated by the government. Yet in *Doctor Zhivago*, his only novel written after years of near silence, there is almost nothing about the terror of the Stalin period and hardly any specific criticism of the regime. The only allusion to Stalin as a 'pock-marked Caligula' passes almost unnoticed. There are a few 'offensive' passages such as the remark about the inefficiency of revolutionaries who are 'ungifted' and 'aren't at home in anything except change and turmoil.' But these remarks are handed down from a lofty distance and Pasternak makes it clear that he *chooses* to have no part in politics and wishes to remain merely human. Political events and sentiments appear in *Doctor Zhivago* as mere aberrations or barbaric atavisms.

This was Pasternak's unpardonable offence, which led to his eventual official disgrace. During the 'new wave' of criticism against Stalin, a book like Solzhenitsyn's *One Day in the Life of Ivan Denisovich* was considered acceptable because it happened to suit the current policies of the leaders. Pasternak, on the other hand, simply dismisses the task of 'denunciation literature' as an endeavour unworthy of his attention and in this way ignores the civic function expected from the writer in a state where everything is determined by politics. *Doctor Zhivago* is, however, unquestionably a political novel. By leaving the unspeakable unspoken and deliberately choosing instead to write about trees, to use Brecht's phrase, Pasternak confirms his life-long assertion that the significance of human life ultimately lies outside of the historical problems of his time and that it is the individual's right to choose his own values. After his initial burst of fervour and subsequent loss of faith, Pasternak consistently refused to acknowledge the importance of the Revolution's mission and this is the reason why, during the Thirties, people were put in prison for disseminating his poetry.

Pasternak's concern to defend man's integrity or individualism (in its original sense of 'in-divisibility' pertaining to a completely self-centred and separate being) lies behind Doctor Zhivago's actions in the novel: Zhivago chooses to abandon the medical profession at a time when his services would be most needed by the community and prefers an underground and fugitive existence. His steady refusal to give up his personal liberty for the sake of any communal interest makes him into the negation, not only of a Soviet 'positive hero,' but also of the *homo politicus* every Russian is expected to be.

What does interest Pasternak's hero is poetry and life. (The name Zhivago comes from the Russian word for life, *zhizn* or more precisely *zhiv(oi)*, alive.) Like Solzhenitsyn's heroes Zhivago has the capacity of enjoying intensely every act of living ('. . . he longed to thank life, thank existence itself, directly, face to face, to thank life in person.') 'Man,' he says, 'is born to live, not to prepare for life,' thus denigrating the revolutionaries who are planning the 'radiant' future. The most memorable scenes in *Doctor Zhivago* are descriptions of everyday life: Zhivago writing poems and his lover Lara attending to housework—gathering fuel, gardening, drawing water. Zhivago is absorbed by his love for Lara, whose simplest act appears beautiful, whether she is peeling potatoes or reading a book. The joy of living which the poet feels in her presence, which leads him to reject every family or communal obligation, is the essence of *Doctor Zhivago*'s moral and spiritual message; the supreme good is man's celebration of the marvel of life, which is an endlessly reiterated challenge to death.

In the same way, the poet is also fascinated by nature, which provides a constant against which the accidents of politics seem irrelevant. As in the case of Solzhenitsyn's heroes, Zhivago's life-celebrating attitude results from his awareness of the existence of a cosmic spiritual power. Pasternak distinguishes this awareness from the emotion provided by the comforts of religion. While attending a funeral, Zhivago feels the presence of this spiritual power: 'and there was nothing in common with devoutness in the emotion he felt of dependence on the supreme forces of earth and heaven, to which he bowed as his true progenitors.' Because he understands that his wholeness—'integrity,' 'individuality'—includes a spiritual dimension, Zhivago is able to become a creative human being. By implication, Pasternak is saying that the life-destroying force of the Revolution is caused by Marxism's ignorance of man's link with the universe.

Basically, this is the same message as Solzhenitsyn's. Although there appears to be a great distance between Pasternak, the unworldly poet living in a state-sponsored dacha in Peredelkino, and Solzhenitsyn, the long-suffering activist (or between Zhivago and, say, Gleb Nerzhin), both writers share the same conception of the artist's mission: he is to understand and reveal man as a *whole* being, related to a cosmic design and unfettered by restrictive political ideologies. This conception is reflected in Pasternak's remarks on writing. Even though, unlike Solzhenitsyn, he says nothing about the utilitarian function of art, there is no doubt about the loftiness of his purpose. In a letter to the translator Eugene Kayden he says the following: 'Art is not simply a description of life, but a setting forth of the uniqueness of being . . . The significant writer of his epoch (and I want no other beside him) is a revelation, a representation of the unknown, unrepeatable uniqueness of reality.'

Is Zhivago only a 'prerevolutionary self-sufficient intellectual, "refined", futile and full of grudges and resentments at the abomination of a proletarian revolution,' as one faction of critics would have it? If this were the case it is unlikely that Pasternak would have had such a large following and been 'seen by many as a last surviving focus of moral resistance to the infinitely cruel and merciless master of the country's destiny.' He owed this position to his idealism and to his obstinate refusal to compromise his integrity by accepting a reduction of his poet's vocation.

Pasternak was, after all, a poet and an intellectual and wrote only about experiences which were familiar to him. Had he been interned in a labour camp, his life-celebrating, soul-searching attitude would probably have made him a brother of 'those who smile while others were serious or while others laughed,' described in Solzhenitsyn's novels. As it is, Pasternak's aloofness is far from being indifference: *Doctor Zhivago*, in which he sets forth precisely the reason for his aloofness—his total disregard for the anti-spiritual Marxist ideology, which he views as an aberration of history—is his testimonial of his concern for Russia's plight. Like Solzhenitsyn he urges men to look inward and to ask themselves fundamental questions about their ultimate values.

The very 'Russian' literary voices of Solzhenitsyn and Pasternak, added to that of Sakharov, the Western-minded scientist, are leading ones in the chorus of dissent that has been heard from the Soviet Union during the past decades. Solzhenitsyn's is that of the mostly self-educated man, whose harsh life has brought him in direct contact with the abuses of human rights in his country. Pasternak is the cultured 'cloud dweller' whose experience is chiefly intellectual. Yet both share the same concern for Russia's problems, and both look for answers not simply at a political level, but at a transcendental one. The spiritual renewal which is taking place in the Soviet Union at the present time owes a great deal to their literary bequest.

The soul-searching questioning of Solzhenitsyn and Pasternak may be what is needed to fulfil what Italo Calvino defines as the function of literature: to 'guarantee the survival of what we call "human" in a world where everything appears inhuman.' Not 'human' in the meaning that Calvino says the word has acquired in the West—that is, 'temperamental, emotional, ingenuous'—but in the sense of 'austere,' introspective and consciously looking for truth.

SOPHIE OLLIVIER

The World of Detention in Dostoevsky and Solzhenitsyn

In the works of literature devoted to detention, Dostoevsky's and Solzhenitsyn's books occupy a special place. They are unique documents for their time, attempts to understand this world made by men who underwent the ordeal of detention. Moreover, they assume a primary importance in so far as they can enable us to grasp the ideological outlook of their authors. A comparison between *House of the Dead*, on the one hand, and *One Day in the Life of Ivan Denisovich* and *The First Circle*, on the other, shows, at a distance of a hundred years, surprising similarities but also striking differences. The aim of this article, on the basis of a comparative study, is to try to bring some light to bear on the Russian messianism of the two authors, which originates in the hell of detention.

One of the great discoveries of convict prison life for Dostoevsky was the unbridgeable gap between the intellectuals and the common people. One day, when he wanted to join in the prisoners' protest, Dostoevsky was greeted with jeers: 'I had never been so bitterly insulted since I was in the place,' he writes. If we are to judge by many passages in *House of the Dead*, there was no close relationship between him and the other convicts—no sense of fraternity, and at the end of his imprisonment, Dostoevsky had not made many friends. In a letter to his brother written after his release from the Omsk stockade (dated 22 February 1854), he underlined the gulf between the social classes:

From *Irish Slavonic Studies* 12 (1991). © 1991 by the author and *Irish Slavonic Studies*.

> Their hatred for the gentry was boundless, and they received us, the noblemen, with hostility and a malicious joy at seeing our misery. . . . 150 enemies never tired of persecuting us, they particularly enjoyed it, it was their main entertainment and occupation, and the only thing which saved us was indifference, moral superiority, which they could not but recognise and respect . . .

The picture he draws of the convicts—'They are coarse, exasperated and irritable people'—is quite similar to the one that can be found at the beginning of *House of the Dead*. Moreover, prison is the place where man becomes corrupt and hardened: 'Whom has convict prison improved, and when?' he wonders later during the Kornilova trial.

However, in the same letter and in *House of the Dead*, especially from the middle of the book onwards, Dostoevsky refers to a quite different experience. Another outlook appears which will come into full bloom in *Diary of the Writer*. The hymn to the Russian people at the end of the book is well known:

> How much joyless youth, how much strength for which use there was none, was buried, lost in those walls! . . . For I must speak my thoughts as to this: the hapless fellows there were perhaps the strongest and, in one way or another, the most gifted of our people.

Dostoevsky—under the cover of the narrator—notes the convicts' skill at work, which he contrasts with his own incompetence, thus in a way approving of the contemptuous attitude of the lower classes towards him. When set a task by the overseer, the prisoners were allowed to return to their barracks if they finished before the working day was over, and they were transformed from reluctant workers into intelligent and hard-working people. If Dostoevsky points out that the prisoners lived money and that they were ready to steal or do anything to get some, he nevertheless explains and justifies this attraction to money: money is necessary for men deprived of freedom—it takes the place of freedom. Furthermore, it is never saved for long, as it is quickly squandered on tobacco and vodka. Dostoevsky shows that the Russian people have no greed, no veneration of riches: they do not experience the thirst for money which the writer indicts in his great novels and which he opposed to the *need* for money.

What is more, these criminals, who at first sight seem so coarse, so cruel, so devoid of a moral sense, are the true upholders of the Christian religion. Aware of their crimes, they feel guilty and accept their sufferings as a purification. Dostoevsky was struck by their simple faith, their piety in church. In those men he found the truth of Christ that the intellectual cannot find in himself because he does not have the spirit of humility and because, unlike the peasant convicts, his faith is unstable and precarious and he is beset by doubt. To reach this understanding, as he pointed out to his brother, he had to remove 'the coarse crust' under which the 'gold' was hidden. Twenty-three years alter he was to speak of 'diamonds' which must be looked for in the 'filth.'

In the convicts, Dostoevsky distinguishes two completely opposite elements: the 'filth'—violence, perversion, cruelty, evil—and also 'diamonds'— a luminous soul, a keen sense of justice, true faith. The famous short story, *The Peasant Marei*, reveals the technique by which Dostoevsky extracts the gold from the filth. Sickened by the sight of drunken prisoners furiously beating Gazin, Dostoevsky rushes out of the barracks and happens to meet a Polish nobleman who looks at him gloomily and mutters 'Je hais ces brigands.' Then Dostoevsky abruptly retraces his steps, goes back to the barracks, and, finding the debauch impossible to bear, lies down and pretends to sleep. A memory comes to him—of a peasant he met during his childhood when he believed he had heard a wolf:

> The encounter was a solitary one, in an empty field, and only God, perhaps, saw from above what profound and enlightened human feeling, what delicate, almost feminine tenderness could fill the heart of a coarse, bestially ignorant Russian serf, who at the time neither expected nor dreamed that he might be free.

When he gets off his bunk and looks around, he feels that, 'as if by some miracle,' all hatred has vanished from his heart: 'That despised peasant with shaven head and brand marks on his face . . . why, he may be that very Marei. Dostoevsky is capable now of facing the Pole with some superior pity: 'He could have no memories of any Mareis.' Before the recollection Dostoevsky felt guilty for experiencing feelings which contradict his former convictions and for sharing them with a foreigner. To resolve his inner conflict he used a type of therapy he had perfected during his convict years: that of involuntary association—erasing the present, he lets his mind wander in the past. Whether the incident is authentic matters little: the main thing is that Dostoevsky used a childhood memory to shape an image of the Russian peasant which allowed him to rid himself of his guilt. Each Russian peasant thus becomes a potential Marei. This vision has been transposed in the field of writing. As Robert Jackson has shown so well, only the artist can feel and display through his art the spiritual beauty of the Russian people.

We are therefore confronted with two opposite experiences, and the first tends to disappear and give way to the second. The writer discovers the Russian common people and, thanks to them, discovers the truth of Christ, which, according to his own words, he had 'lost' for a while. In Turgenev and Tolstoy is found the idealisation of the Russian common people. Dostoevsky, however, is thrown in with the core of the Russian people, represented by criminals, including some of the hardest. He shares their lives: living on top of one another in a stinking room, subjected to hard labour and the threat of the knout. He constantly refers to the time he spent as a convict to assert that he has greater right than others to speak of the Russian common people: 'I have learned to know, if not Russia than at least its people, to know them well, as perhaps few know them.' We have seen that Dostoevsky extracts the gold from the filth. Let us now take a closer look at the reasons which prompted him to do this and at the impact it had on his development as a writer.

Did he share Belinsky's opinion on the atheism of the Russian common people? Did he really lose faith in Christ, as he himself asserted? In his famous letter to Gogol', the reading of which led directly to Dostoevsky's imprisonment, Belinsky had written that the Russian church had moved away from Christ's ideals. Dostoevsky had read the letter several times in the Pal'm–Durov and Petrashevsky circles. He adhered to Belinsky's ideas on religion as an institution, which he did not defend. If we go by his *Petersburg Chronicles*, written before the experience as a convict, he appears to have believed that the faith of the Russian peasants was not founded on real knowledge of Russian history (when they came to Moscow to kiss the thaumaturgical relics) but on lack of education and on inertia. His faith in the Russian *muzhik* was at that time humanitarian. As for his loss of faith in Christ, as Pierre Pascal has written, it was a relative one. It is known that he cried when Belinsky insulted Christ in his presence. The New Testament which Madame Fonvizina had given him was his bedside book while in prison, and he had it in his hands when he died. He had a real veneration for Christ, whom he took to be not the Son of God but the most perfect man, the model towards which humanity must aspire. All his life, he was tormented by God. He remained 'a child of doubt,' but he thirsted for faith.

It was in the Russian peasants that Dostoevsky found irrational faith, not corrupted by the intellect—a faith he had experienced in childhood. For Dostoevsky the writer, the Christian spirit is the prerogative of the Russian common people, which is all the more amazing to him as it coexists with a capacity to do evil, to kill, to dominate others and to enjoy one's own cruelty.

It has often been said that Dostoevsky discovered in prison camp evil buried in the human soul. But in his later works he does not impute evil to the common people but to the intellectuals. Separating the spiritual beauty of the Russian peasant from the 'alluvial barbarism' was of primary importance in helping Dostoevsky to realize the links uniting him with the Russian common people whom he wanted to deliver from oppression. He thus manages to resolve the major problem of the Russian intelligentsia through his knowledge of the Russian common people, which he considers to be irrefutable. He bridges the gap which separates the two classes. His faith is enriched with a new content. It moves from personal faith to a national one. The longing for the purity of childhood, for faith based on feeling (because according to him it cannot be justified by reason), is linked to the love of the Russian common people and of his native land. As he writes to Apollon Maikov in 1856, the great discovery he made in prison is that he was able to understand the peasant convicts because he was Russian.

His time abroad intensified the change that had taken place in Dostoevsky. Before his imprisonment, he favoured opening up Russia to Europe and breaking with traditions which did not meet the requirements of modern life. But after going to Paris and London he was convinced that the West was prey to capitalism and had betrayed the ideals of the French revolution, and that socialism, as it was developing there, was not compatible with Christianity. The solution to the Russian problem is to be found in Russia herself, in the heart of Russia, in its peasants, who bear the Russian Christ within themselves. Dostoevsky therefore distances himself from his master without completely turning his back on him, for the criticism of the milieu of which convicts are the victims—criticism can be found in *House of the Dead* and even in the *Diary*—involves an indictment of the established order. Besides, the oath of allegiance to Belinsky's ideals is always present in his mind. However, the conviction that humility and the acceptance of suffering are superior to violence, separates Dostoevsky from Belinsky, for whom Orthodoxy was not deeply rooted in the spirit of the people and was linked to autocracy, to an order which had to be destroyed. The urge to believe and the discovery of popular faith together bring about an ambiguous shift in Dostoevsky's ideological convictions. At the end of his life, he comes closer to the ruling power and the Church, but in his works he appears as a man who dreams of a spiritualised social and political order, of a spiritual fraternity which would be a Russian socialism, a Christian socialism, a true socialism where men would really live in harmony.

In Solzhenitsyn, too, we find the need to go to the common people—a need dear to the Russian intellectuals of the nineteenth century. For Nerzhin, one of the principal characters in *The First Circle*, the common people are made up not of the proletariat—as they were for the communist Rubin—but of the peasants. In his attempt to encounter them, Nerzhin (in whom Solzhenitsyn has put a lot of himself) goes through various stages. First, the common people as seen through the literature of the nineteenth century appear to him to be full of wisdom and spiritual greatness. Then, after having believed for a time that it was necessary to belong to the intellectual elite, he turns again towards the lower classes, among whom, like Dostoevsky, he is thrown, and whose tragic destiny he shares. But Dostoevsky finds himself among criminals—often terrifying characters—and at the beginning of his detention, and even later, he sees 'monsters' in them. Moreover, he feels inferior to them in the field of physical work, and this inferiority complex is exacerbated by the scornful attitude which the convicts have towards him. For Nerzhin, common people

> were no more firm of spirit as they faced the stone wall of a ten-year term. They were no more farsighted or adroit than he during the difficult moments of transports and bodily searches. They were blinder and more trusting about informers. They were more prone to believe the crude deception of the bosses.

In comparison with the GULag prisoners, the convicts are more intelligent, more skilful, more wary of the authorities. In order to understand the Russian spirit Nerzhin has to meet the peasant Spiridon.

Spiridon had been a communist and had taken part in the dekulakisation drive, then had left with the Germans and subsequently returned to Russia. Just like many Russians who have no understanding of history, he is blind. But in the turmoil of history, he has kept his love of the Russian earth and of his family. In Spiridon, Nerzhin has found that popular wisdom which he was burning to acquire Spiridon has forged his own particular conception of virtue: neither lies nor slander nor stealing; a rejection of violence; moderation; a total lack of egoism and a contempt for material possessions. On leaving the *sharasksha* Nerzhin makes a symbolic gesture: he gives the blind man his copy of Esenin's poems. A deep friendship has grown up between the intellectual and the peasant. Finally Nerzhin comes to the conclusion that

> Not by birth, not by the works of one's hands, not by the wings of education is one elected into the people. But by one's inner self. Everyone forges his inner self year after year. One must try to temper, to cut, to polish one's soul so as to become a human being. And thereby become a tiny particle of one's own people.

Nerzhin will become a part of the common people by forging his soul, by freeing himself from things. Such is the conclusion drawn by Solzhenitsyn from the encounter between Spiridon and Nerzhin.

Ivan Denisovich is the continuation of Spiridon. He is a simple man who is happy to receive an extra bowl of soup and a piece of bread, is not eager to leave the camp, and he works although he is aware that work has no meaning. Michel Heller has written that *One Day in the Life of Ivan Denisovich* is 'the writer's final farewell to faith in the simple muzhik and to populism, these aftermaths of the nineteenth century.' Indeed, Solzhenitsyn does not want to idealise Ivan Denisovich. He studies the life of a *zek* (зэк—convict): how does the Russian man change in the world of the concentration camp? His talents of organisation, of solidarity, of resourcefulness and of observation develop. He is a good worker, he knows how to work in a team and likes to work properly. Solzhenitsyn's companion, D. Panin (Sologdin of *The First Circle*), reproached him for the wall-building scene during which Ivan feels moments of pure joy, claiming that the prisoners in fact sabotaged their work. Solzhenitsyn replied to him that he had experienced this phenomenon himself: work well done gives inner satisfaction. For Shalamov, by contrast, the camp kills man's love of work, just as it kills all feelings of charity, honesty and friendship. In *The GULag Archipelago* Solzhenitsyn will denounce the murderous and destructive camp labour, but here he wants to show that work allows Ivan to apply his ingenuity, not to lose his human dignity, to feel alive. For Ivan has a thirst for life, which, together with a physical resistance, enables him to overcome physical and moral ideals.

The camp thus becomes the place of truth for the Russian man of the people, not the setting of the absurd, as it is in Shalamov's short stories. Ivan does not seem to believe in God, and he tells the Baptist Alesha, 'I don't believe in paradise or in hell . . . .' But, as he himself says, he is not 'against God' and he is ready to believe in Him. He learns to pray, 'O Lord, save me! Don't let them send me to the cells.' And then, when the guard does not examine the mitten containing the broken hacksaw blade, he says a prayer of thanksgiving: 'Glory be to Thee, O Lord.' Ivan understands the prayer, 'Give us this day our daily bread,' in his own way, adapting it to his condition: 'Our ration, you mean?' He also learns to weave a special type of relationship with things. Eating becomes a mysterious and sacred rite for him: 'First he only drank the liquid, drank and drank. As it went down, filling his whole body with warmth, all his guts began to flutter inside him at their meeting with that skilly.' At last, he learns to love his neighbour: he gives Alesha his slice of sausage. In the ordeal, in the experience of destitution, Ivan has shaped his character. Perhaps he does not know which hand to cross himself with, but he has made the Christian discovery of his neighbour: it is the second birth of man in deprivation. The involuntary asceticism in which the GULag man is engulfed helped him to purify his soul. Solzhenitsyn, it seems, speaks through Alesha's mouth when the latter cries out: 'Why d'you want freedom? In freedom your last grain of faith will be choked with weeds. You should rejoice that you're in prison. Here you have time to think about your soul.'

The camp is also the place of truth for the intellectual. It is in prison that scientists meeting in the *sharaksha* found a union of free men: these are the new Decembrists (Abramson quotes fragments of the unfinished Chapter X of *Eugene Onegin*). Nerzhin—like Solzhenitsyn—completes his education in the camp. He holds discussions with the great minds of his time and debates all subjects. This is where he ponders on the mechanism of the totalitarian system which fetters common people along with the most gifted intellectuals. This is where, as noted above, he feels a deep kinship with the long-suffering people and understands that in history man has to make a moral choice.

The central chapter of *The First Circle* is entitled 'The Castle of the Holy Grail.' Apart from commissioned works, Kondrashev pursues his quest for truth in his own private pictures. In one of his best works Kondrashev paints the moment when Parsifal sees the castle. The horseman is ascending a narrow path at the edge of an abyss. 'But the horseman was not looking at the abyss. Amazed, he was looking into the distance where a reddish-gold light, coming perhaps from the sun, perhaps from something purer than the sun, flooded the sky behind a castle.' This castle, which is not represented in the picture, is the unearthly 'image of perfection.' Man has this image in himself, and 'in rare moments, it suddenly emerges before his spiritual gaze.' Only the stronger souls can behold the Grail.

The camp is also the place where the stark horror of the regime is expressed. The stone prison symbolises the solidity of the system. The lights which embody the mechanical world identified with socialism eclipse the stars, and the sun which rises in the grey fog of detention symbolises hope. The camp is the allegorical image of daily life under Stalin. Life outside is not different: the same orders must be obeyed without knowing what they mean (Ivan discovers that the sun must submit to the decrees of the Soviet government!), the same hard labour. Through the thoughts, the memories, the words of prisoners and the letters they receive, Solzhenitsyn constantly draws a revealing parallel between life outside the barbed wire and life inside. The prisoner who does not fulfil the work norms does not receive his ration of bread. Similarly, if the peasant does not fulfil the norms, his garden—which is his sole livelihood—is taken away from him. The indictment of the regime is at the very basis of Solzhenitsyn's work. The writer has 'risen from his knees' to become the historian of his time, to cry in men's faces that the inhuman world of camps, the concentration camp hell, is created by the regime.

Comparing these writings of Dostoevsky and Solzhenitsyn, the superficial similarities between the two writers become obvious: their anti-Semitism (the Jew is depicted in a more attractive light in Dostoevsky); their defence of the old believers; the bath scenes are comparable; the scene between Ivan Denisovich and the Baptist Alesha is reminiscent of that between Alesha and Ivan Karamazov, and so forth. But the main point lies elsewhere. There is the same ambiguity towards the Russian common people, who are both criticised and exalted; there is the same conception of prison as the meeting-place between the intellectual and the lower classes, a blessed place where simple man suffers and where he purifies himself and finds his true nature. Dostoevsky speaks, it is true, of criminals (whereas most of the GULag prisoners are innocent): is he not then considering crime as the direct consequence of an unjust social system? Even if Dostoevsky holds the convicts responsible for their acts, they are at the same time victims of a system, like the GULag prisoners. For both writers, the prison is a symbolic place of suffering and of purification.

One of the main differences between the two writers is to be found in their conception of freedom. The theme of freedom runs all through *House of the Dead*. The moment when the fetters fall and he is leaving the jail forever is an 'unspeakable' one for Dostoevsky: 'New life! Resurrection from the dead!' As for the peasant convicts, freedom to them is something sacred, as is revealed in the beautiful scene of the release of the eagle. Once a convict brings in a wounded eagle. The prisoners look after it, and then in late autumn decide to release it: 'It doesn't suit him being a prisoner; give him his freedom, his jolly freedom.' And they stand for a long time watching it fly away: 'Sure enough, he's free; he feels it. It's freedom!' The convicts, like Dostoevsky himself, are dreamers: they dream of freedom. In an unpublished chapter of the book Dostoevsky depicts a palace of 'marble and gold' but surrounded by a fence: 'Yes, only one thing is missing: free air, freedom! Cherished freedom! . . .' For Solzhenitsyn, there can be only inner freedom, as outside the camp, too, men are deprived of freedom. The whole of Russia is a camp. Dostoevsky also compares life in the convict prison with life outside the prison—through the convicts' biographies, their memories and the stories inserted in the book. As Solzhenitsyn does for Ivan Denisovich, so Dostoevsky shows that the life of the common people was such that they would sometimes prefer to be imprisoned. But the theme of double slavery is emphasised much more in Solzhenitsyn. The concentration camp is the place where man can free himself from the 'brambles' of ideology. Solzhenitsyn wants to indict the regime that has sent him to prison, and his entire work strives towards the denunciation of that regime. Dostoevsky indicted not so much the regime which imprisoned him as the socialism which he supported in his youth.

This is where the two writers come together. Dostoevsky believes that utopia is an unattainable ideal (as he says of Fourierism in the *Explanation* which he writes for the Commission of Inquiry when he is imprisoned), and unsuited to the Russian world. It was because he loved utopia that he went to prison, and he was always to be obsessed by it. Solzhenitsyn saw 'utopia in power' and if he did not have a clear vision of the situation in the 1930s during the great trials (he was nineteen years old in 1937), the scales were quickly to fall from his eyes. He became a writer who confronts socialist ideology. Solzhenitsyn criticises what he knows. Dostoevsky criticises what he foresees: he prophesies. The camp reinforces, enlightens and deepens Solzhenitsyn's political ideas; the prison makes Dostoevsky's ideas waver.

After a century, Solzhenitsyn's message links up with Dostoevsky's. In spite of noticeable differences (for example, the metaphysical revolt is absent from Solzhenitsyn's work, as is the veneration of Christ), the two writers dream of introducing harmony into a chaotic world. Both are haunted by the dream of God's kingdom on earth and give art an eschatological function, that of anticipating that kingdom. Both are influenced by the philosophy of Solov'ev for whom art is the representation of facts of things in the light of the future. In his Nobel prize speech, Solzhenitsyn said that he gave a permanent value to the sentence uttered by Prince Myshkin in *The Idiot*: 'Beauty will save the world.'

CARYL EMERSON

The Word of Aleksandr Solzhenitsyn

Few Nobel laureates alive today are so profoundly identified with their nation's past, yet so disputed a part of its real future, as Aleksandr Solzhenitsyn. This paradox was nicely caught in an article in *Izvestiia* on 23 July 1994, two days after the writer's seven-week journey of repatriation across Siberia ended with his return, after a twenty-year exile, to Moscow. "In an interview at Yaroslavl Station," the byline read, "Aleksandr Solzhenitsyn has confirmed that he would accept no government posts and would try to serve society as a writer. But to be a writer in Russia is traditionally a political calling, and Solzhenitsyn is the most political writer of the last twenty years."

Politics here must be understood in the broadest possible sense. Its parameters were laid down in a country where, for most of this century, top-heavy social commands, totalitarian controls, and the absence of grass-roots civic structures had made *everything* political, even the desire to withdraw from politics itself. The *Izvestiia* article continues: "Before his arrival in Vladivostok, Solzhenitsyn had observed the course of Russian reforms from afar, and thus many could rightly claim more knowledge than he of the facts of Russian life. But one does not expect from a writer merely a simple knowledge of everyday facts. A writer is the voice of the people; it is expected that he have the ability to say what others know but cannot express. He must find the Word."

From *The Georgia Review* 49, no. 1 (Spring 1995). © 1995 by The University of Georgia.

What is Solzhenitsyn's Word? Having matured under Stalinist conditions, can this Word now survive the complexities, compromises, and erosion that freedom inevitably brings? Does a writer-witness of Solzhenitsyn's sort identify so thoroughly with history—the history of his nation as well as his own personal history—that it is difficult for him to accommodate, and perhaps even to envisage, a radically new or different future? For there are two kinds of writers: those with biographies, and those without. If Shakespeare and Emily Dickinson are of the latter category (one need not know their lives to appreciate their Word), then Solzhenitsyn is emphatically of the first. As for Lord Byron, Dostoevsky, and, today, Czeslaw Milosz, the events of Solzhenitsyn's life are the primary ethical and myth-building matter that nourishes the literary texts. That life was of heroic, tragic proportions and tied to Stalinist oppression—the awful reality of which became Solzhenitsyn's master organizing principle, the generator of his personal identity, and the source of his fictional plots.

In considering Solzhenitsyn's Word, then, the present essay attempts three things. First, it aims to suggest to an American audience why the Russian literary word has been so inescapably political for most of Russian history—and thus why Solzhenitsyn intuitively understands that to be a "Russian writer" in the traditional sense is to be much more powerful than a mere holder of a political post. Second, it will survey briefly Solzhenitsyn's major literary works and Nobel Lecture for ethical postulates that come together in the mature programmatic statements *Rebuilding Russia* (1990) and *The Russian Question at the End of the Twentieth Century* (1994). Finally, this essay will assess the "Solzhenitsyn phenomenon" as a whole—for it is a Russian pattern of hero building now very possibly on the brink of a paradigm shift. Solzhenitsyn's public appearances across Russia drew huge and worshipful crowds. But many intellectuals were wary, according to David Remnick, who reported such reactions as, "the time for a single heroic figure is passed . . . I suppose he'll come back and play the role of Tolstoy, the great writer who gives us all advice, the prophet who accepts visitors and wears a great beard. The beard is very important in this role." Americans, from the White House on down, have been suspicious of Solzhenitsyn ever since he settled in Vermont. We watched him depart with few regrets. In the restructured 1990's, can we deal compassionately with the elevated, prophetic voice that Solzhenitsyn has always commanded—and that is so routinely ironized, even made to sound ridiculous, in the West he has left behind? Might we yet learn from him?

I

Solzhenitsyn devoted most of his 1970 Nobel Lecture to the therapeutic and salvational powers of literature. People belong to such different worlds, he noted, with so many different standards of measurement, that individual humans as well as whole cultures can only be confused by—and thus indifferent to—each other's experiences and sufferings. "Words ring out and fade away, they flow off like water—leaving no taste, no color, no smell. No trace." Only one means exists to communicate experience across the barrier of nationality and generation, and that is art. Only art, Solzhenitsyn insists, cannot be based on an error and a lie; politics, philosophy, official history can all lie with elegance and impunity, but a lie in art will invariably be sensed as false and ruin the work. The ancients were right: Beauty, the aesthetic principle, is an inalienable aspect of Truth and Goodness.

Let us pursue the fate of this invigorating, old-fashioned sentiment in post-Communist Russia. Under Soviet tutelage, culture had indeed been shackled and censored. But the literature that survived these filters was "clean," subsidized, secure, and protected from the ravages of a debased popular market. It might have been difficult to get hold of a desired piece of pornography, but one could usually find inexpensive editions of Pushkin, Tolstoy, Shakespeare, Hemingway; and one could be assured—in a country traditionally reverent toward its literary canon and reluctant to alter it—that schoolchildren would be taught the classics. Now the humanities and social sciences, deprived of familiar centralized directives, are in immense disarray. As Solzhenitsyn put it in 1990, the Iron Curtain had protected Russians superbly from all the positive features of the West, but "did not reach all the way to the bottom," permitting the "liquid dung" of popular Western culture to seep in and pollute Russian youth. Even more alarming than the "polluted" content of post-Communist culture, however, is the newly pluralistic context for the Russian word.

Here American secular experience prepares us poorly for Russian realities. For most of Russian culture (at least from the sixteenth century on) the printed word has been associated with something lofty and sacred; it has not been at the disposal of Russian subjects for their own casual or private use. In the words of one historian, among medieval Russians—and in important ways Russia remained medieval until Peter the Great in the early eighteenth century—"writing itself was regarded as a solemn, important action which one must not perform carelessly or without sufficient reason; one was expected to write down only those things that required perpetuation. . . ." As late as the 1830's, the minister of public education of the Russian Empire decreed that "among the rights of a Russian subject, the right to address the public in writing is not included."

Literature written in such a culture must inevitably play a more serious, politicized, and potentially more subversive role than it has had to play in the modern West. In successive Russian Empires, tsarist and Soviet censorship of real-world events tended to make literature the best refuge of honest ideas. This has been a very mixed blessing. Not only did creative writers often consider themselves seers or prophets and (from our Western perspective) assign themselves an altogether inflated task; also, those who interpreted art and culture (the critics) were granted the role of priest, a sort of divine intermediary between the people and revealed Truth. They were the insiders who alone could decode the real meaning of dangerous texts and incomprehensible current events. For how could writers not be martyrs? It was part of one's professional definition in a culture where literature was taken so seriously that its practitioners, readers as well as writers, could be shot for it. And when the writer is at once primary creator, memoirist, witness, and cultural critic, this prototype gains extraordinary moral force. Solzhenitsyn, it could be said, is the perfectly distilled residue of this Russian legacy.

The falling away of the writer's special status is only one unruly fact facing the repatriated Solzhenitsyn. There have been other paradigm shifts as well, ones that directly affect the reception of his huge, mixed-genre, historical chronicles: *The Gulag Archipelago* and the recently completed tetralogy *The Red Wheel*. Solzhenitsyn wishes to serve Russia today not through politics but "through literature," yet the parameters of literature are now under some pressure to become more discriminating. This too could hurt. In oppressive times, the best ideas in many disciplines found a home in literary fiction because they had not been free to constitute themselves as autonomous fields of study: philosophy, theology, economics, politics. Now those professions can construct their own legitimate homes. "Russian literature has always carried out someone else's obligations," the Russian scholar Vyacheslav Ivanov remarked with some dismay in a forum on Dostoevsky in 1990. "Nowadays, Aleksandr Isaevich [Solzhenitsyn] is not really doing his own work, but doing the work of the nonexistent historians of Russia of the modern period. It is indeed time to work for disarmament. But it is also time to give literature the chance to be literature, art to be art."

Many younger Russian writers have come to welcome this reappraisal. "The writer in Russia was for so long like an uncrowned prince," the Petersburg poet Aleksandr Kushner has noted. Now this is gone. But "literature will always have a place, as it does in America. Marginal, but important. Small but beautiful. . . ." Solzhenitsyn is not blind to this new reality. "When I said [in *The First Circle*] that a writer is like a second government, I meant it in the context of a fully totalitarian regime. But in a free society this formula no longer applies. Moreover, literature, like so much else in Russia, is now in a state of terrible degeneration." Implicit in Solzhenitsyn's comment is a question that Russian writers now must ask themselves: Is the enfeeblement of art the price that must be paid for civic freedom?

There is, however, a larger and more troublesome issue at stake than the fate of literature's lofty unifying mission, and here too the Nobel lecture is the starting point. According to Solzhenitsyn in that speech, it is precisely *national cultures*, rather than individuals, that register human experience. The writer is "the articulator of the national tongue, that main tie which holds a nation together." This distinctive role is precious; to erode nationhood "would impoverish us not less than if all men should become alike. . . . Nations are the wealth of mankind, its generalized personalities." Thus Solzhenitsyn evades the issue of differentiated, contradictory experiences and consciousness *within* a single nation by not asking what a nation is that it should leave so uniform a stamp on its people. In a review of Solzhenitsyn's 1994 polemic *The Russian Question*, one Moscow historian pointed out, sadly, that Solzhenitsyn belongs to the deeply conservative, purist, nineteenth-century school of "spiritual nationalism," which viewed a "mixing of cultures and histories as inadmissible." Not surprisingly, Solzhenitsyn despairs over the "mongrelization" of the Russian language with alien terms and categories— even as he must be aware that some concepts crucial to debureaucratization and de-Stalinization (for example, privacy, efficiency, tolerance, pluralism) have no verbal equivalent in his native tongue. He would either find the word in Russia's past, or endeavor to do without it. The possibility that alien languages might *enrich* the Russian consciousness with otherwise unavailable concepts or experiences appears foreign to Solzhenitsyn.

Russians have long been idealists about what language can do. Held captive, the word was assumed to contain the Truth; once freed from censorship, it was supposed to work miracles. Solzhenitsyn had ended his Nobel Lecture in 1970 with his conviction that "one word of truth outweighs the world." Few people in the West, battered by a billion free words per minute, would find such a sentiment persuasive. But back on Russian soil in 1994, Solzhenitsyn (who is a good learner from experience) proved not at all naïve on this question of responsible freedoms. Speaking from Novosibirsk in mid-July 1994, he recalled a statement he had made in 1969 in response to Andrei Sakharov: "It is terrible for a people to lose freedom of the word, as we lost it in 1917. But still more terrible and anguished will be the return of freedom for the word."

II

How did Solzhenitsyn's literary and life experiences combine to shape his own powerful, but now precariously tested, Word? It might be useful, now that the period of "witnessing Stalinist tyranny" has come to an end, to align Solzhenitsyn's major works retrospectively along one axis, namely, the *moral* implications of their plots. Each of his masterpieces can be shown to pose—in literary or fictional form and under maximally unfree conditions—a facet of the larger ethical message that Solzhenitsyn is now, for the first time in his life, wholly free to deliver to his countrymen. Is freedom a hospitable medium for them?

One Day in the Life of Ivan Denisovich, which draws on Solzhenitsyn's experience in the early 1950's in the northern camp of Ekibastuz, develops a theme universal to concentration-camp literature of the twentieth century: the possibility of sustaining human dignity under unspeakably dehumanized conditions. Unhappily, existing English translations rarely reflect the stylistic boldness of this short novel, which is narrated almost exclusively from inside a simple prisoner's head and in his own pungent, practical-minded diction, without metaphysical bitterness or irony. Ivan Denisovich is genuinely gratified to get through the day with his small gains intact.

The First Circle, as intellectual as *Ivan Denisovich* is working-class, is the most political of Solzhenitsyn's "autobiographical" novels. It is modeled after its author's own "employment," in the late 1940's, as mathematician and political prisoner at a research institute which had been assigned a secret project under Stalin's direct patronage. Through its hero, Gleb Nerzhin, Solzhenitsyn investigates the moral dilemma of collaboration with evil in the name of science. Nerzhin's transfer to a more primitive camp at the novel's end suggests that such privileged collaboration, however unfreely contracted, is never ethically neutral.

Cancer Ward is also an intimately autobiographical work. Its symbolism, however, is more organic—or more pathological. In February 1952, near the end of his prison term, Solzhenitsyn was stricken with fast-growing stomach cancer and operated on successfully by fellow convict-surgeons. His all-but-miraculous cure, with its hopeful parallel implications for a diseased body politic, was the inspiration for the hero of *Cancer Ward*, Oleg Kostoglotov—who is released from a Tashkent hospital likewise cured, weakened, and purified. During his treatment, Kostoglotov courts and is courted by two women, a doctor and a nurse, both of whom he succeeds in discouraging by the final chapter. He departs to his place of exile alone, for cancer, he dimly suspects, is a dangerous foe: beginning mysteriously, spreading according to its own laws, it can be stopped only by cutting or killing human tissue almost at random. Until the costs of survival are known, one must convalesce slowly, simplify appetites, not take all that is offered. In this novel of survivorship and spiritual husbandry, Solzhenitsyn explores in a single organism the idea of a "self-limiting economy"—an idea he brings to fruition on a national scale in his 1990 treatise *Rebuilding Russia*.

The huge historical works—*The Gulag Archipelago* (in three volumes) and the five thousand pages of *The Red Wheel* (on the First World War and Revolution, in ten volumes)—present a somewhat different problem. Here the plots are illustrative not solely of personal morality but of the "morality of history" as well; or rather, they indicate how an individual confronted with cataclysmic historical events, can sustain and nourish an ethical dimension. The verdict on *The Red Wheel* is not yet in—the cycle was finished only in 1991 and its final volumes are not due to appear in English translation until 1996 at the earliest—but preliminary reviews have been mixed. *The Gulag Archipelago*, on the other hand, is an established masterpiece. Neither novel nor history, subtitled an "experiment in literary investigation," it grants Solzhenitsyn authority in both realms. The first two volumes are archival and, to an extent, autobiographical: illustrated by the author's own arrest and incarceration, they chronicle the evolution of the hideous administrative machinery of the Terror, its forced-labor system, its psychological impact, and its criminally inefficient economic rationale. Volume three is a more subjective narrative, focusing on the heroism and ingenuity of individual escape attempts and examining the whole psychology of resistance. The first two books are cold with the fury of facts. But the third *Gulag* volume is more complex in its morality; it can serve, in fact, as an instructive laboratory for Solzhenitsyn's paradoxical "authoritarian humanism."

Readers in the West have often taken offense at the lofty and prophetic style of Solzhenitsyn's utterances. As the writer himself has put it, his convictions are cast "at the highest pitch of expression"—a tone of voice he knows is not at all to mainstream America's taste. He was raised in, and forced to confront, a culture that loudly advertised itself as messianic, collectivist, cosmic, teleological, sacrificial; his voice reflects the awful tensions and, as it were, exalted pretensions of that reality. To oppose the tyranny of that culture, Solzhenitsyn endorses values that are recognizably humanist: the dignity and freedom of the individual, the centrality of a moral philosophy over a metaphysics, careful attention to man's integrated place in the natural world. Yet this is not the contemplative, reasonable humanist message with which we feel most comfortable, nor is it delivered in a spirit of tolerance or compassion.

Solzhenitsyn is indeed a humanist, but in a peculiarly authoritarian and heroic sense that has little currency in the modern West. His humanism is to be found in his conviction that the irreducibly individual quality in each of us, as it were our ethical core, is best shaped when tested under totalitarian conditions. This belief is demonstrated, at great and eloquent length, in the third *Gulag* volume's tales of resistance. It is tempting, in the light of that chronicle, to speculate that Solzhenitsyn's censure of consumer capitalism, with its culture of lawsuits and legal rights, falls squarely on this notion of the ethical trial. Goods and services themselves are not necessarily bad or corrupting; but bigness and a greed for things tend to make a society value amalgamation, standardization, and homogenization—all of which destroy the individual risk and the individualized moral response. Recall Oleg Kostoglotov, hero of *Cancer Ward*, on his first day in Tashkent after being released from the hospital. He is savoring his survival and pondering "how easy it was to stir human desires and how difficult to satisfy them, once aroused." Waiting in line in a department store, he overhears a man ask the clerk for a shirt by its collar size. The request "staggered him like an electric shock." "Why return to this life?" Kostoglotov asks himself. "If you had to remember your collar size, you'd have to forget something. Something more important!" Thus does Solzhenitsyn value self-limitation, thrift, and modesty in aim, so that the contours of the answerable individual can always be kept in view. Even if—and perhaps especially if—the individual is Ivan Denisovich, taking pride in aligning his bricks correctly as he builds his own prison wall.

    Such a moral position, however, puts the repatriated Solzhenitsyn at exquisite risk. It has become fashionable in Russia today to condemn the intelligentsia for its idealism, utopianism, self-importance, and fastidious refusal to compromise in practical political tasks. Inevitably, Solzhenitsyn was pulled into this orbit of cultural self-laceration—and resented additionally for his wealth and fame. In a lengthy article published in the newspaper *Rossiiskie vesti* during the month of Solzhenitsyn's return, one political scientist remarked bitterly that normal human life, "normal development, without revolutionary shocks, is in practice always tragic for the intelligentsia." Yet Solzhenitsyn's own experience and its wisdoms make him part of that traditional tsarist/Communist "intelligentsia of unfreedom"—for whom it was, in a sense, a disaster to develop normally. The norms of Western life (which also bring complex challenges) do permit us to recall our collar size; and it is an open question, I believe, whether such knowledge must come at the cost of forgetting something more important.

    There is a final dilemma intrinsic to Solzhenitsyn's prison-camp writings, one that locates him somewhat outside the community of psychologists investigating totalitarian structures. Solzhenitsyn unabashedly applies dramatic, individualistic, even romantic models of "tragic heroism" to concentration-camp experience. The point made by many today, however, is that such old-fashioned models are simply not relevant to holocausts and human exterminations, and that the wholesale depersonalization and disfiguring of consciousness, utterly normal in this context, make such an ideal both cruel and inaccurate. Solzhenitsyn will not sacrifice this ideal—and in his unwillingness to do so, he is perhaps more stubbornly a humanist than those who surpass him in tolerance and modesty of diction.

III

What happens when a prophet returns to his native land? Solzhenitsyn's repatriation occurred in two stages, the order being decreed by the writer himself: first the works and then the man. The return of the man was a modern phenomenon, safe and somewhat staged, a media event. The prior repatriation of the works, in contrast, was marked by all the oppression, high scandal, and heroic resistance that nurtured the comfortable paradigm of the Russian writer. Still, it could be argued that in Solzhenitsyn's case the old repressive paradigm remained in force longer—even under conditions that had become hostile to it—than in the case of any other eminent Russian writer. As late as October 1988, well into Gorbachev's *glasnost*, over a million back covers of the journal *Novy mir* were ripped off—"arrested," as it were—because they had announced the forthcoming publication of the *Gulag* volumes, a move that had not been cleared by the Soviet Politburo. The subsequent outrage among the intelligentsia produced a miracle: the Writers' Union, having rescinded its twenty-five-year-old expulsion of Solzhenitsyn, pulled together with like-minded public figures, faced down the recalcitrant government, and by August 1989 had *Gulag* in print. It was only a matter of months before other long-banned writings went to press, and plans for a Collected Works followed soon after. The path for the writer was open.

But the problematic liberated word had preceded him. In a December 1989 interview, Natalia Solzhenitsyn remarked that her husband would not return to Russia until "every simple man and woman in his motherland had the chance to read *Gulag* and *The Red Wheel*, if they would like to . . ." It probably never seriously occurred to Solzhenitsyn, however, that simple men and women in Russia might not make such reading a priority. "I thought I was returning to a Russia that had read me," he is said to have remarked during his trans-Siberian journey home. But *The Red Wheel*, he sadly acknowledged, had had "no impact whatsoever."

However negligent his currently distracted Russian readership, Solzhenitsyn's return elicited a passionate, widely varied response to his person. Much was made in the Russian press of the fact that America did not like him—and parting shots critical of Solzhenitsyn in the Western media were gleefully (and at times quite misleadingly) translated. Communists and fascist groups despised Solzhenitsyn's anti-imperialism; liberals were made anxious by his authoritarian Slavophile views; and some muckrakers stooped to slander of the most unpalatable sort.

Among the useful byproducts of the repatriation polemic was a fresh look by the Russians at their own "image of the writer as seer." In a major essay by Lev Navrozov entitled "Solzhenitsyn and the West: Farewell without Ovations," America's miscomprehension of the famous Vermont recluse is laid partly at our doorstep, but also partly at Solzhenitsyn's own. Solzhenitsyn, Navrozov observes, has clung to the Leninist myth that there are two Americas, that of the government (allied with the bourgeois press) and that of the *narod*, the common people. Solzhenitsyn assumed that the two must be hostile to each other—and that the *narod* by definition was the more virtuous entity. But Navrozov reminds his Russian readers that "the people" have no special unity or distinguishing marks; one certainly cannot assume that they oppose their government, nor does their government refer to them (in Soviet style) as a singular and undifferentiated mass. It is neither government policy nor the machinations of the press that determines an American citizen's priorities; it is *individual taste*. And these citizens, Navrozov concludes, are utterly indifferent to Solzhenitsyn and haven't read him—or, if they have read him, they hate him; in any case they are much more taken up with scandals like that of Tonya Harding than by the past or future fate of Russia.

There is an additional factor that might have alienated Solzhenitsyn from the "spirit of American ingenuity" and passion for invention that has long been a characteristic of the New World. This is his overall stand against innovation itself. In an important speech delivered in New York City in January 1993, Solzhenitsyn condemned the "relentless cult of novelty" that, in his opinion, had wrecked the twentieth century. If, as he had claimed in his Nobel Lecture, the proper art could save and reunify the world, then surely an improper attitude toward art could prime any culture for its own destruction. Russia in the prerevolutionary, avant-garde 1910's and the West in the postmodernist 1990's resemble each other, Solzhenitsyn argued, in their aggressive pursuit of newness for its own sake. Such a pursuit always leads to a decline in moral values, to an indulgence in "uninhibited self-expression," to a "pessimistic relativism," and to such vacuous substitutes for true art as the "world as text" or a mere "playing on the strings of emptiness." Solzhenitsyn is not alone, of course, in decrying the tedious superficiality and barrenness of Postmodernism. He is perhaps extreme, however, in his rejection of all aesthetic experimentation and all nondidactic forms of art.

There remains the awkward question of Solzhenitsyn's nationalism. By this I mean not only his Russocentrism—although that quality rightly worries some observers—but, more important, his deep belief in cultural difference and national exclusivity as an almost sacred principle. This cultural separatism runs counter to certain myths that have long lain at the center of mainstream American thought. Until quite recently, our dominant ideology taught us that the individual, not the minority group or the nation, is the primary reckoning point. A corollary was that individuals, created equal in opportunity and potential, were all pretty much the same. In contrast, Solzhenitsyn argues that the presumption of sameness among peoples is a mistake. Although we might all be alike in certain biological (and other easily identifiable) ways, we are very, very different in the crucial ways that makes cultures necessary and valuable to one another.

According to Solzhenitsyn, the magic of art enables one nation to intuit another nation's uniqueness and briefly to experience its truth, but we should never strive to fuse or obscure the multiplicity and incompatibility of national truths. Is this a philosophy of life—or of literature—for an angry and divided world on the brink of the twenty-first century? Will Solzhenitsyn himself soften his position, as he continues to live in his homeland on the far side of the Stalinist night? The era of the great writer-witness, when one voice could speak the experience of a nation, is now gone. And yet there are indications that once the repatriation saga has faded, pressure to integrate Solzhenitsyn—his heroic life and heroic works—will reassert itself. One view of his long-term place in Russian literary history was voiced by a participant at a Dostoevsky evening hosted early in 1990 by Jack Matlock, United States ambassador to the Soviet Union during the Brezhnev years. "Solzhenitsyn presents us with that type of artist who begins at the point where Dostoevsky and Tolstoy had ended," the critic remarked. "He is the true continuator of Dostoevsky's cause, only on that level where the spiritual search is finished, the choice has been made, the faith has been found. Now it remains for us to stand firm in the faith."

To be sure, not everyone would endorse such an image of Dostoevsky, that powerful man of doubt who took such care to balance a Father Zosima with a Grand Inquisitor. Nor would all of us welcome such a precommitted, end-determined image of post-Communist moral leadership. It has the ring of that prototype evoked in the *Izvestiia* article on which this essay opened, a Russian writer who has "found the Word." Many today would prefer a more modest, familiar, pluralistic humanism. But it is a role that Solzhenitsyn, if called upon, is surely prepared to play— and perhaps play out, having resumed his position as Russia's greatest (and perhaps *final* greatest) living writer.

HUGH RAGSDALE

The Solzhenitsyn That Nobody Knows

For the second time Alexander Solzhenitsyn last year returned home from exile. He has had a house built in the environs of Moscow, where he plans to take up residence. He foreswears politics, yet he publicly condemns revolutions—both French and Russian—and declares that Russia should be a unified state rather than a "false confederation." He himself has said that the presence of a great writer at home is tantamount to an alternative government in the country. A recent poll in Petersburg found far more sympathy for him than for anyone in Russia's present leadership.

In the past few years, Solzhenitsyn's once remarkably strident views have undergone a kind of lapidary furbishing; the sharper edges have been removed. He has made a sort of accommodation with electoral democracy. More important, he has praised the state of Israel for its stubborn resistance to American popular culture, and he has thus explicitly distanced himself from the anti-Semitism of which he has been suspected, a feature so characteristic of his school of literature. We cannot say of him—as of the Bourbons returned from exile—that he has learned nothing and forgotten nothing. Still, for a poignant synopsis of his thought—and his potential intentions?—the best guide, his most important piece of work, is one of his first, a short story that remains almost unknown in the land of his former refuge.

From *The Virginia Quarterly Review* 71, no. 4 (Autumn 1995). © 1995 by the Virginia Quarterly Review.

"Matryona's Home" ("Matryonin dvor," 1963) is in its way as simple and direct as Hemingway and Pushkin, and yet its modesty is deceptive. It is a composite of different elements. It is most obviously the story of the author's return from his first exile in the Gulag. It is, in addition, a statement of the code of values of the Slavophile creed. Perhaps most provocatively, it is an allegorical history of Russia in fictional form.

Released by the amnesty of 1953 from the Gulag, Ignatich, a mathematics teacher, sought work in a remote vista of rural Russia, "some place far beyond the railroad," some place that would undoubtedly represent to him an asylum from that monster of modernization, the Five-Year Plans and the purges needed to guarantee their appearance of success. Yet even in a region bearing the beautiful name *Vysokoe pole* (High Field), an area once deep and trackless forest, the intrusions of progress had established an ugly little village by the name of *Torfoprodukt* (Peat Product). Farther out and offering perhaps a slightly more sylvan prospect, was *Talnyi* (Hostage). The local school needed a math teacher. Even here, however, the trains ran right through the village, ran right recklessly, as did the whole modern Moloch, the revolutionary monster of devouring materialism.

Travelers and newcomers here were few, and lodging was rarely needed or provided. Someone suggested that Matryona Vasilievna might have room. Matryona's place, Ignatich was warned, would be far from neat. It was old and needed repair. Still the house was large. There was plenty of room for a boarder. Matryona herself was sickly. She did not encourage him. "We are not clever, we don't cook, how shall we suit? . . ." There was a cat and mice and cockroaches, but there was little other choice, and Ignatich was not choosy. He stayed. It was, after all, a microcosm of the kind of refuge that he sought.

Matryona was no modern Soviet woman, "new Soviet person," no Calvinist Communist of the forest. Rather she was an awkwardly proto-Orthodox embodiment of the Biblical beatitudes. An elderly countrywoman, humble and homely Matryona had a lot of worries. Her husband had not returned from the war, and after eight years it was not likely that he ever would. Matryona had only recently received the pension to which she had so long been entitled. Nearing 60 years of age now, when she grew ill, she had been dismissed from the local collective farm. Matryona lived by working her petty garden plot—like everybody else in the region—by poaching fuel from the state peat trust. A single day's supply for her stove weighed 70 or 80 pounds, and she had to fetch it from a distance of two miles. During the 200 days of winter, she had to do it every day. She fed herself on a few meager potatoes and the milk that her goat gave.

In spite of her expulsion from the collective, the farm management was not embarrassed to call on her for help when the harvest was taken in. She grumbled and complained of ill health, but she always went. When her neighbors called on her, she went without hesitation, and she refused their offers of pay. Blessed are the meek, blessed are the pure in heart.

Matryona had typical folk fears. She was afraid of fire, afraid of lightening, and afraid of trains—there was something ominous here about trains. She was religious in the curious half-pagan, fully superstitious fashion of the Russian countryside, more generically religious than specifically Christian. Matryona would not go into the garden on St. John's day for fear of spoiling the harvest. In the weather she found signs of doom or foreboding. She was never seen to cross herself, but she called on God's blessing whenever she undertook any job. She lit an oil lamp before the icons on feast days.

Matryona and her boarder treated each other with respectful reserve. They inquired little into their respective pasts. Ignatich eventually mentioned that he had served time; it was a kind of hurdle crossed. Matryona nodded as if she had apprehended it. How else to explain the sudden appearance of a newcomer in 1953? Slowly in the course of long evenings and snatches of conversation the life of Matronya—and of Russia itself—was sketched out.

Married at 19, she moved into her husband's home, the one in which she now lived. The war came—World War I—and Faddei went to the front. He didn't come back, he disappeared. For years she waited for him. In the meantime, his brother Yefim came courting and proposed marriage. Matryona hesitated and accepted. Within months, Faddei returned. He had been released from a P.O.W. camp in Hungary. Shock engulfed them all. Faddei declared that he would look for another Matryona. Eventually he found one in a neighboring village, and he married her. Two brothers, Yefim and Faddei, and two wives, Matryona Vasilievna and the other Matryona, Matryona II.

Faddei's Matryona, Matryona II, suffered her husband's constant beatings, but she bore him six children. Yefim was a gentler husband. He did not beat his wife, Matryona Vasilievna. He did scorn her country ways. He liked to dress up, and he made fun of her village fashions. He took a mistress in the nearby town, too.

Matryona Vasilievna had a blighted fecundity. She, too, gave birth to six children, but all of them died. Eventually she begged of her sister-in-law, Matryona II, the youngest daughter, Kira. Kira was raised by Yefim and Matryona Vasilievna. Before Ignatich's coming, Kira had married and moved away. In the meantime, the next war had come, World War II. Faddei was exempted this time for poor vision, but Yefim, Matryona Vasilievna's husband, was drafted, and what had happened to Faddei in the first war happened to Yefim in the second—except that he never came back.

This is the story of Russia itself. I have long thought of the relationship of government and people in Russia as that of parent and child. A friend of mine insists that it is rather the relationship of abusing husband and abused wife, and she knows Russia, too. Russian husbands are, in any event, as sovereign as the Russian government.

Matryona is the colloquial variant of the Russian name Matrona, a Latin borrowing meaning wife or matron. In another variation, it is Matryoshka, the name of the nesting dolls that everywhere symbolize Russian folk handicraft. In pure Russian, however, the first syllable of the name, mat, is the Russian word for mother. An author whose opening remarks in this story demonstrate his close attention to the phonology of Russian proper names cannot be suspected of choosing the name of his heroine carelessly. Matryona is Mother Russia.

As there were two Matryonas, so have there been two Russias. Yefim treated Matryona Vasilievna as Peter I treated his Russia. He was not so deliberately abusive as his Soviet successors, but he scorned native culture and went a-whoring after the fashions of Europe. The fate of Faddei's Matryona II was like that of Soviet Russia, more abused and more productive. "Love your wife like your soul, shake her like your pear tree."

The fate of Yefim, the husband who never returned, can only be imagined, but the numbers of graphic possibilities exemplify the tortured history of the nation during his generation. He may have become an MIA. He may have died in a German camp. If he survived captivity, maybe he chose, as so many Soviet "displaced persons" did, not to risk the implacable mercies of Stalin and went West. Or maybe he suffered forced return by Anglo-American repatriation teams and died in the Soviet camps.

In any event his widow, feeling the approach of illness and death, had made out a will. It bequeathed the upper room of her house to her foster daughter, Kira. The rest of the house would be disposed of by the quarrels of the relatives. This process began, however, sooner than anticipated. Kira and her husband discovered that they could acquire a plot of land in their nearby village if they could establish a dwelling on it, and they seized on the idea of persuading Matryona at once to part with her upper room to satisfy their need.

Just as in the case of the trains, there was something foreboding about this particular part of the house. It was not called the upstairs (*naverkh*), the upper story (*verkhnii etazh*), or second floor (*vtoroi etazh*). Rather it was always called the *gornitsa*, a somewhat antiquated word formerly meaning upper room. This is the word which in the Russian Gospel of Luke is used for that upper room in which the first Holy Eucharist took place. Does the ravishing of it suggest the poor quality of the Russian people's commitment to their Orthodox Christianity? Does it suggest the Soviet decapitation of the Orthodox Church? Had the Church, like the upper room, been disposed of so readily because it had come to be regarded by the people as dispensable? In any event, the role of the upper room is heavy with premonition. And even without religious reference, here was a regular witches' brew of greed, materialism, and the civilization of modern mechanical technology that both Matryona and Ignatich so dreaded.

Matryona was troubled. The idea of breaking up the house in which she had lived for 40 years disturbed her. Her relatives knew that in the end she would give in to their entreaties. Their eager solicitation was overwhelming. So the wrecking crew arrived—Kira, her husband, her father Faddei, and a couple of Faddei's sons. They took the room apart board by board, stacking them all beside the house until transport could be arranged.

Ignatich came home from school one day to find the grand enterprise under way. A tractor was there and a large sledge. The sledge fully loaded would not accommodate all the lumber, so Faddei and company were knocking together an improvised home-made duplicate. They disagreed whether the two sledges should be hauled together or separately. The tractor driver insisted that he could take them both at once. His motive was obvious: he was being paid for one trip, and one trip he would make. He had sneaked the tractor our of the motor pool at no little risk. It had to be back in place by morning as if it had never been away, and two round trips of 30 miles in a single night were out of the question. They would take the two sledges at once.

The excitement of the undertaking, the fear of having the heist of the tractor discovered, and the urgency of the timetable all made them nervous. The smell of vodka was in the air. It fortified their resolve and expedited their labors.

Eventually they pulled off. The approach to the rail crossing was up a steep hill. The tractor pulled the first sledge over, but the tow-rope then broke and the second sledge stuck on the tracks. The driver brought the tractor back to get it. Faddei's son and—for some reason—Matryona Vasilievna lent their assistance.

Meantime, two coupled locomotives were backing along the track in their direction. The tractor engine made the approach of the train inaudible. There were no lights on the rear of the nearer locomotive, and the smoke was blowing in the driver's face. Shades of the Five-Year Plan—technology blind, reckless, and backwards! The repair party did not anticipate a train without lights, and the driver of the locomotive could not see through the smoke. Matryona and her companions were crushed between the locomotive on one side and the tractor and crippled sledge on the other. "It smashed them to pieces. Can't find all the parts." The tractor was destroyed, and the locomotives were overturned.

In the midst of all the physical and emotional wreckage, Faddei managed to organize a rescue operation to maintain possession of the dismantled room, and three days later he brought it successfully to his own home. The same day, the priest of the local church officiated at the burial of Matryona and the other victims.

Here is not only a striking piece of fiction. Here is also the Slavophile protest against urbanism, technology, alcohol, against the neglect of old folk values. Solzhenitsyn and his more academic counterpart, Dmitrii Likhachev, the great historian of medieval Russian literature, have said over and over again that without a moral and spiritual regeneration of Russia, no economic and political *perestroika* is possible. "We had all lived cheek by jowl with Matryona and not understood that she was that upright person without whom, according to the proverb, no village can endure. Nor any city. Nor our whole land." Blessed are the poor in spirit.

The writers of the Slavophile school—otherwise known as the *derevenshchiki*, "village prose" writers—are romantic conservatives who share a great deal with the old Southern agrarians of the United States, the contemporary Greens of Germany, and the fundamentalists of the Islamic renaissance of the Middle East. They comprise that camp in the confrontation of "the world and the West" that Arnold Toynbee denominated the Zealots, the super-nativists. They loathe the popular culture of the modern West and all the moral and cultural flotsam that it gurgitates.

The assertion of their cultural values faces a Sisyphean struggle. The Soviets moved mightily to impel Russia along a fantastic route to progress and power. Post-Soviet Russia now joins the international rush to multiply ever more sources—and indices—of wealth and power, in the main without success thus far. Both the Stalinist and the Gorbachev/Yeltsin/Gaidar/Chernomyrdin crash courses in the economy of instant transformation have numbed the sensitivity of the nation to traditional values more intrinsically human, and the suffering that they have produced generates monsters of hyper-nationalistic pseudo-humanism too nearly like those from which Russia is allegedly fleeing.

Solzhenitsyn asks us to consider whether the Russians' folk ethos—or is it a more elemental Christian ethos?—is compatible with the material hype either of Soviet socialism or of Western capitalism. Are they, in the sense of Livy's Romans—damned if they do, damned if they don't—unable alike to endure their former vices or their present remedies?

SVITLANA KOBETS

The Subtext of Christian Asceticism in Aleksandr Solzhenitsyn's One Day in the Life of Ivan Denisovich

The phenomenology of Christian asceticism has long been a part of the Russian literary tradition. It has served Russian writers as a rich source of ideas, images, literary themes, and techniques. Representatives of different types of Russian Christian asceticism (saintly monks, hermits, pilgrims, holy fools, etc. populate the pages of Russian classics of the nineteenth and twentieth centuries. They may exhibit the traditional behavioral modalities of the ascetic (Tolstoy's *Father Sergius*, Leskov's *Ovtsebyk*), be passionate advocates of the ascetic worldview (Ferapont and Zosima in Dostoevsky's *Brothers Karamazov*), exhibit an allegiance to ascetic values without being ascetics in the institutional sense (Sonia in Dostoevsky's *Crime and Punishment*, Leskov's righteous ones in, for example, *Single-Thought* (*Odnodum*) and *The Death-Defying Golovan* (*Nesmertel'nyi Golovan*)), or be fully-fledged bearers or exponents of the ascetic ideal (pilgrim Makar Dolgoruky in Dostoevsky's *Adolescent*, Tolstoy's *Three Hermits*). Gorky's revolutionary matriarch, Nilovna (*Mother*), and Pilniak's visionary-turned-drunkard, Ivan Ozhogov (*Mahogany*) are more recent examples of the representation of the ascetic type in Russian literature.

   As an heir to the great Russian writers of the nineteenth and early twentieth century, Solzhenitsyn continues the exploration of the ideal and practice of Christian asceticism. In many of his works he describes

---

From *Slavic and East European Journal* 42, no. 4 (Winter 1998). © 1998 by AATSEEL of the U.S., Inc.

situations—the subjection of men and women to extremes of poverty, disease, human cruelty, political oppression—in which the ascetic mode of thought and behavior tends to come to the fore. His novella *One Day in the Life of Ivan Denisovich* is a vivid example of this aspect of his *oeuvre*.

Christian *topoi* are scattered throughout the text of *One Day*. They are adumbrated by means of visual images, linguistic formulas, and conventional symbols. These *topoi* function as similes (e.g. an artist renewing the numbers on inmates' caps resembles a priest anointing a man's forehead with holy oil); they are incorporated into the text as temporal landmarks (Shukhov recalls that the outbreak of the war coincided with Sunday Mass in Polomnia); they serve as means of characterization (a Ukrainian, Pavlo, crosses himself after a meal). These *topoi* bring into the text a religious dimension, which acquires a notable verbal and narrative importance as religious *discourse* unity of vocabulary, power, and social allegiance). Religious discourse is incorporated in the direct speech of Alioshka's and Shukhov's prayers, in the expression of their hopes set on God, or in the aesthetic judgment of Soviet art by Tsezar's intellectual interlocutor X-123. These discursive narrative layers serve subtly to introduce a number of religious notions which are central to the story as a whole. In fact, it is possible to argue that *One Day* is an essentially religiously-oriented narrative.

While the novella contains a variety of coded and overtly stated themes relating to Christian cosmogony, mythology, ontology, and ritual, the most dominant theme is that of Christian asceticism. As the author develops this theme he places the ideals of Christian asceticism at the center of the narrative. He endorses these ideals as high ethical norms. Moreover, they serve as criteria for the characterization of the story's protagonist. Ascetic ideals, being inescapably ethical and religious, not only inform the spiritual stance of the story's protagonist, Ivan Denisovich Shukhov, but furthermore are identified in the text as an indispensable condition for survival in the Gulag. Survival in that evil environment, in its turn, will be treated not as a biological issue, but in terms of an individual's spiritual reawakening (or at least the chance for such). The prisoner's survival as a spiritual being stands in opposition to the allegedly free Soviet citizens' spiritual death through allegiance to and espousal of the false and evil values of the totalitarian state. The contrast between the protagonist—who, as I will show, is a carrier of Christian virtues associated with asceticism—and the demonic, hellish environment of the camp is maintained throughout the tale. Shukhov's fortitude in the face of active and rampant evil is truly ascetic. Just like a medieval holy man he resists and overcomes the terrors and blandishments of evil and attains a higher level of spirituality.

It must be noted that the concept and phenomenology of asceticism (from the Greek *askesis*, "spiritual accomplishments") have an inherently radical quality. The two main stances in asceticism comprise the abnegation of one's social self, which is attached to the material world, and the cultivation of one's spiritual self. These two spiritual practices form the core of ascetic doctrines in Christian as well as other religions. An ascetic rejects the values of the profane world and by means of constant prayer and the denial of his physical and social self makes his life a spiritual path to God. He withdraws from society—forms of this withdrawal range from individual seclusion (hermits) to collective seclusion (monks)—and practices the physical austerities of fasting, exposure to heat and cold, lack of sleep, etc., in combination with mental discipline.

Though it is a common belief that a commitment to ascetic ideals is a self-conscious act, there are many examples from ascetic traditions around the world that make it possible to argue otherwise. In Russian Orthodoxy it is not imperative that an ascetic assume his feat with full self-awareness; the latter can be thrust upon him or her. For example, the "Life of Pimen" in the *Kiev Cave Paterikon* indicates that his condition of health provided him with the original motivation for embracing monastic life. To the category of "unintentional" ascetics also belong numerous holy fools (holy foolishness being, according to George Fedotov, "a form of extreme asceticism"), whose health or mental condition often contributes to assuming their feat. Among examples that can be adduced is that of Pelagia Ivanovna Serebrenikova (1809–1884), who had never fully recovered from a childhood disease and eventually became a fool in Christ.

The *topos* of an individual's determination to overcome the ties with the profane plane of existence in order to achieve oneness with the sacred constitutes an important feature of the hagiographies of ascetics. Yet the hero's perseverance in fulfilling this task and maintaining his daily routine is of no less importance. The individual becomes an ascetic through uninterrupted effort and perseverance. In fact, it is possible to argue that the popularity of hagiographic literature has always rested less on the fairy-tale miracles performed by the saints than on their heroic resistance to the lure of mundane life. Hence the Russian term *podvizhnik*, which roughly corresponds to the English "ascetic"; it connotes the meaning of persisting in one's feat. The hagiographies treat as miraculous not only the curing of the sick or the acquisition by the saint of the gift of prophecy, but also the ascetic's persistence in the superhuman effort to overcome his human limitations.

Note that the word *podvizhnik* entered the vernacular Russian as part of the expression "vesti zhizn' podvizhnika" (to lead the life of a *podvizhnik*), which means to accept hardships in one's existence and to humbly deal with them without revolting or falling into despair. Synonymous with the phrase "vesti zhizn' podvizhnika" is the expression "nesti svoi krest" (to bear one's cross). Here the idea of emulating Christ's Passion and accepting one's destiny is employed to describe a person who humbly endures the unendurable. Such a lifestyle is an expression of the kenotic stance.

The kenotic idea, which is the source of all Christian asceticism, comprises meekness, self-abasement, voluntary poverty, humility, obedience, "non-resistance," acceptance of suffering and death. These components of the kenotic mode of being supply the ascetic with a means for purifying his heart and thus bringing himself closer to the Godhead. The central importance of kenosis in the Russian religious consciousness is unanimously accepted by both theologians and philosophers of Russian spirituality. As John Gregerson puts it,

> For many centuries before the Divine Kenosis as such appeared in Russian religious thought and theological writings, there was an almost unconscious application of its far-reaching implication in regard to the spiritual life. Man's salvation was seen as being intimately connected with the degree to which he imitated or one might say shared in and partook of the Divine Self-giving, sacrifice, lowliness, and humiliation. Such an attitude enters into nearly every facet of Russian spirituality; it may be seen in Russian asceticism and general world outlook; it may be seen in the lives of countless saints and ordinary laymen; and among the truly religious it led to a profound recognition of the presence of the indwelling Christ in the "lowliest and least," in beggars, in prisoners, and in the downtrodden—although, of course, in a very different sense than in the fully sanctified kenosis of the holy man.

Thus, the kenotic mode is not only the core and the goal of asceticism but can also be a mark of those who did not formally embark on the ascetic quest. It is suffering that brings about kenosis by degree. Indeed, asceticism was never treated as an end in itself, or as being important per se. Ascetic practices are merely a method employed by the most radical and determined believers for fulfilling their spiritual quest. In other words, the phenomenology of asceticism can be described as a form employed in achieving a certain spiritual content, that of a state of grace or holiness.

One Day in the Life of Ivan Denisovich is set in a Soviet concentration camp which is divided into two incompatible worlds: that of the *zeks* (inmates), represented by the protagonist Shukhov, and that of those in power. The opposition between these two worlds is presented by means of religious images and notions which relate to the antithesis of spirit and materia. As we follow Shukhov's itinerary through one of his better days in the camp, we are shown how the demarcation line between these two worlds is drawn. The lot of the inmates is depicted first of all in terms of physical privations. Every morning they leave the camp "in the dark, in the freezing cold, with a hungry belly, and the whole day ahead."

Just like ascetics whose links with the world have been permanently severed, the inmates are virtually isolated from the outside world. They are outcasts. When Shukhov visits the camp hospital he is impressed—and oppressed—by the clean white furniture, the bright lights, and the sparkling uniform of Vdovushkin, a *zek* appointed to work at the hospital. The hospital is a little island of comfort and warmth in the midst of the icy hell of the camp. Shukhov demonstrates his disquiet and sense of being an intruder by his awkward body language: "Shukhov sat on the very edge of a bench by the wall, just far enough not to tip over with it. He had chosen this uncomfortable place unconsciously, intending to show that he wasn't at home in sick bay and would make no great demands on it."

The antinomical opposition between the Gulag's two worlds is delineated in Christian terms. The world of Soviet officialdom is in control of the material side of human existence and is the diabolical world of materia. This world is that of hell, which is Solzhenitsyn's central, albeit hidden, metaphor for the Soviet regime (cf. the title of *The First Circle*). It is a world founded on lies, the domain of the devil. This world embraces all mortal sins. Murder, anger, theft, pride, greed, and wrongdoing are the sins of those in authority as they kill, torture, humiliate, rob and cheat the *zeks*. They represent the Soviet State, a true Empire of Evil. For the inmates, it goes without saying, the camp is an anti-world, the real world turned inside-out to become hell. Hence the ironic remark about the wrong thermometer: "It doesn't work properly . . . Think they'd hang it where we can see it if it did?"

The incompatibility of the world "outside" and the world "inside" is reflected in Shukhov's query: "Can a man who's warm understand one who's freezing?" And further on, as Alioshka reads aloud from the Gospels, it is epitomized in the evangelical truth: "But let none of you suffer as a murderer, or a thief, or a wrongdoer, or a mischief-maker; yet if one suffers as a Christian, let him not be ashamed, but under that name let him glorify God." This evangelical formula serves not only to identify Christian values embraced by Alioshka. It is also the unstated (and unthought) motto of Shukhov himself, whose stance is thereby defined in Christian terms and put in contrast with the cruelty and depravity of the Gulag's officials. By giving the antagonism of these two worlds an evangelical wording, this maxim elevates it to the religious and universal level. At the same time it implicitly brands the representatives of the Soviet state as "wrongdoers" (*zlodei*), while on the other hand it characterizes the inmates as the Gulag's sufferers (*strastoterptsy*) and martyrs.

From the time of its origins, Christianity regarded martyrdom as the highest good. Martyrs were among the first canonized Christian saints who suffered for their faith (St. Apostles, St. Sebastian, St. Bartholomew, the Forty Martyrs). Martyrdom has always been welcomed by Christian ascetics who, when not subjected to persecution, sought suffering of their own free will (e.g. Alexis, the Man of God). In Russian Orthodoxy the concept of martyrdom, though still seen as being of the utmost importance, was modified, with the emphasis placed on its kenotic aspect. Gregerson writes,

> The "kenotic life" not only involves lowliness and humiliation but also non-resistant acceptance of suffering, both spiritual and physical. This perception has found expression in Russian life in general and especially in the cult of holy "sufferers," a type of saint found only in Russia where they replaced, to a considerable degree, martyrs for the faith in the popular cults.

Thus, the first Russian canonized martyrs, Boris and Gleb (1015), were not martyrs for faith, but innocent victims of a political crime. The canonization of these first two Russian saints as innocent victims and sufferers was an assertion of Russia's predilection for the kenotic ideal. This ideal found its expression in the orientation toward the idea of suffering and imminent death whether the martyrs was a lay member of the religious community or a high ranking member of it. This orientation is clearly seen in a large number of lay people canonized by the Russian Church, which has not been the case in Byzantium. The twentieth century, perhaps, yields the largest number of Russian holy sufferers, both martyrs for faith and laymen.

A distinctive characteristic of martyrdom—as perceived in both Eastern and Western Christian spirituality—is that it allows a Christian to partake of Christ's Passion and thus makes it possible for him to gain an understanding of himself, the Creation, and God. (Note that the English term "martyr" is rendered into Russian as "strastoterpets," the one who experiences Christ's "strasti," Passion). In other words, martyrdom facilitates one's eschatological quest for enlightenment. The theme of enlightenment is related to the theme of martyrdom. There is also a different kind of enlightenment described in the story. It has to do with the individual's awareness of the real situation in the country and the true nature of the regime. Even the possibility of independent thought is viewed by the authorities as a threat to the established order. That is why so many of the prisoners are convicted "spies." Some of the *zeks* were arrested for being in German captivity (Senka Klevshin), while others for simply having met with foreigners (Buienovsky). A man becomes a prisoner of the Gulag because of possessing an awareness, or at least a potential awareness of the truth (in Greek "martyr" means witness). Prison gives him a unique chance to spiritually awaken, to develop his soul, and thereby to escape the net of the devilish world of lies and spiritual death. Thus, martyrdom in the Gulag opens the path to enlightenment for the prisoner. But only those who embrace their suffering and patiently bear their cross become chosen for spiritual fulfillment.

The first sign that a prisoner is undergoing this radical change is when spiritual awareness begins to replace ideological blindness. The camp novice Buienovsky cries out his realization of the truth right to the face of the guards: "You are not Soviet people! You are not communists!" His denunciation of evil is presently confined to the camp authorities and, as indicated by his Soviet discourse, he continues to embrace communist ideals. Yet Buienovsky is starting to see that the world is not what he was told it was and what it seemed to be; he is already embarking on the path to enlightenment through suffering.

The Christian kenotic ideal holds that only a spiritual life is authentic (e.g. Serapion of Thmuis's eucharistic prayer: "make us truly alive"). On many occasions Solzhenitsyn, like the great champion of suffering Dostoevsky before him, pointed to the formative influence of the Gulag on the individual and affirmed that the Gulag offered its prisoners a chance to find, cure, and develop their souls (e.g. "suffering molds the soul"; "[there] soul has a chance to evolve"; *Gulag Archipelago Two*). Therefore the hell of the Gulag becomes a place of initiation, the place "where your soul . . . ripens from suffering" (*First Circle*). Consequently it acquires the meaning of a spiritual birthplace and spiritual homeland. Only those who gain awareness of the real situation in the country become truly alive, hence Tiurin's remark about the happy young Soviet girls on the train: "They didn't know they were living—they'd had green lights all the way." If rendered into English literally, his words mean: They were passing life by. The implication of this remark is that their happiness is but ignorance. Moreover, their life of blindness is but a waste: they exist rather than live. People's lack of awareness of the true state of affairs in the country as well as ignorance inflicted on them by the lies of the ruling ideology make their spiritual selves, or their souls, inarticulate and paralyzed.

For the *zek* his former life, his family and friends, exist on the fringes of his memory. The distance between him and them becomes insuperable. Shukhov no longer yearns for an opportunity to write to his family. Communication with them is completely thwarted. He cannot understand the essence of life in his native village. The values of that world have become completely alien to him. Nor is he eager to tell his family about his life in the camp:

> Writing letters was like throwing stones into a bottomless pool. They sank without a trace. No point in telling the family which gang you worked in and what your foreman, Andrei Prokofyevich Tyurin, was like. Nowadays you had more to say to Kildigs, the Latvian, than to the folks at home.

The common path through the Gulag draws the inmates close because of their shared experiences, values, and vision of life. Together with the other prisoners, Shukhov is part of a cast segregated from the rest of the world, a cast that is given a unique chance to discover and develop its souls. Therefore their camp experience acquires the religious significance of a chance for spiritual restoration, or, in terms of Christian asceticism, a chance for liberating one's soul from the net of the profane world.

Yet spiritual fulfillment does not become the lot of each and every *zek*. It does not offer itself to those *zeks* who persist in their attachment to or rely on the values of the outside world. For example, Tsezar, who regularly receives packages from home and whose interests and thoughts outreach the confines of the camp, does not really share the lot of other *zeks*. He stands in sharp contrast to them and is presented as someone who in his thoughts, tastes, and even appearance (he still wears a mustache) belongs to the outside world. Indeed, Tsezar does not work with the team, he does not depend on camp food, his suffering is minimal, and unlike Shukhov, Tsezar does not fear his return home. A member of the elite in both his pre-camp and camp lives, Tsezar has never known the kind of suffering that makes one embrace ascetic values and consequently facilitates one's initiation into a new awareness. Since Tsezar's thoughts center on his material possessions, which are the source of his well-being, he is not free from the material world. Another exception in the community of *zeks* is Fetiukov, the scavenger. Unlike Tsezar, whose detachment from suffering is supported by his privileged status, Fetiukov is a representative of the camp's lowest depths. While, unlike Tsezar, Fetiukov cannot reduce his suffering by bribing camp authorities, he tries to safeguard his physical existence by all means. In fact, he suffers, but he does not embrace his suffering, nor does he preserve his human dignity. Being outsiders, neither Tsezar nor Fetiukov are granted a chance for spiritual awakening.

Camp space and time present a new ontological reality for the development of one's soul which in *One Day* is the central metaphor for a *zek*. (e.g. "A vot prishla 104-ia. I v chem ee dushy derzhatsia?"; "now Gang 104 had arrived. What kept body and soul together in these men was a mystery"). It is also made explicit by the spokesperson of Christian consciousness Alioshka, who defines the space of the camp as the place where "you have time to think about your soul." On the other hand, time is referred to as eternity: inmates have no watches, there is no past or future, but only an eschatological time of the ascetic, time of here and now. Besides, it is common knowledge that no one has ever been released after serving out his term in this camp. The human soul—which in Christian mythology has always been at the center of the confrontation between God and the Devil, evil and good—in the novella is also at the center of this struggle. The reader comes to this realization when he finds himself in the atemporal dimension of camp life and is forced to see the real borderline between good and evil. In his article "Repentance and Self-Limitation" Solzhenitsyn describes the metaphysical location of this borderline:

> the universal dividing line between good and evil runs not between countries, not between nations, not between parties, not between classes, not even between good and bad men: the dividing line cuts across nations and parties, shifting constantly, yielding now to the pressure of light, now to the pressure of darkness. It divides the heart of every man, and there too it is not a ditch dug once and for all, but fluctuates with the passage of time and according to a man's behavior.

In *One Day* this borderline divides the population of the Gulag, excluding the camp officials and collaborators from the category of those chosen for a spiritual path. This special status of the inmates is acknowledged, however unknowingly, by their enemies, when the sentries refer to the inmates as a flock (*stado*). The word evokes the image of God as the prisoners' shepherd. But those who are in charge of this "flock" are usurpers and imposters. Their nature is reflected in their names, Volkovoi (volk = wolf) and Tatarin (in Russian this is a byword for a hostile invader). They are also mockingly presented as incapable of adequately attending to their assumed responsibility: "Any herdsman can count better than those good-for-nothings. He may not be able to read, but the whole time he's driving his herd he knows whether all his calves are there or not. This lot are supposed to be trained, but it's done them no good."

The failure of camp authorities to adequately perform their duty as "shepherds" is emblematic of the futility of the Soviet system of camps and repressions to subdue the human spirit. It can be further paralleled to Satan's abortive attempt to assume control of God's world. While the religious image of inmates as flock articulates their meaning of spiritual beings, it also accentuates the spiritual import of the path of the Gulag. In *One Day* this path is presented by means of *topoi* of Christian asceticism.

Traditional practices of asceticism entail austerities of life, suffering, and mental discipline, all of which are experienced by the inmates. These physical austerities are directly connected to the monastic values of obedience, brotherhood, and mutual help. In fact, these values of communal asceticism comprise the *zek*'s unwritten code of honor, references to which can be traced throughout the story. Interdependency is the law of the *zek* community. The camp may be seen as a kind of monastery, where evil is the organizing and controlling institutional authority but where the "monks" (*zeks*) have recourse to Christian values and practices. In fact, allegiance to, rejection of, or deviation from the *zek* code of honor, which is based on ascetic (cenobitic) values is directly related to the status of the *zek* in the community and his belonging to the cast of those who follow the path toward spiritual reawakening. The prisoners who do not embark on this path are shown as essentially anti-ascetic.

The anti-ascetic Fetiukov, who constantly violates the rules of this code, stands in opposition to such genuine adherents of ascetic values as Shukhov, Alioshka, Pavlo Tiurin and other members of the work team. Unlike these men, Fetiukov has acquiesced, fallen into despair. He is outside the ascetic paradigm. He licks plates, steals food from others, begs, scavenges. He does not contribute to the community: by slacking off at work, he forces the work team to do his job. He cannot renounce his social self. He truly tries to live by bread alone.

If Fetiukov is the embodiment of anti-asceticism, Yu-81, an old *zek* whom Shukhov admires, is the embodiment of the ascetic ideal. Yu-81 is a camp legend:

> With hunched-over lags all round, he was as straight-backed as could be. He sat tall, as though he'd put something on the bench under him. That head hadn't needed a barber for ages: the life of luxury had caused all his hair to fall out. The old man's eyes didn't dart around to take in whatever was going on in the mess, but stared blindly at something over Shukhov's head. He was steadily eating his thin skilly, but instead of almost dipping his head in the bowl like the rest of them, he carried his battered wooden spoon up high. He had no teeth left, upper or lower, but his bony gums chewed his bread just as well without them. His face was worn thin, but it wasn't the weak face of a burnt-out invalid, it was like dark chiseled stone. You could tell from his big

chapped and blackened hands that in all his years inside he'd never had a soft job as a trusty. But he refused to knuckle under: he didn't put his three hundred grams on the dirty table, splashed all over, like the others, he put it on a rag he washed regularly.

Yu-81, the archetypal ascetic, has retained and affirmed his human identity and has achieved spiritual knowledge. The allegiance to or deviation from ascetic values and mode of life result in the establishing of one's communal and personal identity. In this respect one's choice can be seen as the tool for one of the major tasks of an ascetic: the quest for self-identity and self-knowledge. The truth about a *zek*, like the truth about an ascetic, is revealed through his everyday practices and demeanor, as may be seen in Yu-81's case.

The vices denounced by both Christian ascetics and *zeks* are gluttony, sloth, lust, avarice, melancholy, anger, boredom, vainglory, and pride. The elimination of these vices does not constitute the goal of *zeks*, yet it is an imperative condition for their survival. It is the gluttony and sloth of Fetiukov that make him a despicable figure within the community. On the other hand it is the lack of avarice—perhaps his chief, if not his only, virtue— that makes Tsezar a positive character. To give vent to one's anger and pride, as Buienovsky does during the check-out, means to die or, at best, to completely ruin one's health in the punishment cell. Humility, the highest Christian and ascetic virtue, is the key to survival. It is the force which allows *zeks* to endure the harshest conditions. Shukhov agrees with Senka Klevshin that "Kick up a fuss . . . and you're done for. . . . Best to grin and bear it. Dig in your heels and they'll break you in two." Humility is recognized by the community as one of the most valued qualities: "A meek fellow . . . is a treasure to his gang."

Mental discipline, which comprises silence, meditation, contemplation and prayer, is an integral part of the ascetic experience. It is indispensable for gaining an understanding of the nature of the evil desires and thoughts one has, so that one may rid oneself of them. And of all the ascetic practices, prayer is the single most important one. The *topoi* of prayer and meditation are among the most prominent in the story. The narrative contains petitions (e.g. *zeks* pray for blizzards), benedictions, and references to the inmates' meditative states; it comprises several full-length prayers, and culminates in a discussion between Shukhov and Alioshka about the meaning of prayer. The meditative state is inseparable from the inmates' physical condition and is marked by the quality of permanency: "There they all were, sitting on slabs, on the molds, on the bare ground. Tongues were too stiff for talk in the morning, so everybody withdrew into his own thoughts and kept quiet." The spontaneous meditation of the *zeks* is epitomized in the figure of Alioshka, a true Christian and a man of prayer: "Alioshka sat silent, with his face buried in his hands. Saying his prayers."

The core of meditation is complete mental concentration. By focusing one's attention on a single thought or a particular object, one precludes the mind from wandering, which is otherwise its natural inclination. In everyday situations, the endless chain of associations makes one mentally stray from one thought to the next, e.g. one first sees someone's face, or an object, or hears a certain phrase; one relates it to one's memories, or a recent experience; then one elaborates on these thoughts. Daydreaming is an experience of everyday life. Such endless and aimless chains of thoughts condition a person to constantly participate mentally in the mundane (i.e., profane) life. An ascetic opts to eliminate such thoughts through mental and spiritual concentration, whether by means of meditation or prayer. By means of such practices an ascetic seeks liberation from the ties of the world. As he cleanses his mind from all things extraneous, he endeavors to transfer himself to a sacred dimension and thus to achieve a union with God. One common meditative technique is to focus on one's immediate reality. This mental state is especially characteristic of Shukhov. His thoughts encompass only the immediate: "A convict's thoughts are no freer than he is: they come back to the same place, worry over the same thing continually."

One's mental concentration on a narrowly circumscribed, limited temporal and spatial plane results in the change of one's perception and consequently in the eradication of the import of the mundane. As a result, one's perception of self and of the world is restructured. Thus, Shukhov, who is conditioned by his existential situation to adopt a meditative state of mind, is unburdened by anything irrelevant to his human essence. In his own words, he is an unthwarted combination of body and soul (*grud' da dusha*). Indeed, unlike Tsezar, he does not have any emotional attachment to possessions; unlike Vdovushkin, he does not have any privileged position he would fear to lose; nor can he be threatened by extension of his term, because he does not really count on getting released. As a result, there is nothing which could make him stray from the sacred dimension of existence, which he has unintentionally and unconsciously created for himself. In a large sense, Shukhov is not a prisoner deprived of everything that comprises a conventional human life, but an ascetic freed from the yoke of the material world. This freedom gives him strength. Indeed, Shukhov is not bothered by either melancholy or despair, nor is he overwhelmed by anxiety or envy. On the contrary, like a true ascetic, he is serene, content, and strong in his sense of self and his sense of belonging to a community. He shares his meager food with Alioshka, forgets himself in communal work at the building site, and cares about the people around him (e.g. Buienovsky, Alioshka, Tsezar).

Thereby he achieves the ascetic's goal: he transforms himself to the higher sphere of human existence, where one is unfettered by materia and is ruled by the spirit.

Shukhov engages in constant meditation. The change that is gradually taking place in his understanding of the world is exemplified by his thoughts about food:

> Since he's been in the camps Shukhov had thought many a time of the food they used to eat in the village—whole frying pans full of potatoes, porridge by the cauldron, and, in the days before the kolkhoz, great hefty lumps of meat. Milk they used to lap up till their bellies were bursting. But he knew better now that he'd been inside. He'd learned to keep his whole mind on the food he was eating. Like now he was taking tiny little nibbles of bread, softening it with his tongue, and drawing in his cheeks as he sucked it. Dry black bread it was, but like that nothing could be tastier.

The *topos* of meditation on food is as prominent throughout the text as the theme of food in general. The very process of eating itself turns into a form of meditation which, as any meditation, offers one a recourse to the sacred dimension. Alioshka reiterates the importance of meditating about food by saying: "The Lord's behest was that we should pray for no earthly or transient thing except our daily bread, 'Give us this day our daily bread.'"

The characters of Alioshka and Shukhov, both of whom are presented as carriers of Christian and ascetic values, are juxtaposed throughout the story and can be considered counterparts. They argue, but in fact they are in agreement. Indeed, Alioshka embodies Shukhov's eschatological ideal of a perfect society. In Solzhenitsyn's words: "Never says no, that Alyoshka, whatever you ask him to do. If everybody in the world was like him, I'd be the same. Help anybody who asked me. Why not? They've got the right idea, that lot."

The textual sacralization of the existential experience in the Gulag is expressed by means of the Shukhov/Alioshka parallel, which acquires utmost prominence in their last conversation. This conversation encapsulates the Christian import of the story. Although on first reading it may seem to be an attempt by the believer Alioshka to convert the non-believer Shukhov, in actual fact it is a dialogue between two exponents of high ethical norms and spirituality, two practitioners of asceticism. One of them is a conscious believer, while the other is an unconscious one. We could even say that it is a conversation between a Christian in whose life ascetic practices are supported by the conviction proceeding from his faith and a person whose ascetic form of life brings about his spiritual stance identifiable with a Christian worldview. Thus, comparing the cases Alioshka and Shukhov, we can say that in the first case the form (asceticism) originates from the content (Christian worldview) while in the second one the form generates the content.

The respective spiritual positions of these two heroes are directly related to the two major hagiographical types represented by the *vitae* of "conventional" and secret saints. "Conventional" sanctity has found its expression in the majority of hagiographical works that characterize the hero by means of certain traditional hagiographical *topoi*. Among these *topoi* we invariably find the hero's predisposition from very childhood to embrace Christian ideals, his ascetic exploits, and, finally, his recognition by the community as a miracle-worker and a saint. This narrative pattern can be found in both Eastern (Orthodox) and Western (Catholic) *vitae* of Christian saints. Yet the image of the secret saint, or "God's secret servant," is a distinctive and indeed, a defining feature of Eastern Orthodox Christianity.

Unlike his "conventional" counterpart, the secret saint is an individual who does not deliberately pursue either Christian ideals or holiness. In many cases the secret saint does not even dare to call himself a Christian! See, for example, Leskov's short story "Pamphalon the Mountebank" ("Skomorokh Pamfalon"). He is invariably unaware that he is being pleasing to God or that he has been chosen. His state of grace is unknown not only to himself but also to other members of the Christian community. Moreover, his occupation or social position make him a most improbable candidate for the status of either a righteous one or a saint. Stories about such saints are usually interpolated into the *vitae* describing the life of a committed ascetic who asks God if there is another Christian whose ascetic exploit is equal or superior to his own. After that he has a dream or a vision in which God shows him just such a person. The ascetic sets off to meet this person, who turns out to be anything but what the community would regard as a devoted Christian: he may be a mime, a tax collector, or a brothel-keeper. Yet that person's set of mind and life-style (unnoticed and unappreciated by other people) make him pleasing to God and therefore a saint in absolute (i.e. extra-institutional) terms. Stories about these "God's secret servants" not only show the reader the limitations of human judgment but also express a uniquely Eastern Orthodox worldview, according to which God's creation is a holy place where sanctity perpetually seeks the opportunity to manifest itself.

If Alioshka is explicitly presented as a saintly person then Shukhov's saintliness is far less obvious. In fact, his character reflects the paradigm of God's secret servants. While Shukhov's spiritual stance is presented implicitly, it attains textual prominence through being paralleled and equated to Alioshka's own position. An ardent Baptist believer, Alioshka is visually and verbally God's servant, while Shukhov is God's servant invisibly and mutely. Their last conversation is conducted on two stylistic and lexical levels: the vernacular of Shukhov's uneducated speech, which is saturated by camp jargon, and Alioshka's high-flown evangelical rhetoric. These discursive differences yet again parallel the forms (explicit and implicit) that the two characters' respective allegiance to Christian spirituality has taken. Moreover, Alioshka's Christian ideals are incarnated not only into his own but also into Shukhov's life. Thus, Alioshka says that the only true values are not of this world ("What people prize highly is vile in the sight of God!"), and so are the values embraced by Shukhov. Alioshka teaches that prayer has to be incessant and centered around one's daily bread, and so it is in Shukhov's life. Neither of them believes in the traditional institution of the Russian Orthodox Church. Alioshka is a Baptist, a member of a minority denomination, which in Russia has traditionally been rejected as a sect and has been continuously persecuted since its appearance in the mid-nineteenth century by both Church and State. Shukhov's protest is based on his intuitive rejection of the Church, which in his experience accommodates itself to secular needs and employs corrupt priests.

The Russian Orthodox Church has been repeatedly guilty of involvement in worldly matters and interests and has had a long history of willingly subordinating itself to the state, its policies, and its requirements. In the Soviet era those representatives of the Russian Orthodox Church who were not banished or murdered often collaborated with the state. Indeed, Alioshka accuses the church of collaborating with the Soviets and of being worldly in character. "The Orthodox Church has turned its back on the Gospels—they [Orthodox priests] don't get put inside . . . because their faith is not firm," he tells Shukhov. Church and state are treated in the story as belonging in the same camp because they are both rooted in the profane plane of existence and both serve an evil political system which promotes lies.

Shukhov recognizes that the rigors of camp life do not break the Baptists ("Life in the camp was like a water off a duck's back to them"). But the same is true of Shukhov himself! He not only survives, but also finds in his life a measure of joy and contentment, which stem from his spiritual fulfillment. Shukhov's friend Alioshka is willing to be in the camp and views life outside its perimeter as perilous and evil: "What good is freedom to you? If you're free, your faith will soon be choked by thorns. Be glad you are in prison." These words are not foreign to Shukhov, who does not know any longer if he wants to be set free. Thus in the story the issue of freedom is ultimately transferred onto the metaphysical dimension where it is defined not by the existential criteria of spatial confinement, but as a matter of spiritual integrity and clarity of vision. Survival in the camp acquires the meaning of spiritual survival, as opposed to the spiritual numbness and even death which is the lot of the vast majority of Soviet people belonging to the so-called free life.

In conclusion, we can say that the kenotic meaning of the story is engendered first through the religious themes and allusions in the narrative, and second, through the descriptions of the main character's ascetic mode of being. Such an approach to the novella allows for a conspicuous re-reading. The suffering inflicted on the *zeks* by no means extinguishes their human essence. On the contrary, like the martyrdom of the ascetics, it becomes a step toward the achievement of a higher spirituality. The main character, Shukhov, now comes to be viewed as an unconscious ascetic, one of God's secret servants who transfers himself into the numinous dimension, thereby overcoming the evil of the empirical world.

Chronology

1918   Aleksandr Solzhenitsyn born in Kislovodsk, a spa in the Caucasus, on December 11. His father died in an accident before his birth.

1924   Moves with mother to Rostov-on-Don, where she earns a meager living as a typist.

1938   Enters the University of Rostov-on-Don to study mathematics and physics; wins a Stalin scholarship to pursue post-graduate studies.

1940   Marries Natalya Reshetovskaya, a fellow student; teaches mathematics at a Rostov secondary school.

1941   Graduates from the University of Rostov; completes a correspondence course at the Moscow Institute of Philosophy, Literature and History; joins army on October 18, after outbreak of Soviet-German war.

1942   Begins service as artillery officer in the Red Army during World War II; twice decorated for valor; promoted to captain by 1945.

1945   Arrested in February by Soviet counterintelligence for slandering Stalin in personal letters to a friend; confined in Moscow's notorious Lubyanka prison; in July, while in prison, sentenced to eight years hard labor in a prison camp by a three-man military tribunal, a "troika."

1946–49 Works as a mathematician in a prison research institute, Marvino, outside of Moscow.

1950–53 Serves remainder of sentence at prison camp in Dzezkazgan, in the province of Karaganda, where a network of camps had been built; divorced by wife Natalya Reshetovskaya, who believed he had died in exile; undergoes surgery for cancer.

1953–54 Concentration camp sentence ends, but forced to remain in "perpetual" exile near Dzhambul, in southern Kazakhstan; begins writing; cancer returns and he enters hospital in Tashkent, Uzbekistan; cancer arrested in second series of treatments at Tashkent.

1956   Released from exile.

1957   "Rehabilitated" in post-Stalin rehabilitations; returns to Ryazan, 100 miles southeast of Moscow, to teach mathematics, and is joined by former wife Natalya Reshetovskaya, although she has remarried; begins writing *One Day in the Life of Ivan Denisovich*.

1961   Sends manuscript of *One Day in the Life of Ivan Denisovich* to literary magazine *Novy mir*; meets editor-in-chief Alexander Tvardovsky in December.

1962   *One Day in the Life of Ivan Denisovich* published in November in *Novy mir*, with Nikita Khrushchev's approval. Khrushchev overrides objections of Politburo.

1963   Three short stories, "Matryona's House," "The Incident at Krechetovka Station," and "For the Good of the Cause," published in *Novy mir*; begins writing *The Cancer Ward*.

1964   Editorial in *Pravda* announces that Communist Party has declined to award Solzhenitsyn the Lenin Prize; completes *The First Circle*, and sends the manuscript to the West in October.

1965   Manuscripts and private papers seized by secret police on
            September 11.

1966   *The Cancer Ward* discussed by editorial board of *Novy mir* on June
            18; Solzhenitsyn sends letter of protest against persecution to
            Brezhnev; discussion of *The Cancer Ward* organized by Writers'
            Union on November 16.

1967   Completes first two parts of autobiographical work, *A Calf Was
            Butting an Oak*, in April and November; sends open letter on May
            16 to Fourth Congress of Soviet Writers condemning
            government censorship; calls for Writers' Union to defend and
            protect writers instead of acting as arm of government in
            repression; on June 12 meets with heads of Writers' Union
            without success; on September 12, writes second letter to
            Writers' Union, protesting the suppression of his letter to the
            Fourth Congress of Writers and the government campaign of
            slander and harassment against him; on September 22, Board
            of the Writers' Union insists that he renounce "his role as leader
            of the political opposition" in the Soviet Union and the "anti-
            Soviet" propoganda being "carried on in his name," a demand he
            refuses; on December 1, presents list of eight questions to
            Writers' Union, asking the group to defend him against ongoing
            slander and harassment and to see that his works are published.

1968   Excerpts from *Cancer Ward* published in April 11 *London Times
            Literary Supplement*; on April 16, writes letter to *Le Monde*, *Unita*,
            and *Literaturnaya gazeta* denouncing unauthorized sale of his
            manuscripts outside Russia by the Soviet secret police; on April
            21, writes letter to *Literaturnaya gazeta* denying permission to
            foreign publishers to publish his novels; in May, circulates open
            letter to membership of Writers' Union noting that his eight
            questions had not been answered, the harassment continues, and
            his books remain unpublished in Russia; in September, *The First
            Circle* is translated and published in New York.

1969   In March, rumors that *The Gulag Archipelago*, sequel to *The First
            Circle*, has been smuggled out to the West without the author's
            knowledge or consent; on April 14, Rolf Hochhuth writes open
            letter to President Nikolai Podgorny protesting ban on

Solzhenitsyn's books (the letter is also signed by Heinrich Boll, Arthur Miller, Martin Niemoller, and Giangiacomo Feltrinelli); on November 4, Solzhynitsn is expelled from Ryazan branch of the Writers' Union; eight days later, expulsion confirmed in Moscow; on November 27, writes letter of protest to Writers' Union; on November 30, *Literaturnaya gazeta* suggests he be given an exit visa and allowed to emigrate; in December, Western writers and cultural organizations, and twenty-nine Soviet dissidents, protest Solzhenitsyn's expulsion from the Writers' Union; begins writing *The Red Wheel*. *The Cancer Ward* is translated and published in New York.

1970   In March, appoints Zurich attorney Fritz Heeb to protect his copyrights and interests as an author outside Russia; in June, publicly denounces government detention of writer Zhores Medvedev in a psychiatric hospital; awarded Nobel Prize for literature in October and says he will go to Stockholm to personally accept, if permitted. Although the Soviet press accuses him of presenting a distorted picture of Soviet life and contributing to anti-Soviet propoganda and agitation, thirty-seven Soviet dissidents, including Pyotr Yakir and Zinaida Grigorenko, publicly support the award of the Nobel Prize to Solzhenitsyn and cellist Mitsislav Rostropovich writes letter to Soviet newspapers defending Solzhenitsyn's work and applauding his receiving the Nobel Prize. (The letter is not published in the USSR, and Rostropovich is forbidden to travel abroad on a concert tour.) In November, Solzhenitsyn announces that he will not go to Stockholm to receive the Nobel Prize; Swedish Academy awards it to him *in absentia* on December 10; Solzhenitsyn joins Committee for Human Rights, established in November by physicists Andrei Sakharov, Andrei Tverdokhlebov, and Valery Chalidze; *Stories and Prose Poems* is translated and published in New York.

1971   In May, authorizes publication of *August 1914*, in Russian, by a small press in Paris; *The Love-Girl and the Innocent* translated, published in New York.

1972   Writes letter to Patriarch Pimen of Russia in March; *Nobel Lecture* is translated and published in New York.

1973   August 23, secret police find copy of *The Gulag Archipelago*; Solzhenitsyn grants interview to Associated Press and *Le Monde* the same day. Sends protest letter to Soviet leaders September 5;

contacted by secret police though Natalya Reshetovskaya September 24; Part I of *The Gulag Archipelago* published in Russian in Paris on December 28; translated, published in New York; eventually translated into 30 languages.

1973–74   Writes three articles, published in Paris by Soviet dissidents in collection *From Under the Rubble*; *August 1914* and *Letter to the Soviet Leaders* are translated and published in New York.

1974   Writes appeal to Russian youth through underground press essay, "Don't Live a Lie"; arrested in Moscow on February 12, stripped of Soviet citizenship, and deported to West Germany on February 13.

1976   Settles near Cavendish, Vermont.

1989   Solzhenitsyn's Nobel acceptance speech and selected chapters of *The Gulag Archipelago* published in *Novy mir*.

1990   In March, full version of the *Archipelago, The First Circle, Cancer Ward*, and *One Day in the Life of Ivan Denisovich* published. *Novy mir* editor-in-chief Sergei Zalygin calls 1990 "The Year of Solzhenitsyn," but Russian critics and public now indifferent to his works. Gorbachev restores citizenship on August 15.

1991   *The Red Wheel*, an eight-volume historical saga, published.

1994   On May 27 returns to Russia, for first time since exile, to Kolyma; he tours through the Russian provinces; "The Russian Question Up to the End of the 20th Century" published in *Novy Mir* in August; speaks before session of Duma on October 28, but generates little interest; begins series of television appearances; captures interest of press and public; suggestions that Solzhenitsyn be put forward as presidential candidate; he refuses.

1995   Begins to seem out of touch with contemporary Russian society and politics; television program cancelled.

1995–96   Publishes a dozen short stories and articles in *Novy Mir*.

1997   Russian radio airs 65-part series: Solzhenitsyn reads *The Red Wheel*. With former wife, Natalya Solzhenitsyna, creates annual literary prize of $25,000, funded by royalties from *The Gulag Archipelago*.

Contributors

HAROLD BLOOM is Sterling Professor of the Humanities at Yale University and Henry W. and Albert A. Berg Professor of English at the New York University Graduate School. He is the author of over 20 books, including *Shelley's Mythmaking* (1959), *The Visionary Company* (1961), *Blake's Apocalypse* (1963), *Yeats (1970)*, *A Map of Misreading* (1975), *Kabbalah and Criticism (1975)*, *Agon: Toward a Theory of Revisionism* (1982), *The American Religion* (1992), *The Western Canon* (1994), and *Omens of Millennium: The Gnosis of Angels, Dreams, and Resurrection* (1996). *The Anxiety of Influence* (1973) sets forth Professor Bloom's provocative theory of the literary relationships between the great writers and their predecessors. His most recent books include *Shakespeare: The Invention of the Human*, a 1998 National Book Award finalist, and *How to Read and Why*, which was published in 2000. In 1999, Professor Bloom received the prestigious American Academy of Arts and Letters Gold Medal for Criticism.

EDWARD E. ERICSON JR. is the author of *Solzhenitsyn in the Modern World*; *Solzhenitsyn, the Moral Vision*; and *Radicals in the University*.

JAMES M. CURTIS is the author of *Solzhenitsyn's Traditional Imagination* and *Rock Eras: Interpretations of Music and Society, 1954–1984*.

KENNETH N. BROSTROM is the editor of *Russian Literature and American Critics*.

JOHN B. DUNLOP is Associate Director and Senior Fellow at the Hoover Institution, Stanford University. He is the author of *The Faces of Contemporary Russian Nationalism*.

EDWARD J. BROWN is a professor of slavic languages and literature at Stanford University.

MIKHAIL S. BERNSTAM is the author of *Andropov: New Challenge to the West*.

Q. D. (QUEENIE DOROTHY) LEAVIS (1900?–1981) is the author of many essays of literary criticism; she has lectured extensively on topics of English and American literature. She is the author of *Fiction and the Reading Public* and co-author, with F. R. Leavis, of *Collected Essays: Lectures in America*. Her *Collected Essays* were published in 1985.

ANNA DIEGEL's works include a translation of Mireya Robles's *Hagiography of Narcisa the Beautiful* (1996).

CARYL EMERSON is the author of *Modest Musorgsky and Boris Godunov: Myths, Realities, Reconsiderations*; *The First Hundred Years of Mikhail Bakhtin*; *The Life of Musorgsky*; and editor of *Critical Essays on Mikhail Bakhtin*.

HUGH RAGSDALE is the author of *The Russian Tragedy: The Burden of History*; *Imperial Russian Foreign Policy*; and *Tsar Paul and the Question of Madness*.

Bibliography

Allaback, Stephen. *Alexander Solzhenitsyn*. New York: Taplinger, 1978.

Freeborn, Richard, ed. *Russian Literary Attitudes from Pushkin to Solzhenitsyn*. London: Macmillan, 1976.

Aron, Raymond. "Alexander Solzhenitsyn and European 'Leftism,'" *Survey* 22 (Summer/Autumn, 1976): 233–41.

Barker, Francis. *Solzhanitsyn: Politics and Form*. London: Macmillan, 1971.

Berman, Ronald. *Solzhenitsyn at Harvard*. Washington, D.C.: Ethics and Public Policy Center, 1980.

Bjorkegren, Hans. *Aleksandr Solzhenitsyn*, trans. Kaarina Eneberg. New York: The Third Press, 1972.

Buckley, William F. Jr. "Continuing Presence of Solzhenitsyn," *National Review* 28 (15 October 1976): 1140–41.

Burg, David, and George Feifer. *Solzhenitsyn*. New York: Stein and Day, 1973.

Carlisle, Olga. *Solzhenitsyn and the Secret Circle*. New York: Holt, Rinehart, and Winston, 1978.

Carpovich, Vera V. *Solzhenitsyn's Peculiar Vocabulary: Russian-English Dictionary*. New York: Technical Dictionary Co., 1976.

Casillo, Robert. "Techne and Logos in Solzhenitsyn," *Soundings* 70 (Fall–Winter, 1987): 519–37.

Clardy, Jesse V. *The Superfluous Man of Russian Letters*. Washington, D.C.: University Press of America, 1980.

Clement, Oliver. *The Spirit of Solzhenitsyn*, trans. Sarah Fawcett and Paul Burns. London: Search Press Ltd., 1976.

Diakin, Nadia Odette. "Solzhenitsyn's *First Circle*," *Explicator* 42 (Fall 1983): 59–61.

Dunlap, John B., Richard Haugh, and Alexis Klimoff, eds. *Aleksandr Solzhenitsyn: Critical Essays and Documentary Materials*. Belmont, Mass.: Nordland, 1973.

Fairlie, Henry. "Mother Russia's Prodigal Son," *New Republic* (29 July 1978): 18–20.

Feuer, Kathryn, ed. *Solzhenitsyn: A Collection of Critical Essays* (Englewood Cliffs, N.J.: Prentice Hall, 1976.

Fifer, George. "The Dark Side of Solzhenitsyn," *Harper's* 260 (May 1980): 48–51.

Galler, Meyer. *Soviet Prison Camp Speech: A Survivor's Glossary*. Madison: University of Wisconsin Press, 1972.

Gleason, Abbott. "Solzhenitsyn and the Slavophiles," *Yale Review* 65 (Autumn 1975): 61–70.

Hallett, Richard, "Beneath the Closed Visor: Dimitry Panin and the Two Faces of Sologdin in Solzhenitsyn's *First Circle*," *Modern Language Review* 78 (April 1983): 365–74.

Halperin, David M. "Solzhenitsyn, Epicures, and the Ethics of Stalinism," *Critical Inquiry* 7 (Spring 1981): 475–97.

Jones, Jack. "Solzhenitsyn's Warning: A Secular Reinterpretation," *Chicago Review* 32 (Winter 1981): 141–64.

Kelley, Donald R. *The Solzhenitsyn-Sakharov Dialogue*. Westport, Conn.: Greenwood Press, 1982.

Kodjak, Andrej. *Alexander Solzhenitsyn*. Boston: G. K. Hall and Co., 1978.

Kramer, Hilton. "Solzhenitsyn in Vermont," *New York Times Review of Books* (11 May 1980): 3, 30–32.

Krasnov, Vladislav. *Solzhenitsyn and Dostoevsky: A Study of the Polyphonic Novel*. Athens: University of Georgia Press, 1980.

Lukacs, Georg. *Solzhenitsyn*, trans. William David Graf. Cambridge, Mass.: MIT Press, 1971.

Medvedev, Roy. "A Prophet and His Country," *Russian Life* 40 (November 1997): 22–30.

Medvedev, Zhores A. *Ten Years After Ivan Denisovich*. New York: Alfred A. Knopf, 1973.

Moody, Christopher. *Solzhenitsyn*. New York: Harper and Row, 1973.

Oja, Matt F. "Shamalov, Solzhenitsyn, and the Mission of Memory," *Survey* 29 (Summer 1985): 62–69.

Podhoretz, Norman. "The Terrible Question of Alexandr Solzhenitsyn," *Commentary* (February 1985): 17–24.

Pomorska, Krystyna, ed. *Fifty Years of Russian Prose: From Pasternak to Solzhenitsyn*. Cambridge, Mass.: MIT Press, 1971.

Rancour-Laferriere, Daniel. "The Deranged Birthday Boy: Solzhenitsyn's Portrait of Stalin," *Mosaic* (Summer 1985): pp. 61–72.

Reshetovskaya, Natalya A. *Sanya: My Life with Alexander Solzhenitsyn*, trans. Elena Ivanoff. Indianapolis, Ind.: Bobbs-Merrill, 1975.

Rosefielde, Steven. "The First 'Great Leap Forward' Reconsidered: Lessons of the *Gulag Archipelago*," *Slavic Review* 39 (December 1980): 559–87.

Rothberg, Abraham. *Aleksandr Solzhenitsyn: The Major Novels*. Ithaca, N.Y.: Cornell University Press, 1971.

Rzhevsky, Leonid. *Solzhenitsyn: Creator of Heroic Deeds* (Tuscaloosa: University of Alabama Press, 1978).

Scammell, Michael. *Solzhenitsyn: A Biography*. New York: W. W. Norton, 1984.

Shin, Un-chol. "Conscience, Lie, and Suffering in Solzhenitsyn's *The First Circle*," *Modern Age* 29 (Fall 1985): 344–52.

Ulam, Adam B. *Ideologies and Illusions: Revolutionary Thought from Herzen to Solzhenitsyn*. Cambridge: Harvard University Press, 1976.

Weerakoon, R. *Alexander Solzhenitsyn: Soldier, Prisoner, Writer*. Colombo, Ceylon: Gunaratne and Co., 1972.

Yakovlov, N. *Solzhenitsyn's Archipelago of Lies*. Moscow: Novosti, 1974.

Acknowledgments

"Humanity *In Extremis: One Day in the Life of Ivan Denisovich* and *The Love-Girl and the Innocent*" by Edward E. Ericson Jr. From *Solzhenitsyn: The Moral Vision* by Edward E. Ericson Jr. © 1980 by Wm. B. Eerdmans Publishing Co. Reprinted with permission.

"Solzhenitsyn's Traditional Imagination: Tolstoy" by James M. Curtis. From *Solzhenitsyn's Traditional Imagination* by James M. Curtis. © 1984 by the University of Georgia Press. Reprinted with permission.

"*Prussian Nights*: A Poetic Parable for Our Time" by Kenneth N. Brostrom. From *Solzhenitsyn in Exile: Critical Essays and Documentary Materials*, John B. Dunlop, Richard S. Haugh, and Michael Nicholson, eds. © 1985 by the Board of Trustees of the Leland Stanford Junior University. Reprinted with permission of the publisher, Hoover Institute Press.

"*The Gulag Archipelago*: Alternative to Ideology" by John B. Dunlop. From *Solzhenitsyn in Exile: Critical Essays and Documentary Materials*, John B. Dunlop, Richard S. Haugh, and Michael Nicholson, eds. © 1985 by the Board of Trustees of the Leland Stanford Junior University. Reprinted with permission of the publisher, Hoover Institute Press.

"*The Calf and the Oak: Dichtung* and *Wahrheit*" by Edward J. Brown. From *Solzhenitsyn in Exile: Critical Essays and Documentary Materials*, John B.

Dunlop, Richard S. Haugh, and Michael Nicholson, eds. © 1985 by the Board of Trustees of the Leland Stanford Junior University. Reprinted with permission of the publisher, Hoover Institute Press.

"Solzhenitsyn: The Russian Liberal" by Mikhail S. Bernstam. From *Chronicles* 12 (10 October 1988): 12–18. © 1988 by The Rockford Institute. Reprinted with permission.

"Solzhenitsyn, the Creative Artist, and the Totalitarian State" by Q. D. Leavis. From *Modern Age* 32, no. 4 (Fall 1989): 294–310. © 1989 by the Intercollegiate Studies Institute, Inc. Reprinted with permission.

"Human Rights and Literature: Solzhenitsyn and Pasternak" by Anna Diegel. From *Theoria* 75 (May 1990): 77–85. © 1990 by the University of Natal Press. Reprinted with permission.

"The World of Detention in Dostoevsky and Solzhenitsyn" by Sophie Ollivier. From *Irish Slavonic Studies* 12 (1991): 27–39. © 1991 by the author and *Irish Slavonic Studies*. Reprinted with permission of the author and *Irish Slavonic Studies*.

"The Word of Aleksandr Solzhenitsyn" by Caryl Emerson. From *The Georgia Review* 49, no. 1 (Spring 1995): 64–74. © 1995 by The University of Georgia. Reprinted with permission.

"The Solzhenitsyn That Nobody Knows" by Hugh Ragsdale. From *The Virginia Quarterly Review* 71, no. 4 (Autumn 1995): 634–41. © 1995 by the Virginia Quarterly Review. Reprinted with permission.

"The Subtext of Christian Asceticism in *One Day in the Life of Ivan Denisovich*" by Svitlana Kobets. From *Slavic and East European Journal* 42, no. 4 (Winter 1998): 661–75. © 1998 by AATSEEL of the U.S., Inc. Reprinted with permission.

Index